RELIGION IN SOCIETY

Religion in Society

Social Dimensions of Buddhism, Hinduism and Jainism in India

BIRENDRA NATH PRASAD

MANOHAR
2025

First published 2024

Reprinted 2025

ISBN 978-93-94262-76-8

Published by
Ajay Jain *for*
Manohar Publishers & Distributors
4753/23 Ansari Road, Daryaganj
New Delhi 110002

Typeset by
Ravi Shanker
Delhi 110095

Printed and bound in India by Replika Press Pvt. Ltd.

Contents

Figures and Tables

Figures

Tables

Preface

This book, consisting of a thematic introduction and slightly modified versions of my published research articles/ papers presented in conferences since 2008, is primarily concerned with the theme of social history of religion in India. These research articles are being reproduced here with some modifications, mainly to ensure their easier availability to scholars interested in this theme. Needless to say, but for the support of some friends and well-wishers, it would have been impossible for me to undertake these researches and publish these articles.

The research articles on the theme of social history of religions in early medieval Bihar and Bengal in the present book owe their origin to my fifteen years of research on this theme. All of them were published between 2008 and 2020.

Most of these research articles were published abroad in prestigious peer-reviewed international journals. Getting these articles published in these journals was always a tough task. Comments of anonymous referees were incisive, which forced me to reconsider some of my arguments. Surviving the peer-review process of these journals was always an exercise in learning. I express my thanks to the anonymous peer-reviewers of these research articles and editors of these journals. Prof. Richard Gombrich, Prof. Peter Harvey, Dr Simon Brodbeck, Dr Dermot Killingley, Dr Anna S. King – editors of some of the journals in which my research articles were published – not only entertained the research articles submitted by a young researcher, but also ensured that the peer-review of my research articles did not take more than the stipulated time. For a young researcher, this was a great favour. Prof. Tansen Sen and Prof. Richard Gombrich invited me to the conferences organized by National University of Singapore and Oxford Centre for Buddhist Studies, respectively, in which I shared my researches on the theme of Buddhist revival in contemporary Uttar Pradesh. I thank Prof. Tansen Sen, Prof. Richard Gombrich and Prof. Peter van der Veer for their comments on my paper presentations on this theme.

Much of my ideas owe their origin to my discussions with my MA students in different universities where I taught. I also had the opportunity of supervising many Ph.D. research scholars working on different aspects of social history of religion in different parts of ancient and early medieval India. Their sharp questions forced me to reconsider many ideas. I express my thanks to them. Prof. Heeraman Tiwari and Prof. Umesh Kadam – my esteemed colleagues at the Centre for Historical Studies, Jawaharlal Nehru University, New Delhi – kept me motivated and focused. Dr Umakant Mishra shared my research interests. I express my thanks to them.

Without the unconditional love, help and support of my wife, Mrs Rashmi Prabha, it would have been impossible for me to achieve anything. Our three children – Pragati, Anurag and Aditya – acted as bundles of happiness and joy.

Finally, I thank Mr. Ramesh Jain and Mr. Ajay Jain of Manohar Publishers and Distributors, Delhi, for considering the manuscript of this book for publication, arranging the anonymous peer-review of the manuscript, and ensuring its prompt publication after the process of peer-review. It was always a pleasing exercise to work with their copy-editors.

JNU, New Delhi BIRENDRA NATH PRASAD
15 November 2022

1

Introduction

As one attempts to study the social dimensions of different ancient Indian religions, one feels a certain degree of unease regarding some very terminologies through which this study is attempted. For a historian trained in defining and demarcating religious traditions of ancient and early medieval India into different 'isms' – Buddhism, Brahmanism and Jainism – this unease becomes even more acute. One may begin with highlighting the fact that the religious landscape of almost every part of India was poly-religious in nature, where different religions not only coexisted but also competed for social patronage. This poly-religiosity creates major theoretical issues in any study of religious dynamics of ancient and early medieval (*c.* 600–1200 CE) India. What could have been, say for example, the religious affiliation of *charmakāra* Thisavī, who donated a big stone sculpture of Viṣṇu as his *deyadharma* to the Buddhist monastic establishment of Āpaṇaka Mahāvihāra in the second half of the ninth century CE as an object of worship: Brahmanical or Buddhist?[1] That he mobilized considerable resources to get this stone image of Viṣṇu sculpted has been noted earlier.[2] So this person was, doubtlessly, a devotee of Viṣṇu, but why would he go to a Buddhist *mahāvihāra* to donate and install this stone sculpture as an object of worship? The Āpaṇaka Mahāvihāra and its *bhikṣus*, arguably, commanded sanctity and pilgrimage from *charmakāra* Thisavī. What could have been the religious identity of Śaka, the son of *mūrtikāra* Sāyanabhara, who constructed a shrine dedicated to *Chaumukha* Mahādeva for the good of the *snātakas* of the Mahābodhi: Brahmanical or Buddhist? What could have been the religious identity of Buddhist monastics of Salban Vihara, Mainamati (in the Comilla district of Bangladesh), who kept images of Viṣṇu inside their monastic cells, most probably as objects of personal worship?[3] The religious worlds of these person were, one may infer, not demarcated into two impermeable 'isms'.

Risking oversimplification, one may identify two main constituent elements of religious matrix of ancient and early medieval India: (1) specialized priesthood/monkhood, and (2) the rest of the population which revered the priest/monk traditions of different religions. Indian religious historiography has been dominated by an analysis of textual material, often normative in nature, produced by the specialized priest/monk traditions of different religions. The behaviour of the other end of the spectrum is generally neglected. This behaviour often marked with a certain level of fluidity in terms of religious ideas and their social praxis. It was easily possible for a person to patronize the specialised priest/monk traditions of different religions. This particular feature had some fundamental ramifications for Buddhism, especially in view of the fact that Brahmanism generally provided ideas and institutions for the maintenance of social order.[4] Except in the cases of the Jaina clergy and devotees, Brahmanism had a kind of monopoly over *rites the passage*, even in the case of Buddhist devotees.[5] So, any individual could have multiple, or at least fluid, religious identity.[6]

If this kind of fluidity was a marked feature of the socio-religious dynamics of a significant portion of ancient and early medieval India, then why do we see a peculiar feature in northern India now: an increasing ossification of religious identities, with a determined effort to seal the rather porous boundaries between Buddhism and Hinduism, not only by the monks' tradition of Buddhism, but also by the *upāsaka*s of the same?[7] Clearly, much water has flown down the Ganga River and the socio-religious and cultural landscapes of this area are in a process of significant transition. The present book hopes to be a humble attempt in tracing some of these transitions in the backdrop of some long-term socio-religious developments in the same.

The basic endeavour of the present book is twofold:

(1) to trace the socio-economic and cultic processes which precipitated the decline of Buddhism in its last stronghold – Bihar and Bengal – towards the end of the early medieval (*c.* CE 600–1200 CE) period, and
(2) to trace the pattern of its attempted revival in the neighbouring province of Uttar Pradesh – which is, one will surely agree, the most important stronghold of Hinduism today – where a revival of Buddhism is being attempted in recent years.

The kind of Buddhism being revived now has almost no parallel with any form of Indian Buddhism in any period of its history. Should this be viewed as a continuum of, or a rupture with the past patterns of social history of Indian Buddhism? If it is a rupture, what implications does it have in determining the future trajectories of Indian Buddhism?

The socio-religious churn northern India has been undergoing in recent decades has also resulted in the attempts of revival of another religion, which once had a significant presence in ancient India: Ājīvika-dharma.[8] This revival too, albeit in a changed form, is being attempted by a section of the Dalit population of Uttar Pradesh. Contrary to the received wisdom in a significant section of existing historiography, Ājīvika-dharma had a much longer survival in India than what is generally believed.[9] With this kind of history, it is but to be expected that the influence of this religion would have lingered, if not in its 'pure' and 'original' form, then at least with some fundamental metamorphosis, which may re-emerge at a fortuitous juncture when socio-economic and religious circumstances favour its revival. It is also to be expected that the new followers of this old religion – like the followers of any other Indic religion in India – may modify it fundamentally to suit their contemporary needs. The segment of Dalit population of contemporary northern India, which is more assertive of its Dalit identity, is attempting a revival of Ājīvika-dharma as the 'original' and 'endogenous' religion of Dalits. The current brand of Ājīvika-dharma in Uttar Pradesh does not believe in *niyati* (predetermined destiny). As every religion evolves and this evolution also involves, occasionally, a fundamental revision of some basic concepts of the religion by its adherents, this rejection of the fundamental tenet of *niyati* of the older form of Ājīvika-dharma does not deny the claim of the neo-Ājīvikas as the legitimate legatee of the old one. What kind of repercussions, if any, does this development have for the future of Buddhism and Hinduism in India?

The first five research articles in the present book focus on early medieval Bihar and Bengal areas, which are generally supposed to be the 'last stronghold' of Indian Buddhism during the early medieval period.[10] The aim is to understand the complex issue of the decline of Buddhism in this area, in the backdrop of developments in other competing religions (Brahmanism and Jainism) in the same area and period.

It is imperative to explain the rationale behind attempting a study of the decline of Buddhism in early medieval Bihar and Bengal in the backdrop of developments in other competing religions (Brahmanism and Jainism) in the same area and period. In a significant section of existing historiography on this theme, the preferred attitude has been to study these religions in isolation from one another. Such studies generally place emphasis on textual sources and neglect archaeological sources. This attitude is discernible in a significant section of available scholarship on the history of Buddhism in this area during this period. Thus, it has been argued that Tantric Buddhism was the only practised form of Buddhism in early medieval Bihar and Bengal.[11] Even this Buddhism was confined to its 'parasitical' monastic centres, which were patronized by royal patrons only: Buddhist monks residing in such monasteries and practising Tantric Buddhism had no interaction with other sections of society.[12] It has also been argued that Buddhism had no presence beyond the confines of its monastic centres, hence it was totally unable to resist attempts of Brahmanical appropriation of Buddhism.[13] Hence, Buddhism 'disappeared' from Bihar and Bengal almost immediately after the Turkic destruction of Buddhist monasteries.[14]

Some recent studies on the religious dynamics of early medieval Bihar and Bengal from an 'archaeology of religion' perspective have questioned these arguments. A study of the spatial distribution patterns of Buddhist, Brahmanical and Jaina religious centres across the variegated landmass of early medieval Bihar and Bengal indicated that all three religions – Buddhism, Brahmanism and Jainism – were expanding religions.[15] Barring the tract to the west of the Sone River in south Bihar, where archaeological markers of the presence of Buddhism are meagre, it was an expanding religion in all parts of Bihar during the Pāla period.[16] Similarly, in the context of Bengal, barring the tract of Bangladesh bounded by the River Jamuna/Brahmaputra in the west, marshes of Sylhet in east and northern portions of Dhaka district in the south, Buddhism was an expanding religion in all parts of Pāla period Bengal.[17] In the non-monastic religious space of Bihar and Bengal, the practised form of Buddhism generally emphasized non-esoteric forms.[18] This expansion of Buddhism, however, occurred in a milieu of a more pronounced expansion of Brahmanism in Bihar and Bengal during the same period.[19]

Jainism expanded in some parts of Magadha, Jharkhand and adjoining portions of Bengal (i.e. western parts of Vardhaman district, and all parts of Bankura, Purulia and West Medinipur districts). Brahmanism, on the other hand, barring the tract of Bangladesh bounded by the River Jamuna/Brahmaputra in the west, marshes of Sylhet in east and northern portions of Dhaka district in the south, expanded in all parts of Bihar and Bengal during the eighth-early thirteenth century CE period, leading to a kind of 'universalization' of Brahmanism in these areas during the same period.[20] In this kind of situation, the trajectories of cultic encounters between Buddhism and Brahmanism in early medieval Bihar and Bengal were bound to be different from what has been reconstructed through purely textual studies of Buddhism: Buddhism was not a religion 'waiting to be appropriated' by Brahmanism. There were multiple patterns of cultic encounters between Buddhism and Brahmanism in early medieval Bihar and Bengal, ranging from peaceful coexistence, violent confrontation, and attempted subordinate integration of Brahmanism by Buddhism. Two research articles in the present book, titled 'Cultic Relationships between Buddhism and Brahmanism in the "Last Stronghold" of Indian Buddhism: An Analysis with Particular Reference to Votive Inscriptions on the Brahmanical Sculptures Donated to Buddhist Religious Centres in Early Medieval Magadha' and 'Merchants and Their Family Members as Donors of Inscribed Buddhist and Brahmanical Sculptures in Early Medieval Bihar and Bengal' respectively look into some aspects of these complex cultic encounters. In the context of early medieval Bihar and Bengal, what has been overlooked is the issue: how did the common population, most of which did not have any fixed religious identity, perceive these cultic encounters? Did their perception remain unchanged over a period of time: say from one generation to the next generation? These two papers offer a new interpretation of these issues.

The first research article notes that the attempts of the Buddhist Saṅgha in Magadha to appropriate Brahmanism failed in the long run as this development came at the cost of exposing its own flank for Brahmanical counter-appropriation. In some cases, in the case of family of successful merchants, their commitment to Buddhism would continue from one generation to another; but when an economic decline set in, some of them changed their religious commitment.[21] The process of religious change was more dynamic than what is presented in the existing scholarship on the subject.

The third research article, titled 'Women as Donors of Inscribed Buddhist Sculptures in Early Medieval Bihar and Bengal' looks into the issue of evolution of patterns of female patronage to Buddhist religious centres in early medieval Bihar and Bengal and spatial variations in the same through an analysis of dedicatory inscriptions on Buddhist sculptures donated by women to different Buddhist religious centres of this area. An important spatial variation is discernible. Buddhist religious centres of Magadha made determined efforts of attracting and retaining patronage from such donors. The pattern in the Kiul-Lakhisarai area of Aṅga in South Bihar appears to be similar. In both Magadha and Kiul-Lakhisarai area of Aṅga, women from diverse social backgrounds donated sculptures to Buddhist religious centres as objects of worship. Not unrelatedly, the survival of bhikṣuṇīsaṅgha in the Kiul- Lakhisarai area as late as the late twelfth century CE is attested to in epigraphic records. But the pattern changed to the east of the Kiul-Lakhisarai area in general, and Bengal in particular. In these areas, Buddhist religious centres seem to be reluctant to enter into ritual engagements with their non-monastic non-aristocratic women devotees.

Two other research articles in the present book, titled 'Monarchs, Monasteries and Trade on an "Agrarian Frontier": Early Medieval Samataṭa-Harikela, Bengal' and 'Jaina and Brahmanical Temples and Political Processes in a Forested Frontier of Early Medieval South-Western Bengal: A Study of Purulia' respectively, look into the issue of complex interplay between the processes of agrarian expansion, trade and state formation and its legitimation, and their impact on religious institutions – Buddhist, Brahmanical and Jaina – in two peripheries of early medieval Bengal. These research articles highlight a peculiar feature of the history of religions in early medieval Bengal: while Brahmanical religious institutions were present in all parts of Bengal – in the core, nuclear areas and peripheral areas alike – and Jainism had a significant presence on the tribal frontiers of South-western Bengal, Buddhism lagged behind. Buddhist monasteries, despite being active on the agrarian frontiers of Samataṭa-Harikela, failed to enter into institutional collaboration with the state in the process of agrarian expansion, detribalization and the socio-economic and cultural integration of marshy and forested areas to the core areas of the state. Brahmanical religious institutions, in contrast, were successful in these processes: a factor, which, in the long run, entailed the decline of Buddhism in this area. Similarly, on the tribal frontiers of Purulia area in south-western Bengal, Buddhism was almost absent. Here, in the complex and interrelated developments of state formation, large-scale Jaina and Brahmanical temple construction, and detribalization, both Jaina and Brahmanical temples played significant roles. Political elites of the local state that emerged in this area patronized Śaiva temples, but Jaina temples provided the primary avenue for the legitimation of local heroes dying in battles related to cattle raids, etc. Hero stones were raised in the memory of many such heroes. Jaina temples were more enthusiastic in accolading hero stones in the temple precincts. Jaina temples, thus, served as the primary avenue for the legitimacy of the dead heroes and their surviving family members.

The last research article in the book, titled 'Buddhist Revival in Contemporary Uttar Pradesh, *c.*2005 CE–2011 CE: Some Aspects of Ambedkarite and Ājīvika Discourses on Buddhism and Hinduism in Hindi Print Media', analyses the interrelated processes of socio-political mobilization of some Dalit and Other Backward Classes (OBC) castes, revival of Buddhism, and dissemination of a particular kind of discourse on Buddhism and Hinduism in the most populous province of India. In recent decades, Uttar Pradesh – the most populous province of India, having an enormous clout in national political and cultural discourses – has witnessed significant socio-cultural, religious and political churnings. A significant aspect of this churning has been the attempted revival of Buddhism among a section of Dalit and OBC castes of Uttar Pradesh. This Buddhism, claiming its legitimacy from Gautam Buddha and Dr B.R. Ambedkar, appears to be somewhat different from earlier forms (i.e. Theravāda, Mahāyāna, Vajrayāna, Sahajayāna) of Indian Buddhism, particularly in its relationship with Hinduism. Protagonists of this Buddhist revival, to disseminate their ideas and also to bring more and more people under the fold of this form of Buddhism, have undertaken the publications of books and popular journals, largely on spontaneous basis. Buddhist religious institutions – temples, open-air shrines and *vihāra*s – have also been established. However, another segment of Dalits, not satisfied with Buddhism, are trying to revive another ancient Indian religion – Ājīvika-dharma – albeit with some modification to suit the contemporary circumstances. Protagonists of the Ājīvika revival too have undertaken the publications of books and journals to disseminate their ideas. In this process, protagonists of both religions (Buddhism and Ājīvika-dharma) have offered interesting discourses on Buddhism and Hinduism. In the present paper, an attempt has been made to report some aspects of Ambedkarite and Ājīvika discourses on Buddhism and Hinduism through an analysis of published ideas in some of the books and journals published by such groups. These books and journals are intended for mass-circulation and they are having some fundamental implications for the religious dynamics of the most populous province of contemporary India. This research article, despite having some obvious limitations, attempts to report some glimpses of religious contestations and dialogues in contemporary Uttar Pradesh.[22]

If this book generates future researches, I will consider myself amply rewarded.

NOTES

1. For an analysis of the dedicatory inscription on this sculpture, see Birendra Nath Prasad, 'The Socio-Religious Dimensions of Dedicatory Inscriptions on Sculptures Donated to a Buddhist Establishment in Early Medieval Magadha: Kurkihar, *c*.800-1200 CE', *Journal of the Oxford Centre for Buddhist Studies*, vol. 7, 2014, pp. 121-5. With some

modifications, this article was reprinted in Birendra Nath Prasad, *Rethinking Bihar and Bengal: History, Culture and Religion*, Routledge, London and New York, 2021, pp. 41-84.
Āpaṇaka Mahāvihāra was a part of the Buddhist monastic establishment at the site of Kurkihar in the Gaya district of Bihar. This site deserves a systematic archaeological excavation, though the explored data has been reported and analysed in various publications. See Pratapaditya Pal, 'A Forgotten Monastery of Ancient Bihar', *South Asian Studies,* vol. 4, 1988, pp. 83-8; Birendra Nath Prasad, 'The Socio-Religious Dimensions of Dedicatory Inscriptions on Sculptures Donated to a Buddhist Establishment in Early Medieval Magadha: Kurkihar, *c.*800-1200 CE', *Journal of the Oxford Centre for Buddhist Studies*, vol. 7, 2014, pp. 116-52; Claudine Bautze-Picron, *The Forgotten Place: Stone Images from Kurkihar, Bihar*, Archaeological Survey of India, Delhi, 2015.

2. Pratapaditya Pal, op. cit., p. 86; Birendra Nath Prasad, 'The Socio-Religious Dimensions of Dedicatory Inscriptions on Sculptures Donated to a Buddhist Establishment in Early Medieval Magadha: Kurkihar, *c.*800-1200 CE', *Journal of the Oxford Centre for Buddhist Studies*, vol. 7, 2014, p. 125.
3. Birendra Nath Prasad, *Archaeology of Religion in South Asia: Buddhist, Brahmanical and Jaina Religious Centres in Bihar and Bengal, c.* AD *600-1200*, Routledge, London and New York, 2021, p. 566.
4. This feature has been noted even in the case of the Pāla empire of early medieval Bihar and Bengal. The Pāla dynasty was one of the last major dynasties of India to patronize Buddhism. Most of the kings of this dynasty claimed to be *paramasaugata* in their official copper-plate charters. Yet an overwhelming percentage of their patronage, as recorded in their official copper-plate charters, went in favour of Brahmins (Birendra Nath Prasad, op. cit., pp. 381-489). Not only that, many such *paramasaugata* Pāla kings claimed to be upholders of *varṇāśramadharma* in their copper-plate charters (Suvira Jaiswal, 'Caste, Gender and Ideology in the Making of India', *Social Scientist,* vol. 36, no. 1-2, 2008, p. 16).
5. P.S. Jaini, *Collected Papers on Buddhist Studies,* Motilal Banarsidass, Delhi, 2001, p. 144; K.T.S. Sarao, *The Decline of Buddhism in India: A Fresh Perspective*, Munshiram Manoharlal, New Delhi, 2012, p. 130; Birendra Nath Prasad, 'Evolution of the Patterns of Cultic Encounters

between Buddhism and Brahmanism in the Religious Space of Some Excavated Buddhist Religious Centres of Early Medieval Bihar and Bengal: A Study Based on an Analysis of the Published Archaeological Data', *Religions of South Asia*, vol. 12, no. 3, 2018, p. 319; Birendra Nath Prasad, *Archaeology of Religion in South Asia: Buddhist, Brahmanical and Jaina Religious Centres in Bihar and Bengal, c.AD 600-1200*, Routledge, London and New York, 2021, p. 241.

6. Birendra Nath Prasad, *Archaeology of Religion in South Asia: Buddhist, Brahmanical and Jaina Religious Centres in Bihar and Bengal, c.AD 600-1200*, Routledge, London and New York, 2021, pp. 347, 567, 612.
7. For details, see the research article titled 'Buddhist Revival in Contemporary Uttar Pradesh, *c.*2005 CE–2011 CE: Some Aspects of Ambedkarite and Ājīvika Discourses on Buddhism and Hinduism in Hindi Print Media' in the present book.
8. For a reconstruction of the history of the *Ājīvika*s, see A.L. Basham, *History and the Doctrines of the Ājīvikas: A Vanished Indian Religion*, Motilal Banarsidass, Delhi, 2009 (reprint; originally published in 1951, London). Also see, A.L. Basham, *The Origins and Development of Classical Hinduism*, Motilal Banarsidass, Delhi, 2016, pp. 64–5.
9. For an analysis of the survival of this religion in the Comilla area of eastern Bengal during the fifth and sixth centuries CE, see R. Furui, 'Variegated Adaptations: State Formation in Bengal from the Fifth to the Seventh Century', in B.P. Sahu and H. Kulke (eds.), *Interrogating Political Systems: Integrative Processes and State in Pre-Modern India*, Manohar, Delhi, 2015, pp. 261–2; R. Furui, 'Ājīvikas, Maṇibhadra and Early History of Eastern Bengal: A New Copperplate Inscription of Vainyagupta and Its Implications', *Journal of the Royal Asiatic Society*, vol. 26, no. 4, 2016, pp. 657–81. For an analysis of the history of this religion in Tamil Nadu, see A.L. Basham, *History and the Doctrines of the Ājīvikas: A Vanished Indian Religion*, Motilal Banarsidass, Delhi, 2009, pp. 278–9. Basham has noted that 'Ājīvika ascetics reached the Tamil country probably in the Mauryan period, and the communities which they founded survived at least until the fourteenth century, though often heavily taxed by orthodox kings and village communities' (p. 278).
10. Andre Wink, *Al-Hind: The Making of the Indo-Islamic World*, vol. II, Oxford University Press, Delhi, 1999, pp. 340–50.

11. Ronald M. Davidson, *Indian Esoteric Buddhism: A Social History of the Tantric Movement*, Columbia University Press, New York, 2002, pp. 114-5; K.T.S. Sarao, op. cit., p. 140.
12. R.S. Sharma, *Urban Decay,* Munshiram Manoharlal, Delhi, 1987, p. 131.
13. K.T.S. Sarao, op. cit., pp. 258-9; Kunal Chakrabarti, *Religious Process: The Purāṇas and the Making of a Regional Tradition*, Oxford University Press, New Delhi, 2001, pp. 109-64.
14. N.N. Bhattacharyya, *Buddhism in the History of India Ideas,* Manohar, Delhi, 1993, p. 238.
15. Birendra Nath Prasad, *Archaeology of Religion in South Asia: Buddhist, Brahmanical and Jaina Religious Centres in Bihar and Bengal, c.AD 600-1200,* Routledge, London and New York, 2021, pp. 602-10.
16. Ibid., pp. 602-5.
17. Ibid., pp. 143-230.
18. Ibid., pp. 602-10.
19. Ibid.
20. Ibid., p. 604.
21. And, in contrast, an upwardly mobile peasant in eleventh-century CE Magadha continued to be a person with an expressed Buddhist identity. For details, see Birendra Nath Prasad, 'The Socio-Religious Dimensions of Dedicatory Inscriptions on Sculptures Donated to a Buddhist Establishment in Early Medieval Magadha: Kurkihar, *c.*800-1200 CE', *Journal of the Oxford Centre for Buddhist Studies*, vol. 7, 2014, pp. 142-3.
22. Some limitations of my present article on Buddhist revival in contemporary Uttar Pradesh must be put on record here only. I do not claim that I have gone through all such books and journals. The books and journals referred to in my article have been published mostly through individual initiative of different persons. I could access only some of them, so the inferences I arrived at are tentative in nature. I also put it on record here that my aim is basically to report what others have written and published. I, in no way, intend to comment on their truth or falsity, moral excellence or otherwise. Nor do I intend to hurt the sentiments of any individual, group or caste. My reportage, far from being complete or exhaustive, rather, reflects my very modest effort towards introducing the potentials of such materials to the

English-language speaking intelligentsia, with the hope that someone in future will take up a detailed study of religious and social transitions northern India is undergoing now. To the best of my knowledge, these materials are largely unknown to the English-language speaking intelligentsia.

2

Cultic Relationships between Buddhism and Brahmanism in the 'Last Stronghold' of Indian Buddhism

An Analysis with Particular Reference to Votive Inscriptions on the Brahmanical Sculptures Donated to Buddhist Religious Centres in Early Medieval Magadha[1]

Introduction

Buddhism, it has been rightly argued, contains a hierarchy of teachings and it has co-existed with other systems in a structured hierarchy.[2] It may be added that the relative positioning of elements in this 'structured hierarchy' and fluctuations in this evolved with the interplay of various interrelated processes: socio-economic and religious. Buddhism, being just one of the religious systems in the poly-religious landscape of India, had to negotiate the presence of other religious systems in general and Brahmanism in particular. It also had to negotiate various animistic cults, which formed an important part of the religious life of ancient and early medieval India. Trajectories of its encounters with animistic cults and Brahmanism were not uniform in different parts of India. That is true even in the context of early medieval Bihar and Bengal. Within these, Magadha offers a particular kind of encounter between Buddhism and Brahmanism: it was only in Magadha where we see a regular donation of inscribed Brahmanical sculptures to Buddhist religious institutions by those donors who have recorded their names in such inscriptions. At the available stage of our knowledge and database for early medieval Bihar and Bengal, this practice largely appears to be a Magadha-specific phenomenon.[3] This development in the 'last stronghold of Indian Buddhism'[4] raises some interesting questions regarding cultic relationships between Buddhism and Brahmanism. In this paper, an attempt will be made to understand such cultic relationships through the prism of dedicatory inscriptions on Brahmanical sculptures donated to Buddhist religious centres in early medieval Magadha. Most of such sculptures have been discovered in definite archaeological contexts: in archaeological excavations and explorations within or nearby important monastic centres, so they can be correlated with developments within important Buddhist religious centres of Magadha (Nālandā, Bodh-Gayā and Kurkihar) with greater certainty. We will also try to situate our analysis in the theoretical debate on the ritual aspects of the decline of Indian Buddhism in eastern India.[5]

Cultic Relationships between Buddhism and Brahmanism in Early Medieval India: A Historiographical Overview

Broadly speaking, four models have been postulated for the cultic relationship between Buddhism and Brahmanism during the early medieval period (*c.*600–1200 CE): peaceful coexistence; congenital incompatibility and protracted conflict between Buddhism and Brahmanism till the final 'defeat' of Buddhism by Brahmanism; Brahmanical appropriation of a passive Buddhism; and the Buddhist attempts of integrating rival religions in a manner of subordinate union through the agency of the Saṅgha. We shall analyse these models briefly.

The first model, advocated by R.C. Mitra and Rama Chatterjee, emphasizes the peaceful coexistence of Buddhism and Brahmanism, and frequent borrowing of cultural idioms and practices between the two.[6] To some extent, this appears to be true in the context of early medieval Bihar and Bengal, where we see a simultaneous presence and expansion of both religions in most of the sub-regions. We have noted the same thing in the archaeological landscape of big monastic centres such as Nālandā.[7] This feature has been noted even in a village that was officially donated to the Nālandā Mahāvihāra,[8] or in the archaeological landscape of Bodh-Gayā.[9] But the simultaneous presence and expansion of these religions does not negate the possibility of sectarian rivalry and conflict.

The second model, advocated by Gail Omvedt, D.C. Ahir and G. Verardi, postulates that Buddhism and Brahmanism had some congenital incompatibility due to their differing attitudes to the institution of caste, hence peaceful co-existence was out of question.[10] They were in a state of protracted conflict in which Buddhism was finally 'defeated' and destroyed due to many factors. In the context of early medieval Bihar and Bengal, while not denying the possibility of sectarian confrontation and rivalries, the theory of 'congenital incompatibility' and 'protracted conflict to the finish of Buddhism' does not appear to be tenable. Had confrontation been the only element in the encounters between Buddhism and Brahmanism and had 'congenital incompatibility' been such a pronounced phenomenon, Buddhist institutions in early medieval Magadha would not have accepted inscribed Brahmanical sculptures in the first place.

The third model is provided by those scholars who, while not negating the elements of conflict and sectarian rivalries between Buddhism and Brahmanism, place more emphasis on the peaceful Brahmanical appropriation and assimilation of a largely passive Buddhism.[11] Buddhism did not even attempt a counter-appropriation of Brahmanical deities, perhaps being incapable of doing so, to guard its own ritual and institutional identity vis-à-vis a hegemonic and assimilative Brahmanism. The question was not *whether* Buddhism would be appropriated by Brahmanism but *when* it would be appropriated, as its eventual assimilation into Brahmanism was just a matter of time.[12] This argument is erroneous. We should not believe that Buddhism was totally incapable of attempting an appropriation of Brahmanical deities. As we shall see later in the present essay, Buddhism did try to do this in early medieval Magadha.

The fourth model is provided by those scholars who, while accepting the elements of conflict and sectarian rivalries between Buddhism and Brahmanism, do not treat Buddhism as a dormant, passive recipient of Brahmanical hegemonic appropriation and eventual assimilation.[13] Buddhist institutions attempted a similar appropriation of Brahmanical deities through the concept of *maṇḍala.* If the cult of some Hindu deity was very popular in a particular area, efforts were made to integrate the cult into Buddhism through a policy of subordinate integration, portraying the relevant deity as an attendant of the Buddha, performing some mundane tasks for Buddhism.

One of the best examples of this process is provided by the evolution of the cult of 'Buddhist Viṣṇu' in medieval Sri Lanka, which has been brilliantly analysed by John Clifford Holt.[14] Given the significance of the paradigm developed by John Clifford Holt in understanding the evolution of cultic encounters between Buddhism and Brahmanism in early medieval Magadha, it is imperative to analyse his study in some detail. Holt has argued that the penetration of the cult of Viṣṇu in Sri Lanka was a collateral development of the conquest of parts of Sri Lanka by the Chola rulers of Tamil Nadu. But Viṣṇu could not become a major figure in the Sinhala religious life until the early eleventh century when Sri Lanka regained its sovereignty from the Hindu Tamils of Tamil Nadu. Tamil rule on the island implanted certain ideas of kingship, which the Sinhala rulers tried to assert even after regaining sovereignty. The Sinhala kings began to style themselves as avatars of Viṣṇu, in continuation of Hindu notions of kingship, while retaining the traditional Buddhist archetype of a king being the defender and regulator of the (Buddhist) Dharma. This entailed invitations to the Brahmin priests to consecrate the semi-divine status of the Sinhalese monarchy. Popularization of the cult of Viṣṇu was the natural corollary. Despite the initial monastic antipathy to the popularization of the cult of Viṣṇu, veneration of Viṣṇu was a firmly entrenched phenomenon in the Sinhala culture by the end of the sixteenth century. It was embraced by the great majority of Buddhist monks and Sinhala peasantry. The Saṅgha, as a means of safeguarding the institutional and ritual identity of Buddhism, embarked upon the task of establishing a subordinate union and eventual appropriation of Viṣṇu. Viṣṇu was made the protector of the (Buddhist) Dharma, but stripped of any soteriological significance. Thus, the Sinhala Buddhist theology reduced Viṣṇu to the material domain, identifying him with such mundane things as the ability to cure sickness and exorcise evil spirits, and the conferring of boons. Thus, by the end of the sixteenth century, as Holt has shown, 'Viṣṇu's powers have not been reconceived in the process; rather they seem to have been reoriented and placed at the service of the Buddhist worldview'.[15] Holt's analysis, thus, indicates that Buddhism was not bereft of the capacity to integrate rival religions and cults in a manner of subordinate union. This must be, however, put on record that the success or failure of this process depended on many socio-economic factors also.

This process of subordinate integration may not have been peaceful in all cases. In some, as we see in the imagery of Trailokyavijaya, Saṁvara and Aparājitā, a powerful Brahmanical deity was portrayed as submitting to Buddhism after a violent conflict with a Buddhist deity. This was just the first step in their eventual integration into Buddhism in a manner of subordinate union. It has been claimed that:

> The process can be understood as having three steps. First, the Saṅgha questioned the existence of these Brāhmaṇa gods and the utility of worshipping them. Second, it degraded and insulted them by considering them the source of all evil, and often had them killed by a minor Buddhist deity.

And third, a Buddhist deity would then revive them, and accord them a respectable albeit subordinate position within the Buddhist pantheon.[16]

Once integrated into the Buddhist pantheon in a manner of subordinate union, these Brahmanical deities, as brilliantly analysed by Claudine Bautze-Picron, were supposed to perform an important function in Buddhism as 'Buddhist deities'. It is imperative to quote Claudine Bautze-Picron here:

> The Hindu gods are perceived as demons and as such they are conquered by the Buddha, which allows them to go back to their original divine nature. They go through a similar experience when they are trampled by Buddhist ferocious deities who assimilate their divine power by mastering them: their destruction becomes positive inasmuch as they are assimilated by the one who tramples them and inasmuch as their dark aspects are destroyed. For the frightening and eventful sculptures of great Buddhist gods lead the path to and open the ways to Enlightenment. These Hindu gods thus share an ambivalent nature. They are at the threshold of two worlds: the one being the Buddhist way, symbolized by the inner mansions of the *maṇḍala*s which they have to protect from the second where chaos rules. Similarly, the Hindu gods occupy the outer mansions of the *maṇḍala*s and combine both the wildness and ignorance of the external world and peace of the inner world.[17]

Which Brahmanical deity would be peacefully made the attendant of some Buddhist deity, and which deity would be made to submit to Buddhism after a violent confrontation? Among many factors, this would also be influenced by the popularity of the cult of a Brahmanical deity in a particular area. Thus, in the context of some Buddhist sculptures of south-eastern Bengal, where the cult of Durgā was very strong, it has been observed that 'Durgā is included among the Hindu deities that attack the Buddha'.[18] But in the context of early medieval Magadha, where Śaivism had a diffused presence, rendering it to be the main competitor of Buddhism, it is the family of Śiva (Śiva, Pārvatī or Gaṇeśa) that is shown to be trampled upon by Buddhist deities (Trailokyavijaya,

Saṁvara or Aparājitā). But Indra or Brahmā, who were no match to Śaiva deities in terms of actual following among the masses in early medieval Magadha, could be directly relegated to the position of attendant deities of the Buddha in Buddhist sculptures.[19]

Let us recapitulate. These studies expect us to believe that whenever the image of a non-Buddhist deity was donated to a Buddhist institution, and whenever the Saṅgha accepted such a donation, it was generally motivated by the desire for a Buddhist maṇḍalic appropriation of the cults of rival deities.

The same logic has been extended to the pattern of interactions between Buddhism and various animistic cults: Buddhism, as an institutional religion, would attempt a hegemonic appropriation of animistic (Nāga, etc.) and local cults,[20] which would, after being integrated to Buddhism in a subordinate capacity, lose their status of independent cults. Animistic deities would become attendants of the Buddha or some other Buddhist deity or they would be transformed into 'protector deities', guarding and protecting Buddhist religious institutions at vital points.[21]

These studies, giving a vivid picture of attempts of cultic appropriation and counter-appropriation by both Buddhism and Brahmanism, somehow miss a vital element of the whole matrix: the common person who generally did not have any fixed religious identity. Buddhism and Brahmanism tried to appropriate each other and Buddhist sculptures depicted Brahmanical deities in attendant positions or as trampled upon figures. Buddhist institutions also accepted donation of Brahmanical sculptures from common persons to accomplish a subordinate integration of the cult of these deities to Buddhism. But what was the perception of the person who actually donated these sculptures? Did he/she donate these sculptures as representatives of a subordinated cult? Or did he/she donate them as representatives of independent cults? It is in addressing this question that the role of epigraphy becomes important. Hence, we will now examine in some detail votive inscriptions on Brahmanical sculptures donated to Buddhist institutions in early medieval Magadha.

Epigraphy and the Questions of the Cultic Identity of Donors of Sculptures and the Subordinate Integration of Non-Buddhist Deities to Buddhism

In the context of early historic and early medieval Indian Buddhism, epigraphic sources have generally been used for the reconstruction of the evolving patronage base of Buddhist religious institutions.[22] In some other cases, we see an interesting use of dedicatory inscriptions on sculptures in reconstructing religious affiliations, identities and expectations of donors of sculptures.[23] We also see the use of dedicatory inscriptions on sculptures in tracing the evolution of a particular cult or tradition within Buddhism.[24] Schopen's studies of the dedicatory inscriptions on Buddhist sculptures have convincingly shown that many traditions within Buddhism devised their own dedicatory formulas to be recorded in votive inscriptions on sculptures. The adoption of a particular form of dedicatory formula in votive inscriptions on Buddhist sculptures was generally not an eclectic choice on the part of the donor, but a conscious adherence to a particular tradition of Buddhism. Thus, in the dedicatory formula on the sculptures donated by those donors who opted to identify themselves as the followers of the Mahāyāna, there are recorded some characteristic technical and definitive words. In many inscriptions, they recorded themselves as *pravara-mahāyāna-anuyāyina* (follower of the excellent Mahāyāna). In many cases, the donor did not categorically identify himself/herself as *pravara-mahāyāna-anuyāyin*, but the occurrence of some characteristic technical, and definitive, words indicated that the donor wished to be identified as a follower of the Mahāyāna. Schopen has noted that in dedicatory inscriptions on sculptures, the words *paramopāsaka* and *paramopāsikā* respectively signified a man and a woman who was a Mahāyāna lay worshipper. Similarly, *śākyabhikṣu* and *śākyabhikṣuṇī* signified a Mahāyāna monk and nun respectively.[25] Similarly, the expression of the aim of attainment of *anuttara jñāna* by all sentient beings, the donor's parents, or the donor him/herself was almost exclusive to the Mahāyāna dedicatory formula on sculptures.[26] Similar was the case with the formula *yad atra puṇyama*, which was 'virtually the exclusive property of Mahāyāna'.[27]

It may be noted that in the dedicatory inscriptions on the Buddhist sculptures of early medieval Bihar and Bengal, generally whenever a donor wished to identify himself/herself with any tradition of Buddhism, that tradition happened to be Mahāyāna. That remained the case till the very end of this period. In such cases, we may discern the Mahāyāna affiliation of the donor either directly (by the use of the title *pravara-mahāyāna-anuyāyin* by the donor) or indirectly (by the use of the technical words *paramopāsaka*, *paramopāsikā*, *śākyabhikṣu* and *śākyabhikṣuṇī* by the donor). That remained the situation even in the case of donation of those sculptures which may be technically designated as Vajrayāna sculptures. The word 'Vajrayāna' did not occur even once in the corpus of dedicatory inscriptions on sculptures of early medieval Bihar and Bengal, nor did a Vajrayāna dedicatory formula ever evolve.[28]

The same remained the situation even in the context of the donation of inscribed Brahmanical images donated in Buddhist contexts. If the donor wished to be identified as a follower of the Mahāyāna, he/she generally used the Mahāyāna dedicatory format. If a donor wished to identify himself/herself as a follower of Mahāyāna Buddhism (either as a monk/nun or a lay worshipper), he/she either claimed to be a *pravara-mahāyāna-anuyāyin* or used the technical words *śākyabhikṣu/śākyabhikṣuṇī/paramopāsaka/paramopāsikā*. Or the stated motive for donating the image was for the attainment of *anuttara jñāna* by all sentient beings, the donor's parents, or the donor him/herself.

Besides, when the subordinate integration of an animistic cult to Buddhism was attempted, that was generally reflected in the dedicatory inscription on such sculptures: in such cases, as has been shown in the case of early historic Mathurā where we have many examples of the donation of Nāga sculptures and figurines to Buddhist institutions, these sculptures were generally inscribed with a Buddhist dedicatory formula.[29] Similarly, if some Brahmanical deity-image was donated in a Buddhist context — as of a deity integrated to Buddhism in manner of subordinate union — that was also reflected in the dedicatory inscription on the sculpture. In such cases, the donated sculpture was inscribed with the dedicatory formula of some Buddhist tradition. One of the best examples in this context, is provided by the inscription on a sculpture of Gaṇeśa, datable to *c.*952 CE, that was discovered at Mandhuka in the Comilla district of eastern Bengal: the dedicatory inscription on this sculpture records that it was donated for the purpose of the attainment of *anuttara jñāna* by the parents of the donor. This goal (attainment of *anuttara jñāna* by a donor's parents) is generally met in the developed form of Mahāyāna dedicatory inscriptions on sculptures.[30] In some cases, only the Buddhist Creed Formula (*ye dharmā hetu-prabhavā hetunteṣān tathāgatohyavadatteṣāñca yo nirodha evamvādi mahāśramaṇaḥ*) was inscribed on a non-Buddhist deity. We may consider the example of a sculpture of Haragaurī that was discovered at Sringirikh near Kajara in the Munger district of Bihar. This Śaiva sculpture was inscribed with the Buddhist Creed Formula.[31] It is apparent that this is an example of an attempted Buddhist appropriation of the cult of a Śaiva deity.

Let us summarize our arguments now. In the context of inscribed Brahmanical sculptures donated to different Buddhist religious centres of early medieval Magadha, we will not consider any inscribed Brahmanical image as Buddhistic unless it is inscribed either with the Buddhist Creed Formula or it includes the dedicatory formula of some Buddhist tradition. In early medieval Bihar and Bengal, where the Mahāyāna dedicatory formula was generally the most prevalent form in votive inscriptions on Buddhist sculptures, we may legitimately expect its use in the dedicatory inscriptions on those sculptures whose donors did wish to be identified as followers of the Mahāyāna. In general, we may expect to find the use of any of the characteristic terms (*pravara-mahāyāna-anuyāyin, paramopāsaka, paramopāsikā, śākyabhikṣu, śākyabhikṣuṇī*) or motive (for the attainment of *anuttara jñāna*) for undertaking the donation of an image by them.

One more issue should be addressed here. Most of the dedicatory inscriptions on the Brahmanical sculptures donated to Buddhist religious centres in early medieval Magadha record that donated images were the *deyadharma* of different donors. From the Gupta period onwards, this term (*deyadharma*) was used in the donation of Buddhist sculptures.[32] But in early medieval Bihar and Bengal, this term was used in the donation of both Buddhist and Brahmanical sculptures. Hence, the mere occurrence of this term in the dedicatory inscription on a sculpture will not be sufficient to brand the sculpture Buddhist.

This discussion provides us the necessary background for understanding the significance of dedicatory inscriptions on the Brahmanical sculptures donated to some of the Buddhist institutions in early medieval Magadha.

Votive Inscriptions on Brahmanical Sculptures Donated to Buddhist Religious Establishments in Early Medieval Magadha: The Evolving Pattern

So far, eleven inscribed Brahmanical sculptures donated to different Buddhist religious centres in early medieval Magadha have been reported. Three sculptures have been attributed to Nālandā, one to the Mahābodhi area of Bodh-Gayā, and seven to Kurkihar. At Kurkihar, these sculptures occur with striking consistency: for every century, there is reported at least one such sculpture here. Barring the ninth century example, Bodh-Gayā has not reported any other inscribed image of the previous or later centuries. If we see the cultic breakdown of such sculptures, we have three inscribed sculptures of Viṣṇu; two of Sūrya; three of Balarāma; and two of Umāmaheśvara. Also, one inscribed sculpted lintel contains the depictions of Śiva, Sūrya, Viṣṇu and Lakulīśa.

The practice of donation of inscribed Brahmanical sculptures to Buddhist monasteries was not confined to any particular section of society. We see the donation of such sculptures by a senior Buddhist monk on behalf of a non-monastic member; by a royal officer; by the wife of a village chief; by a member of a 'low' caste (*charmakāra*); by the son of a sculptor, and also by a blacksmith. That is to say, this trend permeated practically all sections of contemporary society. Theatres of such donations were among the most important centres of early medieval Indian Buddhism: Nālandā, Mahābodhi and Kurkihar.

A brief summary of votive inscriptions on such sculptures have been provided in Table 1.

The first instance of donation of an inscribed Brahmanical sculpture to a Buddhist institution in early medieval Magadha is provided by the votive inscription on a sculpture of Sūrya that was discovered at Shahpur in the modern Nālandā district. This inscription is dated to the year 66, probably of the Harṣa era. In this inscription, we are informed that Sālapakṣa, the *balādhikṛta*, installed this sculpture as *deyadharma* in the great *agrahāra* of Nālandā (*nālandā mahāgrahāre*) for the purpose of increasing the religious merit of himself and his parents.[33] This is the only one of the inscriptions listed in Table 1 in which a motive for the donation is expressed. This inscription refers to the regime of Ādityasenadeva. The donor was apparently serving under this king.

Here two things must be considered. The first recorded instance of donation of any sculpture to the Nālandā Mahāvihāra is this one, and it records the donation of a Brahmanical sculpture. Nālandā has not been referred to as a *vihāra* or *mahāvihāra*, but as a great *agrahāra* (*mahā-agrahāra*). This word (*agrahāra*) is, undoubtedly, of

TABLE 1: INSCRIPTIONS ON BRAHMANICAL SCULPTURES DONATED TO BUDDHIST RELIGIOUS ESTABLISHMENTS IN EARLY MEDIEVAL MAGADHA

	Cultic affiliation of the sculpture	*The place where the sculpture was discovered*	*Donor*	*Social back-ground of the donor*	*Places where donors came from*	*Period*
1.	Sūrya	Shahpur, in modern Nalanda district	Sālapakṣa, the *balādhikṛta*	A royal official	–	Year 66 (of the Harṣa era??), i.e. 672–3 CE?)
2.	A sculpted lintel containing the depictions of Śiva, Sūrya, Viṣṇu and Lakulīśa	Mahābodhi area, Bodh-Gayā	Śaka	Son of a sculptor Sāyanabhara	–	*c.*809–10 CE
3.	Balarāma	Nālandā	By Mahāthera Da or Ujjaka, for Padmadāna-siṁha	Monk	–	The regime of Devapāladeva (first half of ninth century)

4.	Balarāma	Excavated out of the northern veranda of Monastery Site No. 1, Nālandā.	Nisiṅghikā, wife of Śauje	–	Mallapore	Ninth century
5.	Balarāma	Kurkihar	Ajhuka	Rural aristocracy (wife of a village chief)	Madhugrāma in Vāhiravana	in the 9th RY of Devapāla, *c.*819 CE
6.	Viṣṇu	Kurkihar	*Charmakāra* Thisavī	Probably from untouchable background	–	The year 12 of Surapāla (i.e. second half of the ninth century)
7.	Umāmaheśvara	Kurkihar	Mulūka, wife of Gopala Mahiaru	–	–	The year 32 of Rājyapāla, *c.* 935 CE
8.	Sūrya	Kurkihar	Padaka, son of Bhaṭa	–	Not mentioned	Eleventh century
9.	Viṣṇu	Kurkihar	Subalamati	–	–	Eleventh century
10.	Umāmaheśvara	Kurkihar	Kalāṇḍa	–	–	Twelfth century
11.	Viṣṇu	Kurkihar	Mangane	A blacksmith (*karmakāra*)	–	Twelfth century

Source: Table prepared by the author by collating data from earlier publications.

Brahmanical origin and it generally referred to the tax-free land granted to an individual Brahmin or a group of Brahmins. It is apparent that for the donor, there was hardly any difference between this Buddhist *mahāvihāra* and a *mahā-agrahāra*. This was the perception of at least one donor regarding the nature of the *mahāvihāra*. The *mahāvihāra* accepted this donation in a phase when Brahmanical sculptures were quite rare in the archaeological landscape of Nālandā.[34] But also in the seventh century, the *mahāvihāra* accepted not only the donation of a Brahmanical sculpture by a non-monastic member, but incorporated Brahmanical themes and sculptures in its monastic architecture also: on the outer walls of the Temple Site 2 of the *mahāvihāra*.[35] This iconographic programme has been explained as an example of a Buddhist attempt at maṇḍalic appropriation of rival cults.[36] One may be tempted to offer the same reasoning in the acceptance of the donation of the sculpture of Sūrya donated by Sālapakṣa. We don't know why the *mahāvihāra* needed to be so active in a phase when Brahmanical sculptures were yet to proliferate in the immediate neighbourhood of Nālandā. True, Nālandā Mahāvihāra was not a local institution and it had to respond to distant (pan-Indian) challenges as well, hence this attempt at maṇḍalic appropriation. This attempt, of course, could evoke an altogether different impression for persons like Sālapakṣa, who perceived the *mahāvihāra* as not radically different from contemporary Brahmanical religious institutions. Sālapakṣa donated this sculpture as the representative of an independent cult. He did not donate it as the image of a deity of a cult that was being or to be integrated into Buddhism in a relationship of subordinate integration. That was quite natural from a person who did not claim to be a committed lay follower of Buddhism.

The second example of donation of an inscribed Brahmanical sculpture to a Buddhist institution in early medieval Magadha is provided by the votive inscription on a sculpted lintel that was discovered amidst the ruins of the Mahābodhi by Alexander Cunningham. This lintel contained depictions of Sūrya, Viṣṇu and

Lakulīśa, so we may assume that this might have formed part of a Brahmanical temple or the outer walls of a Buddhist structure. This inscription is dated to the 26th regnal year of the Pāla king Dharmapāla. Given the importance of this inscription, it is important to quote it fully:

For the endless virtue, and for the good of the inhabitants of the Mahābodhi, an image of the four-faced Mahādeva was consecrated by Saka, the son of the noble sculptor Sāyanabhara (?). A tank, holy as the river born of the feet of Viṣṇu, was also excavated by him at a cost of three thousand *dramas*[37] in the 26th year of the great king Dharmapāla.[38]

R.R. Mukheji and S.K. Maity's reading of the inscription is a little different, but they too have noted that this sculpture was installed for the benefit of the monks of the Mahābodhi.[39] This inscription is one of the biggest evidences of the penetration of Brahmanical cults to the holiest of Buddhist shrines. At Mahābodhi, a sculpture of Śiva was installed, 'for the good of the inhabitants of the Mahābodhi' by invoking the name of the ruling Pāla king who took pride in being *paramasaugata* (great devotee of the Buddha). A tank was also constructed for the benefit of the monks of the Mahābodhi by mobilizing a sum of money by the donor. This could have been very useful in a dry region like Gaya. But this tank too was described in a typical Brahmanical motif (*viṣṇupadīsamā*).

The significance of this inscription has been read in different ways, as an indication of: the religious tolerance of the ruling Pāla king and the peaceful coexistence of Buddhism and Brahmanism, even at the holiest Buddhist spot; the multi-religious character of the sacred site of Bodh-Gayā;[40] the superimposition of Śaivism on a Buddhist site;[41] and, recently, as an attempt at the Buddhist maṇḍalic appropriation of Śaivism[42]. As we have analysed the theories of peaceful coexistence of Buddhism and Brahmanism, and multi-religious character of the sacred sites of Indian Buddhism in the previous section, let us now analyse the arguments of Mishra and Amar.

In framing his arguments, Mishra has not taken into account the social background of the donor of this sculpted piece. Son of an ordinary sculptor, without any kind of backing by the state, he could hardly have the power to forcefully impose a Śaiva cult on the holiest of Buddhist spots. So, the theory of 'superimposition of Śaivism on a Buddhist site' is not sustainable. That leaves us with the issue of attempted Buddhist maṇḍalic appropriation of Śaivism. Let's see this proposition in some detail. It has been claimed that:

> Previous studies have failed to analyse the inscription's context or its implications for Buddhist–Śaiva relations. Why did the monastic centre at Bodh-Gayā allow the installation of a four-faced Mahādeva and a lintel with other Brahmanical gods within the Mahābodhi complex? A contextual reading of the inscription suggests that the Buddhist *saṅgha* attempted to appropriate Śiva and Śaivism within their own order. This was widely practised within Buddhist monastic complexes and village-shrines, the installation of statues of Umāmaheśvara within the Buddhist shrines being deliberately undertaken to prove Buddhist superiority and the subordination of Śiva as a lay-follower.[43]

This is another example of Saṅgha-centric historiography. For the Buddhist Saṅgha, acceptance of this sculpture could have been a method of appropriating Śaivism in a relationship of subordinate union. But what about the donor? Was he even remotely aware that he was donating a sculpture whose cult was to be reduced to the position of a subsidiary cult of Buddhism? If we read the inscription, the opposite appears to be the case. The donor was not only proud of his Śaiva leanings, but was also attempting to do some favour to the Buddhist monks of Mahābodhi by installing this sculpture 'for the good of the inhabitants of the Mahābodhi'. This is what he inscribed on the sculpture.

In our third example from Table 1, the votive inscription on a sculpture of Balarāma that was discovered during the excavation of the Nālandā monastic complex, we have unmistakable evidence of a senior monk donating and installing a Brahmanical sculpture on behalf of a donor from a non-aristocratic background. This inscription, datable to the regime of Devapāla, records that this sculpture of Balarāma was a gift from Mahāthera Dajjaka or Ujjaka and was made for Padmadānasiṁha.[44] We don't see the use of titles such as *paramopāsaka* or *mahāyāna-anuyāyina* for Padmadānasiṁha, so we may assume that he was not willing to be identified as a lay follower of Buddhism. Nothing has been recorded of the social background of Padmadānasiṁha. Those donors who have not recorded their social status in dedicatory inscriptions were most probably from the non-aristocratic, non-monastic section of society, so we may assign the same status to Padmadānasiṁha. Mahāthera Dajjaka or Ujjaka could have hoped to actualize a subordinate integration of the cult of Balarāma and expected to attract donations from the followers of this cult to the Nālandā Mahāvihāra. But for many common persons, this could have resulted in the blurring of institutional boundaries between Buddhism and Brahmanism.

If the previous inscription indicates a close cooperation between a Buddhist monk and a common person in the installation of a Brahmanical sculpture within the Mahāvihāra, another inscription (Table 1, no. 4) on a bronze sculpture of Balarāma, which was excavated out of the northern veranda of the Monastery Site No.1, Nālandā, reveals another important trend: independent initiative of a woman in donating a Brahmanical sculpture to the monastery. We are informed that Nisinghikā, wife of Śoujeka, who probably belonged to Mallapore, donated this sculpture as her *deyadharma* at Nālandā.[45] Nālandā is referred to by her as *śrī-dēvapāladēva-haṭṭa*.[46]

What are the implications of the installation of this Brahmanical sculpture in the northern veranda of the Monastery Site no. 1, an important monastery within the *mahāvihāra*, where the resident monks must have encountered it regularly? A woman, who has not even claimed to be a lay follower of Buddhism (no such title as *paramopāsikā*, etc., has been used for her), donated it to the *mahāvihāra* and the *mahāvihāra* accepted it due to diverse factors, either to attempt a maṇḍalic appropriation of this cult; or simply not to show disrespect to an entrenched religious tradition of the area. There was, presumably, no compulsion on the part of the authorities of the *mahāvihāra* to install this sculpture, or to allow the installation of this sculpture, at a place where monks had to encounter it day and night. In the maṇḍalic schema, figures of appropriated cults are generally placed on the outer periphery of monastic architecture. This does not appear to be the case here, as this inscribed sculpture is installed deep inside the monastery. One wonders if it represented a case of ritual concession to the laity or a deep penetration of Brahmanical deities into the 'greatest centre for Buddhist learning' during the regime of those kings who officially claimed to be *paramasaugata*s.

Another example of the installation of a sculpture of Balarāma in an important Buddhist monastery through non-monastic initiative is shown by the votive inscription on a sculpture of Balarāma discovered at Kurkihar (Table 1, no. 5). This inscription, dated to the ninth regnal year of the Pāla king Devapāla, records that this sculpture was donated to Mallapore (possibly a monastery) by the wife of Sidhmaka, who was a resident of Saddhu village in Vāhiravana.[47] Sidhmaka appears to be a village chief.[48] Mallapore may refer to some Buddhist establishment at Kurkihar.

It was not the case that only the privileged members of society donated inscribed Brahmanical sculptures to Buddhist institutions in early medieval Magadha. The votive inscription on a stone sculpture of Viṣṇu (Table 1, no. 6), probably discovered at Kurkihar, but now kept in the Gaya Museum, informs us that this sculpture was the *deyadharma* of *charmakāra* (cobbler) Thisavī at the illustrious Āpaṇaka during the twelfth regnal year of the Pāla king Surapāla.[49]

A similar pattern is visible in a votive inscription on a metal sculpture of Umāmaheśvara (Table 1, no. 7), dated the 31st or 32nd regnal year of the Pāla king Rājyapāla. This sculpture was discovered at Kurkihar. Its inscription states that it was the religious gift of Mulakā, the wife of Mahiaru, who was a resident of the Āpaṇaka

Mahāvihāra (*śrīmada-āpaṇaka-mahāvihāre–vāstavya-mahiaru-bhāryā-mulakāya-devadharmakṛtama*).[50] The question which demands some explanation is: in what capacity was a married man living in the monastery? Was he an *ārāmika,* a person associated with the management of the monastery? This inscription doesn't throw any light on this issue, but it has nothing to suggest that the donor had any notion that the sculpture was that of a cult figure that was to be integrated into Buddhism in a subordinate capacity.

Evidences of donation of inscribed Brahmanical sculptures to Buddhist religious centres in eleventh- and twelfth-century Magadha are confined to Kurkihar (Table 1, nos. 8-11). Donors have generally not left any detail of their social background, but we may assume that they were from non-aristocratic and non-monastic backgrounds. None of them has opted to assume an explicit Buddhist identity in dedicatory inscriptions. In all probability, these images were donated as representatives of independent cults. Subalamati, the donor of the image of Viṣṇu (no. 9), has not left any detail of his/her social background, so much so that we are not even sure of the gender of the donor.[51] The dedicatory inscription on an image of Sūrya (no. 8) records that this image was the *deyadharmma* of Bhaṭaputra-Padaka.[52] We are not sure if 'Bhaṭaputra' is an incorrect rendering of 'Bhaṭṭaputra' (son of a Bhaṭṭa, a title commonly used by the Brahmins). During the twelfth century, we see the donation of an image of Viṣṇu (no. 11) by a blacksmith (*karmakāra*) named Mangane.[53] That is evidence of flow of artisanal patronage to the monastic complex of Kurkihar. Kalāṇḍa, the donor of an image of Umāmaheśvara (no. 10)[54] has also not left any detail of his/her social background.

Conclusion

Before we wrap up this chapter, we may proffer some tentative generalizations. One may note that, barring the example of Mahāthera Dajjaka or Ujjaka, none of the donors — including the wife of a resident of a monastery — has claimed a Buddhist identity: none of the donors has claimed *paramopāsaka/paramopāsikā* or *mahāyāna-anuyāyina* status for himself/herself. In none of the cases was the attainment of *anuttara jñāna* the stated motive for undertaking the donation of image. None of the inscriptions betray any influence of the dedicatory formula of any other Buddhist tradition. Similarly, no Buddhist influence is visible in their names either. Most probably, these donors did not have any fixed religious identity. For them, there was hardly any perceived institutional or cultic differentiation between Buddhism and Brahmanism cults. They donated these sculptures as independent cult figures and not as representative of cults that were to be integrated into Buddhism in a manner of subordinate union. In the long run, the end result was somewhat similar to what Kunal Chakrabarti has argued on the basis of analysis of textual sources of early medieval Bengal:

> In popular understanding, Buddhist and Brahmanical icons came to perform the same function. Even in the realm of underlying metaphysical premises, Tantricism brought the Buddhist and Brahmanical ways of worship close. When both the religions began to receive royal patronage irrespective of the personal faiths of the rulers, it carried the universal message that the differences between them, if any, were marginal and that both were entitled to be venerated in almost equal manner.[55]

On the whole, these inscriptions indicate an increasing chasm between the expectations of the Saṅgha and the end result that was produced by its decision to allow the installation of these Brahmanical sculptures in important Buddhist centres of early medieval Magadha. The Saṅgha expected to induce a Buddhist maṇḍalic appropriation of Brahmanical cults, but for the masses this development indicated a gradual blurring of ritual and institutional boundaries between Buddhism and Brahmanism. The eventual result, for the common masses, was a slow metamorphosis of Buddhism. With the Turkic destruction of big monastic centres of Magadha and elsewhere in Bihar and Bengal, Buddhism was left without any institutional nucleus to resist its slide towards merger in the popular mind with various animistic and Brahmanical cults.[56]

Attempting a subordinate integration of Brahmanical deities to Buddhism by accepting the donation of inscribed Brahmanical sculptures in early medieval Magadha was an ambitious, and adventurous endeavour on the part of the Buddhist Saṅgha. But it came with the risk of exposing its own flank to Brahmanical appropriation. In the long run, this adventure backfired. Instead of repeating a 'Buddhist Viṣṇu' phenomenon of the type we see in medieval Sri Lanka, the Saṅgha ended up inducing a process by which the Buddha ultimately became an avatar of Viṣṇu in Magadha.

NOTES

1. This is a slightly modified version of my paper originally published with the same title in *Buddhist Studies Review*, vol. 30, no. 2, 2013, pp. 181–99. I am thankful to Prof. Peter Harvey for his comments on my 2013 paper.
2. David N. Gellner, *The Anthropology of Buddhism and Hinduism, Weberian Themes*, Oxford University Press, Delhi, 2003, p. 51.
3. The inscribed image of Gaṇeśa, discovered at Mandhuk in the Comilla district of Bangladesh, is probably the only exception. For an earlier analysis of votive inscription on this image, see Birendra Nath Prasad, 'Votive Inscriptions on the Sculptures of Early Medieval Samataṭa-Harikela, Bengal: Explorations in Socio-religious History', *Religions of South Asia*, London, vol. 4, no. 1, 2010, p. 33.
4. We have borrowed this term from Andre Wink. Wink has argued that by the eleventh century CE, Islam replaced Buddhism as the 'greatest trading religion of Asia' while the agrarian world within India was gradually lost to the Brahmins by the Buddhists. This simultaneous loss of agrarian and mercantile space precipitated a systemic crisis within Indian Buddhism, which led to the spatial contraction of Buddhism into select areas of strength: some portions of Bihar, Bengal and Orissa. Within this area too, there were spatial variations: Magadha emerged as the 'Well of Buddhism', the last stronghold of Indian Buddhism (Andre Wink, *Al-Hind: The Making*

of the Indo-Islamic World, vol. II, Oxford University Press, Delhi, 1999, pp. 340-50). While we largely agree with his characterization of Magadha being the last stronghold of Indian Buddhism, his theory of a generalized loss of mercantile and agrarian space by Indian Buddhism by the eleventh century needs some revision. For a review of his arguments, see Birendra Nath Prasad, 'Major Trends and Perspectives in Studies in the Functional Dimensions of Indian Monastic Buddhism in the Past One Hundred Years: A Historiographical Survey', *Buddhist Studies Review* (Journal of the U.K. Association for Buddhist Studies, London), vol. 25, no. 1, 2008, p. 78; idem, 'Monarchs, Monasteries and Trade on an "Agrarian Frontier": Early Medieval Samataṭa-Harikela, Bengal', *South and Southeast Asia: Culture and Religion*, vol. 2, 2008, pp. 160-1.

5. For some earlier analysis of functional aspects of the decline of Buddhism in different parts of early medieval Bihar and Bengal, see Birendra Nath Prasad, 'Major Trends and Perspectives', pp. 80-3; idem, 'Monarchs, Monasteries and Trade on an 'Agrarian Frontier', pp. 160-77; idem, 'Votive Inscriptions on the Sculptures of Early Medieval Samataṭa-Harikela*:* Explorations in Socio-religious History', *Religions of South Asia*, London, vol. 4, no. 1, 2010, pp. 27-43; idem, 'Votive inscriptions on the Sculptures of Early Medieval Aṅga, South Bihar: Explorations in Socio-religious History', paper presented at the National Conference of Indian Association for Buddhist Studies. Ahmadabad, 17-20 September 2010; idem, 'Patronage and Societal Linkages: Buddhist Monasteries in Early Medieval Bihar and Bengal', paper presented at the International Conference on Buddhist Heritage—Gujarat, M. S. University, Vadodara, 15-17 January, 2010; idem, 'Brahmanical Temples, *Maṭhas, Agrahāras* and a Buddhist Establishment in a Marshy and Forested Periphery of Two "Frontier" States: Early Mediaeval Surma Valley (Sylhet and Cachar), *c.*600 CE–1100 CE', *Religions of South Asia*, London, vol. 6, no. 1, 2012, pp. 33-60.
6. R.C. Mitra, *The Decline of Buddhism in India*, Vishva Bharati Studies, Calcutta, 1954; Rama Chatterjee, *Religion in Bengal during Pāla and Sena Times: Mainly on the Basis of Epigraphic and Archaeological Sources,* Punthi Pustaka, Calcutta, 1985.

7. Birendra Nath Prasad, 'Nālandā Mahāvihāra in its Archaeological Landscape: Archaeology of Religious Transformation in Early Medieval Bihar', paper presented at the Twentieth World Congress of the International Association for the History of Religions, University of Toronto, 15-21 August 2010; idem, 'Art and Archaeology of a Village Pratibaddha to the Nālandā Mahāvihāra: A Note on the Socio-economic and Cultural Dynamics in the Hinterland of Nālandā Mahāvihāra', paper presented at the National Seminar on 'Recent Researches in Buddhist Art', The Bihar Purāvid Pariṣad, Patna, 19 December 2010; idem, 'Cultural Processes in the Hinterland of the Monastery: A Case Study of a Village in the Neighborhood of Nalanda', paper presented at the National Seminar on 'Heritage of Nalanda: Icons and Symbols, Thoughts and Literature', Nava Nālandā Mahāvihāra, Nalanda, 13 February 2011; idem, 'Recent Archaeological Explorations in the Neighbourhood of Nalanda', paper presented at the ICHR sponsored National Seminar on Recent Archaeological Excavations and Explorations in the Ganga Valley, organized by the Bihar Purāvid Pariṣad, in collaboration with the Archaeological Survey of India, Excavation Branch III, Patna, 28 February 2012; idem, 'Rethinking the Decline of Buddhism in the Nālandā Area: An Analysis in the Light of Some Recently Discovered Sculptures', paper presented at the 10th International Congress of Bengal Art, Patna, 21-24 February 2013; Birendra Nath Prasad, 'Some Recently Discovered Archaeological Sites in the District of Nālandā: Preliminary Notes from the Field', *Prag Samiksha,* Gwalior, vol. 2, no. 1, 2014, pp. 82-93.
8. Birendra Nath Prasad et al., 'Bārā: A Recently Discovered Site in Nālandā District and its Bearings on the Decline of Indian Buddhism', in B. Labh (ed.), *The Ocean of Buddhist Wisdom,* vol. 4, New Bharatiya Book Corporation, Delhi, 2009, pp. 225-34. Also see Birendra Nath Prasad (ed.), *Monasteries, Shrines and Society: Buddhist and Brahmanical Religious Institutions in India in their Socio-Economic Context*, Manak Publications Pvt. Ltd., Delhi, 2011, pp. 81-3.
9. A.S. Amar, 'Buddhist Responses to Brāhmaṇa Challenges in Medieval India: Bodhgayā and Gayā', *Journal of the Royal Asiatic Society,* Third Series, vol. 22, no. 1, 2012, pp. 160-75.

10. Gail Omvedt, *Buddhism in India: Challenging Brahmanism and Caste,* Sage, Delhi 2003; D.C. Ahir, *Buddhism Declined in India: How and Why*, B.R. Publishers, Delhi, 2005; G. Verardi, *Hardships and Downfall of Buddhism in India,* Manohar, Delhi, 2011. For a combined review of Omvedt and Ahir, see Birendra Nath Prasad, 'Dilemmas of Revival of Buddhism in India (a combined Review of Gail Omvedt, *Buddhism in India: Challenging Brahmanism and Caste,* Delhi, 2003; and D.C. Ahir, 'Buddhism Declined in India: How and Why', Delhi, 2005), *Indian International Journal of Buddhist Studies,* Varanasi, vol. 7, 2006, pp. 171-5.
11. K.T.S. Sarao, *The Decline of Buddhism in India: A Fresh Perspective*, Munshiram Manoharlal, New Delhi, 2012, pp. 258-9; Kunal Chakrabarti, *Religious Process: The Purāṇas and the Making of a Regional Tradition*, Oxford University Press, New Delhi, 2001, pp. 109-64.
12. One of the best examples of this approach is provided by Kunal Chakrabarti, op. cit. See particularly the fourth chapter of his book, which analyses the gradual establishment of Brahmanical hegemony in early medieval Bengal and the assimilation of Buddhism by Brahmanism. Despite acknowledging that the two religions (Buddhism and Brahmanism) 'borrowed from and influenced each other, although Buddhist absorption of Brahmanical deities was more pronounced' (p. 140), he finds it 'ironic' that many of the Vajrayāna divinities, called 'defenders of the faith' (*dharmapālas*) were taken from the Brahmanical pantheon (p. 141). This is due to his reluctance to see this process as an attempt by the Buddhist Saṅgha to accomplish a subordinate integration of Brahmanical deities. It may also be due to this reason that in this chapter we don't see any analysis of the measures taken by the Buddhists to safeguard their ritual and institutional identity and resist appropriation by Brahmanism.
13. Claudine Bautze-Picron, 'From God to Demon, from Demon to God: Brahmā and Other Brahmanical Divinities in the Late Buddhist Art of Eastern India', *Journal of Bengal Art*, Dhaka, vol. 1, 1996, pp. 109-35; Rob Linrothe, 'Beyond Sectarianism: Towards Reinterpreting the Iconography of Esoteric Buddhist Deities Trampling on Hindu Gods', in C.P. Sinha (ed.), *Art, Archaeology and Culture of Eastern India, Dr B.S. Verma Felicitation Volume,* The Bihar Purāvid Pariṣad, Patna, 1997, pp. 193-8; A.S. Amar, op. cit.

14. John Clifford Holt, *The Buddhist Viṣṇu: Religious Transformation, Politics and Culture*, Columbia University Press, New York, 2005.
15. Ibid., p. 125. For a review of Holt, see Birendra Nath Prasad, 'The "Hindu Buddha" and the "Buddhist Viṣṇu": Divergent Trends in Buddhist Encounters with Brahmanism (A combined Review of Allen Trevithick, *The Revival of Buddhist Pilgrimage at Bodh Gaya: Anagaraika Dhammapala and the Mahābodhi Temple*, Delhi, 2006; and John Clifford Holt, *The Buddhist Viṣṇu: Religious Transformation, Politics and Culture*, Columbia University Press, 2005)', *Indian International Journal of Buddhist Studies,* vol. 10, Varanasi, 2009, pp. 189-94.
16. A.S. Amar, op. cit., p. 180.
17. Claudine Bautze-Picron, op. cit., p. 131.
18. Ibid., p. 129.
19. A reviewer of this article suggested that Indra and Brahmā were already Buddhist deities. However, it is more appropriate to see them as Brahmanical deities previously appropriated by Buddhists to prove the superiority of Buddhism over Brahmanism. Magadha was not the only land where such an appropriation was attempted, nor was this process confined to the early medieval period. Even if Indra and Brahmā played a significant role in both Buddhist literature and iconography, as far back as we have evidence they remained Brahmanical deities.
20. For a recent analysis of the process of integration of a local cult — Puṇḍeśvarī/Pūrṇeśvarī/Puṇyeśvarī — represented by the sculptures of a seated Goddess having a child, who is shown touching her breast on the left side of her lap, in the Kiul-Lakhisarai area of early medieval Bihar, see Birendra Nath Prasad, 'A Folk Tradition Integrated into Mahāyāna Buddhism: Some Observations on the Votive Inscriptions on the Sculptures of Puṇḍeśvarī/Pūrṇeśvarī/Puṇyeśvarī Discovered in the Kiul-Lakhisarai Area, Bihar', in G. Mevissen (ed.), *Berlin Indological Studies*, vol. 21, 2013, pp. 299-306.
21. Richard S. Cohen, 'Nāga, Yakṣhiṇi, the Buddha: Local Deities and Local Buddhism at Ajantā', *History of Religions*, vol. 37, no. 4, 1998, pp. 360-400; Robert DeCaroli, *Haunting the Buddha: Indian Popular Religions and the Formation of Buddhism*, Oxford University Press, New York, 2004; J. Shaw, 'Nāga Sculptures in Sanchi's Archaeological Landscape: Buddhism, Vaiṣṇavism and Local Agricultural Cults in

Central India, First Century BCE to Fifth Century CE', *Artibus Asiae*, vol. 64, no. 1, 2004, pp. 5-59.

22. Kumkum Roy, 'Women and Men Donors at Sanchi: A Study of the Inscriptional Evidence', in L.K. Tripathy (ed.), *Position and Status of Women in Ancient India,* Banaras Hindu University, Benares, 1988, pp. 209-23; Vidya Dehejia, 'The Collective and Popular Basis of Early Buddhist Patronage: Sacred Monuments, BC 100–AD 250', in Barabara S. Miller (ed.), *The Powers of Art: Patronage in Indian Culture,* Oxford University Press, Delhi, 1992, pp. 35-50; Romila Thapar, 'Patronage and Community', in Barbara S. Miller (ed.), op. cit., pp. 19-34; Upinder Singh, 'Sanchi: The History of Patronage of an Ancient Buddhist Establishment', *Indian Economic and Social History Review*, vol. 33, no. 1, 1996, pp. 1-35; Birendra Nath Prasad, 'Votive Inscriptions on the Sculptures of Early Medieval Samataṭa-Harikela, Bengal: Explorations in Socio-religious History', *Religions of South Asia*, London, vol. 4, no. 1, 2010, pp. 27-43.
23. Gregory Schopen, 'Filial Piety and the Monk in the Practice of Indian Buddhism: A Question of "Sinicization" Viewed from the Other Side', *T'oung Pao*, Second Series, 70, Livr. 198, 1(3), 1984, pp. 110-26; idem, 'On Monks, Nuns and "Vulgar" Practices: The Introduction of the Image Cult into Indian Buddhism', *Artibus Asiae*, vol. 49, no. 1/2, 1988-9, pp. 153-68; J. Kim, 'Unheard Voices: Women's Roles in Medieval Buddhist Artistic Production and Religious Practices in South Asia', *Journal of the American Academy of Religion*, vol. 80, no. 1, 2012, pp. 200-32.
24. Gregory Schopen, 'Mahāyāna in Indian Inscriptions', *Indo-Iranian Journal*, vol. 21, 1979, pp. 1-19; idem, 'The Inscription on the Kuṣān Image of Amitābha and the Character of Early Mahāyāna in India', *Journal of the International Association of Buddhist Studies,* vol. 10, 1987, pp. 99-137; Birendra Nath Prasad, 'A Folk Tradition Integrated into Mahāyāna Buddhism', pp. 299-306.
25. For a different perspective on the significance of these terms, see L.S. Cousins, 'Sākiyabhikkhu/Sākyabhikkhu/Śākyabhikṣu: A Mistaken Link to the Mahāyāna?', *Nagoya Studies in Indian Culture and Buddhism*, vol. 23, 2003, pp. 1-27. For our refutations of the arguments of Cousins, see Birendra Nath Prasad, *Archaeology of Religion in South Asia: Buddhist, Brahmanical and Jaina Religious Centres in Bihar and*

Bengal, c.AD 600-1200, Routledge, London and New York, 2021, pp. 233-40.

26. Gregory Schopen, 'Mahāyāna in Indian Inscriptions', pp. 3-5.
27. Ibid., p. 12.
28. In fact, the use of the Mahāyāna dedicatory formula on the images generally believed to be the product of the Vajrayāna, and the use of the term *pravara-mahāyāna-anuyāyina* by the donors of such images in early medieval Bihar and Bengal, has puzzled scholars of Buddhism for quite some time. One may see, for example, G. Bhattacharya's observations: 'It is known to the students of Buddhism that in Eastern India during the Pāla period the Mahāyāna form of Buddhism developed into the Vajrayāna form. But strangely enough, invariably in all the dedicatory inscriptions, the donor is described as the follower of excellent Mahāyāna (Pravara-Mahāyāna) Buddhism. We, therefore, think that the expression Pravara-Mahāyāna most probably refers to Vajrayāna. But still one may ask what was the harm to call it as such?' (G. Bhattacharya, *Essays on Buddhist Hindu Jaina Iconography and Epigraphy*, ICSBA, Dhaka, 2000, p. 53.)
29. Chandreyi Basu, 'Patronage and Representation at the Huvishka Vihāra: A Kuṣāṇa Period Buddhist Monastery', *Studies in History*, vol. 22, no. 2, 2006, p. 174.
30. Gregory Schopen, 'Mahāyāna in Indian Inscriptions', pp. 4-6.
31. D.R. Patil, *The Antiquarian Remains of Bihar*, K.P. Jayaswal Research Institute, Patna, 1963, p. 552.
32. It is better to quote G. Bhattacharya here: 'The Buddhist donative formula is finalized during the Gupta period. From now onwards, in the whole of northern India, the stereotyped text is written in connection with a donation. The object of donation is not mentioned, it is called *deyadharma* now, a meritorious gift' (G. Bhattacharya, op. cit., p. 397).
33. H. Sastri, *Nālandā and Its Epigraphic Material*, Memoirs of the Archaeological Survey of India, No. 66, Delhi, 1942, pp. 82-3.
34. Frederick Asher, *The Art of Eastern India, 300-800*, University of Minnesota Press, Minneapolis, 1980, pp. 46-51; Birendra Nath Prasad, 'Nālandā Mahāvihāra in its Archaeological Landscape: Archaeology of Religious Transformation in Early Medieval Bihar', paper presented at the Twentieth World Congress of the International Association

for the History of Religions, University of Toronto, 15-21 August 2010; idem, 'Some Recently Discovered Archaeological Sites in the District of Nālandā: Preliminary Notes from the Field', *Prag Samiksha,* Gwalior, vol. 2, no.1, 2014, pp. 82-93.

35. Frederick Asher, op. cit., p. 49; Susan L. Huntington, *The 'Pāla-Sena' Schools of Sculpture*, E.J. Brill, Leiden, 1984, p. 24.
36. Susan L. Huntington, op. cit., p. 24; Rob Linrothe, op. cit., p. 194.
37. As per Cunningham, 'the *dramma* was a silver coin, the descendant of the Greek *drachma*, and of the same weight' (A. Cunningham, *Mahābodhi or the Great Buddhist Temple under the Bodhi Tree at Buddha-Gaya*, W.H. Allen, London, 1892, p. 64). As per his observations, as the sum of three thousand *drammas* was a small one so the tank excavated by Saka 'must have been a mere pond' (p. 64).
38. R.L. Mitra, 'Transcripts and Translations of Two Inscriptions from Buddha-Gayā', *Asiatic Society of Bengal Proceedings* 1880, p. 80; A. Cunningham, op. cit., p. 64.
39 R.R. Mukherji and S.K. Maity, *Corpus of Bengal Inscriptions Bearing on History and Civilisation of Bengal*, Firma KLM, Calcutta, 1967, p. 112.
40. Frederick Asher, op. cit., pp. 79, 119; Nayanjot Lahiri and Elisabeth A. Bacus, 'Exploring the Archaeology of Hinduism', *World Archaeology,* vol. 36, no. 3, 2004, pp. 321-2.
41. Umakant Mishra, *Vajrayāna Buddhism: Study in Social Iconography*, Pratibha Prakashan, Delhi, 2009, p. 79; idem, 'Imitation or Syncretism or Selective Appropriation?: Studying Religious Equations between Brahmanical Religions and Buddhism in the Poly-religious Landscape of Early Medieval Orissa', *Lokaratna: An E-folklore Journal,* 2009, pp. 124-5.
42. A.S. Amar, op. cit., p. 178.
43. Ibid.
44. H. Sastri, *Nālandā and Its Epigraphic Material*, Memoirs of the Archaeological Survey of India, No. 66, Delhi, 1942, pp. 88-9.
45. A. Ghosh, 'A Bronze Image Inscription from Nālandā', *Epigraphia Indica*, vol. 25, 1939-40, pp. 334-5.
46 Ibid. It may be noted that an inscription from Kurkihar refers to Mallapore. As per A. Ghosh: 'it is tempting to regard the word as an indirect derivation of Mallapura and to take it to mean a 'resident of

Mallapura', but this meaning is hardly possible in the Kurkihar inscription, though it may suit the present record' (A. Ghosh, op. cit., p. 335).

47 Ananta Prasad Banerji-Sastri, 'Ninety-Three Inscriptions on the Kurkihar Bronzes', *Journal of the Bihar and Orissa Research Society*, vol. 26, no. 3, 1940, p. 251.

48. Ibid.

49. S.L. Huntington, op. cit., p. 211, has referred to this image inscription on the basis of a personal letter from D.C. Sircar. This image is now kept in the Gaya Museum and its accession number is 76.1.

50. Ananta Prasad Banerji-Sastri, op. cit., p. 250; P.L. Gupta, *Patna Museum Catalogue of Antiquities,* Patna Museum, Patna, 1965, p. 153.

51. Ibid., p. 247; ibid., p. 153.

52. Ibid., p. 247; ibid., p. 153.

53. Ibid., p. 251; ibid., p. 153.

54. P.L. Gupta, op. cit., p. 153.

55. Kunal Chakravarti, op. cit., p. 142.

56. For an analysis of this process with reference to a village donated to the Nālandā Mahāvihāra, see Birendra Nath Prasad et al., 'Bārā: A Recently Discovered Site in Nālandā District and its Bearings on the Decline of Indian Buddhism', in B. Labh (ed.), *The Ocean of Buddhist Wisdom,* vol. 4, New Bharatiya Book Corporation, Delhi, 2009, pp. 225-34.

3

Merchants and their Family Members as Donors of Inscribed Buddhist and Brahmanical Sculptures in Early Medieval Bihar and Bengal[1]

Introduction

Over the years, Indian historiography has witnessed an important debate on the nature of economy during the early medieval period (*c.*600–1200 CE). The proponents of 'Indian Feudalism' school of historiography, who preferred to build pan-Indian models, have generally argued that this period was largely marked with a decline in long distance trade, commerce and urbanization. This theorization gradually impacted some studies on the decline of Indian Buddhism as well. Thus, in a significant study, Ronald Davidson has argued that during the early medieval period, Indian Buddhism entered into a spiral of 'Systemic Crisis', which had its genesis in a combination of factors: evaporating mercantile patronage due to decline in the long distance trade and the Arab domination of the high seas, rendering it increasingly dependent on royal, feudal patronage; lessening participation of women in Buddhism[2]; militant Śaiva competition; and a serious dent in the 'previous Buddhist monopoly of dealing with the barbarians, outcastes, tribals, and foreigners' made by the Brahmins who were now willing to travel great distances in search of land and patronage.[3] All this resulted in a gradual spatial shrinkage of Buddhism, and its contraction to select areas of strength. Thus, there was a creeping realization within the Indian Buddhist community that their faith was a 'tradition in duress'[4] and the evolution of esoteric Tantric Buddhism was the result of adaptations by a 'tradition in duress' to feudalism for its very survival.

Some other studies on the decline of Indian Buddhism emphasize the Buddhist monastic failure on agrarian frontiers and in the detribalization process.[5] Andre Wink has added one more variable: by the eleventh century CE, Islam replaced Buddhism as the 'greatest trading religion of Asia' while the agrarian world within India was gradually lost to the Brahmins by the Buddhists. This simultaneous loss of agrarian and mercantile space precipitated a systemic crisis within Indian Buddhism.[6] More recently, K.T.S. Sarao has argued that the decline of urbanization and long distance trade were among the central factors that precipitated the decline of Indian Buddhism.[7]

As more micro studies of select regions and sub-regions of different parts of India were undertaken by historians, these pan-Indian theorizations were increasingly challenged. In the context of early medieval Bihar and Bengal, it has been generally argued that the Samataṭa-Harikela sub-region of early medieval Bengal, comprising the areas to the east of the Surma-Meghna rivers, witnessed the continuation of long-distance trade and high-quality metallic currency in gold and silver.[8] B.N. Mukherjee has extended this argument further. He has argued that in the whole of early medieval Bihar and Bengal, there was 'no sign of unusual decline of trade and commerce in the period and zone under study; but evidences for brisk trading activities in the area'.[9]

It may be stated here that the issue of trade has been looked into in some available studies on the economy of early medieval Bihar and Bengal, but the issue of the religious behaviour of merchants and their family members remains understudied. Which religion did they patronize? How did the pattern evolve as we move from Bihar to Bengal? What implications did these issues have, if any, in the decline of Buddhism in early medieval Bihar and Bengal? In the present chapter, an attempt will be made to understand the evolving pattern of mercantile patronage to Buddhism and Brahmanism as reflected in dedicatory inscriptions on sculptures. We will also try to situate our inferences in the broader debate on the decline of Buddhism in early medieval Bihar and Bengal.

Some limitations of our study must be put on record at the very outset. As this study is based solely on the use of only one genre of database (dedicatory inscriptions on sculptures), it has some limitations of its own. Most of the dedicatory inscriptions on sculptures we will analyse in the present paper come in a very short dedicatory format, just recording that the donated image was the *deyadharma* of a particular donor. Very few of them are inscribed with the regnal year of the king when the donation was made. Only these inscriptions can be dated on a surer footing. Other inscriptions, assigned to a particular century on the basis of palaeographic features, do not offer this kind of surer dating. In this kind of situation, we cannot be sure if some inscription of the same century were spaced by decades, years, months or days. Due to these reasons, it is difficult to trace the transitions taking place within a particular century.[10] The inferences arrived at through this study need to be contrasted with other kind of sources.

The Donation of Sculptures by Merchants and their Family Members in Early Medieval Bihar and Bengal: The Evolving Pattern

The data from the published examples of donations of images by persons from mercantile backgrounds in early medieval Bihar and Bengal is summarized in Table 2.

An analysis of this table offers some interesting inferences. The total number of sculptures donated through mercantile patronage, which happens to be just thirteen, is certainly not impressive, especially given the fact that during the Pāla period Bihar and Bengal witnessed an impressive proliferation of sculptures inscribed

TABLE 2: DONATIONS OF SCULPTURES BY PERSONS FROM MERCANTILE BACKGROUNDS IN EARLY MEDIEVAL BIHAR AND BENGAL

	Cultic identity of the image	*The place and sub-region where the image was discovered*	*Donor and his/her gender*	*Social background of the donor*	*Places where donors came from*	*Expressed motive behind donation*	*Period*
1.	Tārā	Mahābodhi (Magadha)	Nattukā	A merchant's wife, without expressed Buddhist identity	Not mentioned	None expressed	Early eighth century CE
2.	Vāgīśvara	Kurkihar, Gaya district (Magadha)	Vaṇika Māṇeka, son of Jānu	Male donor without an expressed Buddhist identity	Not mentioned	Do	Ninth century CE
3.	Seated Buddha	Guneri, Gaya district (Magadha)	Paramopāsaka Śrīpā(la), son of Vaṇika Haridatta	Male donor with an expressed Buddhist identity	Not mentioned	Do	Latter half of the ninth century CE
4.	Aparājitā	Some unspecified site of Magadha	Krodhanandin, son of Vaṇika-Śreṣṭhī Kalyanandin	Male donor with an expressed commitment to Vajrayāna	Not mentioned	Do	Late ninth or early tenth century CE

contd.

TABLE 2: (*contd.*)

	Cultic identity of the image	*The place and sub-region where the image was discovered*	*Donor and his/her gender*	*Social background of the donor*	*Places where donors came from*	*Expressed motive behind donation*	*Period*
5.	Dvādaśā-ditya	Rajauna or Valagudar (Aṅga)	Ranoka, son of Vaṇika Śrīdhara	Non-aristocratic; from a mercantile background	Not mentioned	Do	Ninth century CE
6.	Gaṇeśa	Mandhuk, Comilla district (Samataṭa)	Vṛddha Sārtha Jambhalamitra	Mercantile, with an expressed Buddhist identity	Apparently from within Samataṭa	*Anuttara Jñāna* by all creatures	*c.*967 CE
7.	Viṣṇu	Baghaura, Comilla district (Samataṭa)	Lokadatta	Mercantile	From within Samataṭa	For the increase of religious merit of his parents and himself	*c.*995 CE
8.	Vināyaka	Narayanpur, Comilla district (Samataṭa)	Buddhamitra, son of Jambhala-mitra	Mercantile, with an expressed Paramavaiṣṇava identity	Bilakandha-ka in Samataṭa	For the religious merit of his parents and himself.	*c.*996 CE

9.	Pedestal of an unidentified image	Arma in Munger district (Aṅga)	Sonikā, wife of a merchant	Mercantile	Not mentioned	None expressed	Eleventh century CE
10.	Mahāśrī Tārā	Lakhisarai (Aṅga)	Jaśadevaka, son of merchant Cāju	Male donor without expressed Buddhist identity	Not mentioned	Do	Twelfth century CE
11.	Khasarpaṇa Avalokiteśvara	Chandimou, Nalanda district (Magadha)	*Paramo-pāsaka pravara-mahāyāna-anuyāyin vaṇika sādhu* Saharaṇa	Male donor with an expressed Buddhist identity	Not mentioned	Do	*c.*1129 CE
12.	Khasarpaṇa Avalokiteśvara	Giriyek, Nalanda district (Magadha)	Dānapati Sādhu Śrīkara and Sādhu Dāgonmata	Male donor without expressed Buddhist identity	Mathurā	Do	First quarter of the twelfth century CE
13.	Maitreya	Unspecified site of Magadha or Aṅga	Sādhu Chamvivra	Male donor without expressed Buddhist identity	Not mentioned	Do	Twelfth Century CE

Source: Table prepared by the author by collating data from earlier publications.

with the names of donors.[11] In the reported assemblage of thirteen inscribed sculptures donated by merchants or their family members, six sculptures have been reported from Magadha, three from Aṅga, one from an unspecified site of either Magadha or Aṅga, and three from the plains of Comilla in Samataṭa. No such sculpture has been reported from North Bihar, Varendra, Rāḍha and Vaṅga as yet.

Out of the thirteen reported sculptures, three sculptures (nos. 5, 7-8 in Table 2) are Brahmanical and nine sculptures (nos. 1, 2, 3, 4, 6, 10-13 in Table 2) are Buddhist. The cultic affiliation of one sculpture (no. 9 in Table 2) is difficult to determine due to the fragmentary nature of the sculpture. In the available state of our database, Buddhist sculptures seem to have been more successful in attracting mercantile donation than the Brahmanical sculptures.

Out of the thirteen inscribed sculptures donated by merchants or their family members, only one (no. 1 in Table 2) was donated in the pre-Pāla period. In the Pāla period, four were donated in the ninth century, three in the tenth century, one in the eleventh century, and four in the twelfth century.

The earliest available example of donation of a sculpture by a person from a mercantile background is the eighth century sculpture of Tārā (no. 1 in Table 2), whose provenance has been traced to the Bodh-Gayā area on stylistic grounds. The dedicatory inscription on this image records that this image was the *deyadharma* of *vaṇijakī* Nattukā.[12] G. Bhattacharya has rightly argued that the term *vaṇijakī* has been used in the sense of 'merchant's wife' in the present inscription.[13] This is the only epigraphically recorded example of female participation in the donation of any image at Bodh-Gayā.

It must be noted here that the name of the husband or father of *vaṇijakī* Nattukā is not recorded in the dedicatory inscription, indicating that she had access to wealth and she utilized that wealth in donating an image on her independent initiative. Given the fame of Tārā as a saviouress, it was but natural that Nattukā donated her sculpture, most probably to some shrine or sanctuary in Bodh-Gayā.

Reported examples of donations of sculptures during the ninth century are the donation of an image of Vāgīśvara (no. 2 in Table 2) as the *deyadharma* of Vaṇika Māṇeka, son of Jānu, to the Buddhist establishment of Kurkihar[14]; and an image of the seated Buddha discovered at Guneri in Gaya district (no. 3 in Table 2). The dedicatory inscription on the image of the seated Buddha records that this image was the *deyadharma* of Paramopāsaka Śrīpā(la), son of Vaṇika Haridatta.[15] This image was donated in the ninth regnal year of the Pāla king Mahendrapāla at the illustrious Guṇacarita (Śrī-Guṇacarita).[16] Guṇacarita was, most probably, the name of the Buddhist establishment where this image was donated. The modern name of the place (Guneri) is obviously derived from that, indicating that the Buddhist establishment of this site attracted patronage from a person from a mercantile background. In early medieval Magadha, Buddhism was successful in attracting patronage from such donors not only in the case of its famous monastic and pilgrimage centres (Mahābodhi, Nālandā and Kurkihar) but also in the case of lesser-known Buddhist religious centres like Śrī-Guṇacarita.

An interesting trend is seen in the dedicatory inscription on a big inscribed stone sculpture of Aparājitā (no. 4 in Table 2), attributed to late ninth or early tenth century Magadha on stylistic grounds and palaeographic features.[17] Given its big size, this stone image was most probably enshrined in a public religious centre; it was not just an object of worship in a home shrine. The dedicatory inscription on this image, besides recording the Buddhist Creed Formula, records that this image was the *deyadharma* of Krodhanandin, son of Vaṇika-śreṣṭhī Kalyānanandin.[18] Bhattacharya interprets *Vaṇika-śreṣṭhī* in the sense of a 'leading merchant of his times of the area'.[19] But, as has been noted in some other studies, *śreṣṭhi* also functioned as bankers.[20] Krodhanandin, the son of a leading merchant-banker, patronized the donation of the image of a Buddhist deity (Aparājitā) that displayed an overt triumph of Buddhism over Śaivism after a violent conflict, to a public religious centre. In the context of early medieval Magadha, where Śaivism had an entrenched presence, Krodhanandin's patronage of the cult of Aparājitā was a very audacious act: in early medieval Magadha, the general pattern was the coexistence of Buddhism and various Brahmanical sects (Vaiṣṇavism, Śaivism) at the sites located away from Buddhist monastic sites, and attempts at subordinate integration of Saivism to Buddhism within the religious space of important monastic centres. An open display of violent conflict between Buddhism and Śaivism was not the general pattern in early medieval Magadha and Aṅga.[21] Brahmanism was not without mercantile support either.

This will be amply clear through the analysis of dedicatory inscriptions of some ninth- and tenth-century sculptures of Aṅga and Samataṭa. A ninth-century inscribed sculpture of Dvādaśāditya (no. 5 in Table 2), discovered at Rajauna or Valgudar near Lakhisarai, records that 'these Dvādaśāditya were set up by Ranoka, son of Vaṇika Śrīdhara, a resident of Kṛmilā, during the fifth regnal year of the illustrious Surapāla'.[22] This image was an object of public worship, most probably in the shrine/temple caused to be constructed by Ranoka, to gain social prestige for his family. This image inscription may be contrasted with the inscription on a fragmented image of Vasudhārā, which was discovered at Naulagarh in Begusarai district. This inscription records that this image was donated by Āśokā, wife of Dhāmmajī, and the daughter of *śauṇḍika* (vintner) Mahāmati of Kṛmilā, in the 24th regnal year of the Pāla king Vigrahapāla (latter half of the eleventh century).[23] The daughter of a *śauṇḍika* donated an image of a Buddhist goddess (Vasudhārā), who was believed to offer material wealth and prosperity. We may presume that her father too could have been devoted to this deity. Apparently, the mercantile class in the city of Kṛmilā patronized both Buddhism and Brahmanism.

A similar pattern is discernible in the tenth-century inscribed sculptures discovered in the plains of Comilla district in Samataṭa. So far, five inscribed sculptures containing the names of donors have been reported from the plains of Comilla district, out of which merchants appear as donors in three instances.[24] All sculptures donated by merchants are datable to the tenth century. Dedicatory inscriptions on them show the evolution of an interesting pattern. In the earliest example of this century (no. 6 in Table 2), we see a *vṛddha* (senior) *sārtha*[*vāha*] Jaṁbhalamitra donating an image of Gaṇeśa (discovered at Mandhuk) in the first regnal year of the Pāla king Gopāla II (i.e. *c.*967 CE) for the attainment of *anuttara jñāna* by all creatures but firstly by his parents.[25] This senior *sārthavāha* (leader of the caravan of merchants) was, as indicated by the use of the developed format of Mahāyāna dedicatory formula in the dedicatory inscription on sculpture donated by him, was a Mahāyāna *upāsaka*. The image donated by him was also donated as a Buddhist image. Gaṇeśa had an ambivalent character in Buddhist art: Gaṇeśa was worshipped as the remover of obstacles (*vighna-hartā*) and at the same time as the creator of obstacles (*vighna-kartā*) or the obstacle incarnate (*vighna*).[26] This Mahāyāna *upāsaka* most probably worshipped Gaṇeśa as *vighna-hartā*.

It may be noted that Jaṁbhalamitra appears in another dedicatory inscription on a stone image of Gaṇeśa/Vināyaka (no. 8 in Table 2), dated to the fourth regnal year of the Pāla king Mahipāla I (i.e. *c.* 996 CE), which was discovered at Narayanapur in Comilla district. The dedicatory inscription on this image informs that this image of Vināyaka was caused to be established by Vaṇika Buddhamitra, son of Vaṇika Jaṁbhalamitra, for the religious merit of his parents and himself.[27] It has been rightly argued by D.C. Sircar that the Jaṁbhalamitra mentioned in this inscription is identical with the one mentioned in the Mandhuk image inscription.[28] Vaṇika Buddhamitra belonged to the village Vilikandhaka of Samataṭa.[29] We may assume that his father too belonged to the same village.

If contrasted with the previous inscription, we get some interesting inferences. The name of the donor – Buddhamitra – like his father shows Buddhist influence. But this influence seems to be confined to his name only. Unlike his father, he did not use a Mahāyāna dedicatory formula in the dedicatory inscription on the sculpture, nor do we have any indication to suggest that the image donated by him was a Buddhist image. His father was no longer a *sārthavāha*, and Buddhamitra too did not claim this status. In other words, this family of merchants witnessed an economic decline and this decline made Buddhamitra less emphatic in claiming an expressed Buddhist identity.

These two image inscriptions need to be contrasted with the dedicatory inscription on a stone image of Viṣṇu discovered at Baghaura (no. 7 in Table 2) dated to the third regnal year of the Pāla king Mahipāla I (i.e. c.995 CE). This inscription records that this image was donated by the Paramavaiṣṇava Vaṇika Lokadatta, a resident of the village Vilakīndaka in Samataṭa, in the kingdom of Śrī Mahipāladeva, for the increase of the religious merit of his parents and himself.[30] D.C. Sircar has rightly argued that Vilakīndaka and Vilikandhaka referred to the same village.[31] The three merchants – Jaṁbhalamitra with an expressed Buddhist identity, Buddhamitra without any expressed Buddhist identity and Paramavaiṣṇava Lokadatta – belonged to the same village. What we noted in the context of the urban centre of Kṛmilā in Aṅga was true for a rural centre of Samataṭa as well.

No eleventh century inscribed sculpture donated by persons from mercantile background has been reported as yet. Five such sculptures have been reported from the twenfth century, all belonging to either Magadha or Aṅga. Four of them are Buddhist, but the cultic affiliation of one image is not known due to its fragmented nature. Thus, the dedicatory inscription on the pedestal of a fragmented, unidentified image, discovered at Arma in Munger district (no. 9 in Table 2), records that this image was donated by Sonikā, wife of the merchant Vāmbha.[32] Due to the fragmented nature of the image, it is not possible to identify its cultic affiliation (Brahmanical or Buddhist). However, a short dedicatory inscription on an image of Mahāśrī Tārā discovered at Lakhisarai (no. 10 in Table 2) informs us that this image was donated by Vaṇika Jaśadevaka, son of *māthura-vaṇika dānapati* Cāju.[33] As per G. Bhattacharya, who deciphered this inscription, the term *'māthura'* may mean a person from Mathurā or may indicate the kāyastha caste of the donor.[34] The use of the term *dānapati* for Cāju indicates that this image was donated by his son Jaśadevaka to fulfil the religious vow of his father.

How did the merchants perceive their profession? Two twelfth-century image inscriptions from Magadha help in looking into this issue. The dedicatory inscription on an image of Khasarpaṇa Avalokiteśvara (no. 11 in Table 2), besides recording the Buddhist Creed Formula, record the donation of this image in the 42nd regnal year of Rāmapāla (i.e. *c.*1129 CE) by *pravara-mahāyāna-anuyāyin vaṇika sādhu* Saharaṇa, son of *sādhu* Bhādūlva, for the attainment of *anuttara jñāna* for all creatures, keeping his *ācārya*, *upādhyāya* and parents in the forefront.[35] *Sādhu* Saharaṇa was originally an inhabitant of Rājagṛha.[36] Similarly, the dedicatory inscription on another image of Khasarpaṇa Avalokiteśvara (no. 12 in Table 2), discovered at Giriyek, records that this image was donated as the *deyadharma* of two merchants (*vaṇika*s) from Mathurā: *dānapati sādhu* Śrīkara and *sādhu* Dāgonmata.[37] As four *vaṇika*s – two from within Magadha (*vaṇika sādhu* Saharaṇa and *sādhu* Bhādūlva) and two from distant Mathurā (*sādhu* Śrīkara and *sādhu* Dāgonmata) – have used the epithet *sādhu* for themselves, it may be reasonably inferred that the use of this epithet in the twelfth century Magadha was a common trend. These *vaṇika*s believed that they were in a noble profession and trading was a pious work, hence they adopted this epithet.

The case with *sādhu* Chamvivra, who donated a miniature metal image of Maitreya, either from southern Magadha or Aṅga area of south Bihar[38] could have been similar.

Some Concluding Observations

It may be difficult to attempt any macro theorization on the basis of thirteen dedicatory inscriptions on sculptures spread across Bihar and Bengal, and donated over a period spanning not less than five hundred years. Yet some broad trends stand out. We see an overwhelming preference to Buddhist sculptures in the donation of sculptures by persons from mercantile background. Brahmanism too attracted mercantile patronage in the donation of inscribed sculptures. But at the available state of our database on inscribed sculptures, Buddhism seems to be the primary beneficiary of mercantile patronage in the donation of inscribed sculptures, especially in Magadha, where it also had assertive patrons like Krodhanandin, who used their weight in favour of Buddhism in the Buddhist-Brahmanical sectarian rivalry and conflict. This pattern demands some explanation.

Some clues to the factors behind mercantile preference for Buddhism in the donation of inscribed sculptures may be found in the dedicatory inscriptions on the sculptures donated by merchants, who used the *sādhu* epithet for themselves. In the early medieval phase, when the Brahmanical normative texts equated the ritual status of a Vaiśya with that of a Śūdra, the donation of sculptures provided a mechanism to traders for claiming that they were in a noble profession.

NOTES

1. This is a slightly modified version of my paper originally published with the same title in the *Journal of the Oxford Centre for Buddhist Studies*, vol. 18, 2020, pp. 123-35.
2. Ronald Davidson, *Indian Esoteric Buddhism: A Social History of the Tantric Movement*, Columbia University Press, New York, 2002, pp. 91-8.
3. Ibid., p. 85.
4. Ibid., pp. 111-12.

5. R.S. Sharma, *Urban Decay,* Munshiram Manoharlal, Delhi, 1987, p. 131. For a review of this approach, see Birendra Nath Prasad, 'Major Trends and Perspectives in Studies in the Functional Dimensions of Indian Monastic Buddhism in the Past One Hundred Years: A Historiographical Survey', *Buddhist Studies Review* (Journal of the UK Association for Buddhist Studies, London), vol. 25, no. 1, pp. 78-9.
6. Andre Wink, *Al-Hind: The Making of the Indo-Islamic World*, vol. II, Oxford University Press, Delhi, 1999, pp. 349-50.
7. K.T.S. Sarao, *The Decline of Buddhism in India: A Fresh Perspective*, Munshiram Manoharlal, Delhi, 2012, p. 208.
8. Birendra Nath Prasad, 'Votive Inscriptions on the Sculptures of Early Medieval Samataṭa-Harikela, Bengal: Explorations in Socio-religious History', *Religions of South Asia*, London, vol. 4, no. 1, 2010, pp. 29-30; idem, 'Brahmanical Temples, *Maṭha*s, *Agrahāra*s and a Buddhist Establishment in a Marshy and Forested Periphery of Two "Frontier" States: Early Medieval Surma Valley (Sylhet and Cachar) , *c.*600 CE-1100 CE', *Religions of South Asia,* London, vol. 6, no. 1, 2012, pp. 36-7.
9. B.N. Mukherjee, 'Commerce and Money in the Western and Central Sectors of Eastern India (*c.*AD 750-1200)', *Indian Museum Bulletin*, vol. XVII, 1982, p. 75.
10. In an earlier study, similar problems were noted in the analysis of dedicatory inscriptions on sculptures donated to the Buddhist establishment of Kurkihar in early medieval Magadha. See Birendra Nath Prasad, 'The Socio-Religious Dimensions of Dedicatory Inscriptions on Sculptures Donated to a Buddhist Establishment in Early Medieval Magadha: Kurkihar, *c.*800-1200 CE', *Journal of the Oxford Centre for Buddhist Studies*, vol. 7, 2014, p. 118.
11. The reported dedicatory inscriptions on the sculptures of early medieval Bihar and Bengal were analysed in Birendra Nath Prasad, *Archaeology of Religion in South Asia: Buddhist, Brahmanical and Jaina Religious Centres in Bihar and Bengal, c.AD 600-1200,* Routledge, London and New York, 2021, pp 231-380. Most of the inscriptions discussed in the present paper were also discussed in the same, but without analysing the evolving pattern of mercantile patronage to the donation of images. The present paper hopes to fill that gap.

12. G. Bhattacharya, *Essays on Buddhist Hindu Jaina Iconography and Epigraphy*, ICSBA, Dhaka, 2000, p. 464.
13. Ibid.
14. P.L. Gupta, *Patna Museum Catalogue of Antiquities,* Patna Museum, Patna, 1965, p. 142, Inscription no. 90.
15. R.D. Banerji, *Pālas of Bengal*, Memoirs of the Asiatic Society of Bengal 3, Calcutta, 1915, p. 110.
16. Ibid.
17. G. Bhattacharya, 'An Inscribed Stone Image of the Buddhist Deity Aparājitā', *Journal of Bengal Art*, vol. 8, 2003, pp. 95-101.
18. Ibid., p. 99.
19. Ibid., p. 100.
20. Birendra Nath Prasad, 'Urbanisation at Early Historic Vaiśālī , *c.*600 BCE-CE 400', in D.N. Jha (ed.), *The Complex Heritage of Early India: Essays in Memory of R.S. Sharma*, Manohar, Delhi, 2014, pp. 229-31; Birendra Nath Prasad, 'Some Observations on the Inscribed Stone Sculptures of Aparājitā and Trailokyavijaya from Early Medieval Magadha', *Kalā* (Journal of Indian Art History Congress), vol. XXV, 2019-20, pp. 77-82; Birendra Nath Prasad, *Archaeology of Religion in South Asia: Buddhist, Brahmanical and Jaina Religious Centres in Bihar and Bengal, c. AD 600-1200,* Routledge, London and New York, 2021, pp. 259-60.
21. For an analysis of these patterns, see Birendra Nath Prasad, *Archaeology of Religion in South Asia: Buddhist, Brahmanical and Jaina Religious Centres in Bihar and Bengal, c. AD 600-1200,* Routledge, London and New York, 2021, pp. 544-69.
22. Priyatosh Banerjee, 'Some Inscriptions from Bihar', *Journal of Ancient Indian History*, vol. VII, 1-2, 1973-74, pp. 107-8.
23. D.C. Sircar, 'Some inscriptions from Bihar', *Journal of Bihar Research Society*, vol. XXXVII, no. 3-4, 1951, p. 4.
24. Birendra Nath Prasad, 'Votive Inscriptions on the Sculptures of Early Medieval Samataṭa-Harikela, Bengal: Explorations in Socio-religious History', *Religions of South Asia*, London, vol. 4, no. 1, 2010, pp. 27-43.
25. D.C. Sircar, 'Pāla Rule in the Tippera District', *Indian Historical Quarterly*, vol. XXVIII, 1952, p. 57.

26. G. Bhattacharya, *Essays on Buddhist Hindu Jaịna Iconography and Epigraphy*, ICSBA, Dhaka, 2000, pp. 97-106.
27. D.C. Sircar, 'Narayanpur Vināyaka Image Inscription of King Mahipāla, Regnal Year 4', *Indian Culture*, vol. IX, 1942-3, p. 125.
28. D.C. Sircar, 'Pāla Rule in the Tippera District', *Indian Historical Quarterly*, vol. XXVIII, 1952, p. 57.
29. D.C. Sircar, 'Narayanpur Vināyaka Image Inscription of King Mahipāla, Regnal Year 4', *Indian Culture*, vol. IX, 1942-43, p. 125.
30. N.K. Bhattasali, 'Some Image Inscriptions from East Bengal', *Epigraphia Indica,* vol. XVII, 1923-4, p. 355.
31. D.C. Sircar, 'Narayanpur Vināyaka Image Inscription of King Mahipāla, Regnal Year 4', *Indian Culture*, vol. IX, 1942-3, p. 123.
32 *Indian Archaeology: A Review,* 1960-1, p. 44. The full inscription has not been published. Only the summary of the same has been provided, so we do not know the exact Sanskrit term for 'merchant' used in this inscription.
33. G. Bhattacharya, op. cit., p. 467.
34. Ibid.
35. R.D. Banerji, 'Four Inscriptions from Chandimou', *Annual Report of the Archaeological Survey of India,* 1911-12, pp. 161-2.
36. Ibid.
37. Priyatosh Banerjee, 'Two Medieval Inscriptions', *Journal of Asiatic Society Letters*, vol. XIX, 1953, p. 107. This inscription records the name of the *saṁvata* of an unspecified era. Dating has been done on stylistic grounds.
38. S.L. Huntington and John. C. Huntington, *Leaves from the Bodhi Tree: The Art of Pāla India (Eighth-twelfth Centuries) and Its International Legacy*, Dayton Art Institute in association with the University of Washington Press, Dayton, Ohio, 1990, pp. 176-7.

4

Women as Donors of Inscribed Buddhist Sculptures in Early Medieval Bihar and Bengal[1]

Introduction

In some pan-Indian theorizations on the decline of Indian Buddhism during the early medieval period (*c*.600–1200 CE), it has been argued that the lessening participation of women in Buddhism was one of the central factors in precipitating this decline.[2] One would hardly underestimate the role of female patronage in the institutional survival of any religion: women devotees play a great role in inculcating affiliation to any particular religion not only in their own generation but also in the next generation. For this reason, a study of evolving feminine patronage of Buddhism from a regional and sub-regional perspective assumes significance. This kind of study may force us to question some commonly held pan-Indian theorizations. In this paper, an attempt will be made to understand the issue of patronage to Buddhism by women in early medieval Bihar and Bengal through an analysis of dedicatory inscriptions on Buddhist sculptures donated by them.[3]

A study of participation by women in Buddhism in this period through an analysis of dedicatory inscriptions on Buddhist sculptures donated by them has some important bearings on the issues of social bases of patronage of Buddhism and its eventual decline. The donation of sculptures to Buddhist religious centres involved considerable monetary expense on the part of the donor: the donor needed to find a sculptor and pay him for making the sculpture. As these Buddhist images were donated to Buddhist monasteries, shrines and sanctuaries as objects of worship, the donor also needed to pay something to the ritual specialist who would perform the *prāṇapratiṣṭhā* ritual for the donated image, without which it would not acquire the required sanctity to become an object of worship.[4] Even with the involvement of this kind of monetary expenses by the donors of sculptures, only some Buddhist religious centres in early medieval Bihar and Bengal were able to attract or willing to accept donations of sculpture by women donors. The question which needs to be explored, then, is: which Buddhist religious centre was willing to accept donations from women donors? Which part of the religious space of such religious centres was made available to women donors? How did the pattern evolve as one moves from Bihar to Bengal? What kind of bearing did it have on the decline of Buddhism in this area in the long run? In some pan-Indian theorizations, it has been argued that not only the *bhikṣuṇīsaṅgha* declined by the seventh century CE, but 'more broadly, though, the early medieval period saw the dramatic deterioration of support for and involvement of women in Buddhist activities at any and every level, whether in the monastery, in the lay community, or in the newly evolving Siddha systems'.[5] Do the patterns observed in early medieval Bihar and Bengal conform to this broad pattern? This paper hopes to explore some of these issues.

So far, 19 Buddhist sculptures inscribed with the names of their women donors have been reported from early medieval Bihar and Bengal. None of them indicate donation of sculpture by any woman from a royal background. The data from them is summarized in Table 3.

It has been noted elsewhere that in the Pāla-Sena period (*c.*750-1210 CE) Bihar and Bengal witnessed a significant proliferation of Buddhist and Brahmanical sculptures.[6] One hundred fifty-eight Buddhist sculptures, inscribed with the names of their donors, have

TABLE 3: BUDDHIST SCULPTURES DONATED BY WOMEN DONORS IN EARLY MEDIEVAL BIHAR AND BENGAL

	Cultic identity of the image	*The place where the image was discovered*	*Donor*	*Social background of the donor*	*Places where donors came*	*Expressed motive behind donation*	*Period*
1.	Tārā	Mahābodhi	Nattukā	A merchant's wife, without expressed Mahāyāna identity	Not mentioned	Not mentioned	Early eighth century CE
2.	Pancika, Bronze	Nālandā	Vikhākā (Viśākhā?)	Probably from aristocratic background, without expressed Buddhist identity	Village Purika in the Viṣaya of Rājagṛha	None expressed	*c*.813 CE
3.	Buddha in BSM*, stone	Nālandā	Paramopāsikā Gaṅgākā, a woman	Non-monastic, non-aristocratic, with expressed Mahāyāna identity	Not mentioned	*Anuttara jñāna* by all creatures	Eighth or ninth century CE

*BSM stands for *Bhūmisparśamudrā.*

4.	Tārā	Kurkihar	Śākyabhikṣuṇī Guṇamati	A Mahāyāna nun	Not mentioned	None expressed	Ninth century CE
5.	Buddha in BSM	Kurkihar	Paramopāsakī Mañju	A female Mahāyāna lay follower	Not mentioned	None expressed	Ninth century CE
6.	Tārā	Kurkihar	Umādukā, wife of Iddāka	Non-monastic, non-aristocratic, without expressed Buddhist identity	Not mentioned	None expressed	Ninth century CE
7.	Avalokiteśvara	Kurkihar	Bhadevī (?)	Non-monastic, non-aristocratic, without expressed Buddhist identity	Not mentioned	None expressed	Tenth century CE
8.	Tārā	Kurkihar	Upāsakī Gopāli-Sāuka	Female Mahāyāna lay follower	Not mentioned	None expressed	Tenth century CE
9.	Tārā	Kurkihar	Upāsakī Duvajha	Female Mahāyāna lay follower	Not mentioned	None expressed	Tenth century CE
10.	Vasudhārā	Kurkihar	Vāṭukā, wife of Gopālahino	Female without expressed Buddhist identity	Not mentioned	None expressed	Tenth century CE

contd.

TABLE 3: (*contd.*)

	Cultic identity of the image	*The place where the image was discovered*	*Donor*	*Social background of the donor*	*Places where donors came*	*Expressed motive behind donation*	*Period*
11.	Vasudhārā	Kurkihar	Gāukā, another wife of Gopālahino	Female without expressed Buddhist identity	Not mentioned	None expressed	Tenth century CE
12.	Crowned Buddha	Kurkihar	Yekhokā, wife of Mahattama Dūlapa	Wife of a Mahāyāna lay worshipper	Not mentioned	None expressed	Eleventh century CE
13.	Avalokiteśvara	Kurkihar	Upāsakī Duvajha	A female Mahāyāna lay worshipper	Not mentioned	None expressed	Eleventh century CE
14.	Mañjuśrī Kumārabhūta	Kurkihar	Jākhyā	Non-monastic, non-aristocratic, without expressed Buddhist identity	Not mentioned	None expressed	Eleventh century CE
15.	Avalokiteśvara	Nālandā	Apparikā, daughter of Rambhu	Non-monastic, non-aristocratic, without expressed Mahāyāna identity	Not mentioned	None expressed	Late tenth or eleventh century CE

16.	Vasudhārā	Naualagarh, Begusarai district	Āśokā, wife of Dhāmmajī	Non-aristocratic non-monastic without expressed Buddhist identity	Daughter of a merchant of Kṛmilā	None expressed	Latter half of the eleventh century CE
17.	Puṇḍeśvarī	Lakhisarai	*Pravara-mahāyāna-yāyinyā-paramopāsikā* Śoma	Non-aristocratic non-monastic with expressed Buddhist identity	Not mentioned	None expressed	Eleventh century CE
18.	Buddhist Tantric Siddhāchārya	Somewhere in Varendra (North Bengal)	Ālasī	Non-monastic non-aristocratic woman without expressed Mahāyāna identity	Not mentioned	None expressed	Eleventh century CE
19.	Khasarpaṇa Avalokiteśvara	Kiul-Lakhisarai area	Śākya-sthavirā Vijayaśrī-bhadrā	A nun with expressed Mahāyāna identity	Not mentioned	None expressed	Twelfth century CE

Source: Table prepared by the author by collating data from earlier publications.

also been reported from this area and period.[7] Of these, dedicatory inscriptions on 19 Buddhist sculptures record the names of their women donors, which forms 12 per cent of reported Buddhist sculptures inscribed with the names of their donors. It is apparent that women were not the dominant group of donors of Buddhist sculptures in early medieval Bihar and Bengal. We may infer that it was not easy for women to access wealth and it was probably more difficult for them to come out of their home. This paper is about those women who could mobilize wealth to visit some Buddhist religious centres and install Buddhist sculptures there as objects of worship, and record their names in inscriptions.

Out of the 19 reported Buddhist sculptures inscribed with the names of their women donors, 15 have been reported from Magadha, one from North Bihar, two from the Kiul-Lakhisarai area of Aṅga, and one from Varendra (north Bengal). No such inscribed sculpture has been reported from other sub-regions (i.e. Rāḍha, Vaṅga or Samataṭa-Harikela) of early medieval Bengal. It may also be noted that all pre-eleventh-century examples are confined to Magadha. Within Magadha, Kurkihar has reported the highest number of inscribed sculptures donated by women, followed by Nālandā and Mahābodhi. It must, however, be noted that such sculptures reported from Kurkihar are mostly miniature bronze sculptures, and, unlike big stone sculptures, they were unlikely to have been prominent cult-objects of public worship.

In terms of cultic preferences, Tārā was the most preferred deity (5 examples), followed by different forms of Avalokiteśvara (4 examples), Vasudhārā (3 examples), Buddha in *bhūmisparśamudrā* (2 examples), Puṇḍeśvarī (1 example), a Buddhist Tantric *siddhācārya* who was devoted to Tārā (1 example), Crowned Buddha (1 example), Pancika (1 example), and Mañjuśrī Kumārabhūta (1 example). Tārā was a saviour deity par excellence, especially in her *aṣṭamahābhaya* form.[8] Vasudhārā was a bestower of wealth and prosperity. Buddha in *bhūmisparśamudrā* basically signified the Māravijaya episode of the life of the Buddha Śākyamuni and represented a continuation of Mahāyāna.[9] Puṇḍeśvarī was a local goddess in the Kiul-Lakhisarai area of Aṅga, who was gradually integrated into the institutional form of Mahāyāna Buddhism, most probably as a goddess who protected children and bestowed fertility to women.[10] Pancika as a deity is often depicted in the company of Hārīti in the sculptural art of early medieval Bihar and Bengal. The Crowned Buddha was regarded as a form of Vairocana.[11] It is apparent that the Buddhist goddesses associated with protection, wealth, prosperity and fertility were preferred objects of worship and donation by epigraphically recorded women donors of early medieval Bihar and Bengal.

None of the women donors have recorded their *varṇa-jāti* background. The same of their male relatives is not recorded either.

In Bihar and Bengal, the earliest epigraphically recorded instance of the association of a woman in the donation of an inscribed Buddhist sculpture is provided by the fragmentary dedicatory inscription on a stone image of a seated Buddha, dated to the year 64 of Mahārāja Trikamala of an unknown dynasty, and found near the Mahābodhi Temple. On stylistic grounds, this sculpture has been dated to fourth century CE by Frederick Asher.[12] Asher has also shown convincingly that this sculpture, despite being heavily influenced by the Kuṣāṇa period Mathurā idioms, was made locally at Bodh-Gayā by local sculptors. In other words, patrons who donated this sculpture to the Mahābodhi undertook a pilgrimage to the Mahābodhi and installed this stone sculpture as an object of worship with the help of some monks. Thus, the dedicatory inscription on this sculpture records that a *vinayadhara* (expounder of the *Vinaya*) *bhikṣu*, who was the companion of another *vinaya-dhara bhikṣu*, caused one Siṁharatha to dedicate this image of the Bodhisattva in the year 64 of Mahārāja Trikamala.[13] We are also informed of another *vinayadhara bhikṣu* and an *upāsikā,* whose name is also not recorded.[14] This sculpture was donated with the aim of *mātā-pitunāma-pujāye-bhavatu-upādhyāye.*[15] Gregory Schopen has shown that this dedicatory formula is generally found in the cases of donation of sculptures by persons associated with some tradition of Hīnayāna.[16]

The much-mutilated nature of this inscription does not allow us to draw many inferences. It is, though, very interesting to note that the names of the three *vinayadhara bhikṣus* and an *upāsikā* are not recorded, despite the fact that they all had some role in the dedication of the sculpture. Only the name of Siṁharatha, who actually funded the installation of the sculpture, has been recorded. A woman with an expressed Buddhist identity (i.e. the *upāsikā* referred to in the inscription) was present, but her role was considered not important enough to be recorded in the dedicatory inscription. We are also not informed what kind of relationship, if any, she had with Siṁharatha.

If contrasted with the next epigraphically recorded instance of the donation of a Buddhist sculpture by a woman donor, we see some fundamental changes in the initiative and agency of woman vis-à-vis her male relatives and monks. Thus, the dedicatory inscription on a stone image of Tārā (no. 1 in Table 3), attributable to the eighth-century Bodh-Gayā area on stylistic grounds, records that this image was the *deyadharma* of *vaṇijakī* (merchant's wife) Nattukā.[17] The name of the woman donor was recorded, but that of her husband was not recorded. Similarly, the name(s) of monks, who must have helped her in the *prāṇapratiṣṭhā* rituals of the donated image, were also not recorded. This woman had access to wealth and agency, which were utilized in the donation of this image.

Among the ninth-century donors, Paramopāsakī Gaṅgākā, the donor of a massive stone sculpture of the Buddha in *bhūmisparśa-mudrā* (no. 3 in Table 3), Śākyabhikṣuṇī (i.e. Mahāyāna nun) Guṇamatī, the donor of an image of Tārā, Kurkihar (no. 4 in Table 3), Paramopāsakī Mañju, the donor of a bronze image of the Buddha in *bhūmisparśamudrā*, Kurkihar (no. 5 in Table 3), indicate the independent agency of women in donation of images and their access to wealth. None of them have recorded the names of their male relatives or the name of any monk. Barring the inscription on the image donated by Gaṅgākā, other dedicatory inscriptions are in a very short dedicatory format, just recording that these images were *deyadharma* of Śākyabhikṣuṇī Guṇamatī and Paramopāsakī Mañju respectively.[18] In none of the cases, are the names of the male relatives (father or husband) of the donor women mentioned.

Among these donors, Paramopāsikā Gaṅgākā and Śākyabhikṣuṇī Guṇamatī stand out. The donation of an image of Tārā by Śākyabhikṣuṇī Guṇamatī indicates the survival of *bhikṣuṇīsaṅgha* in the ninth century as well and contradicts those pan-Indian theorizations that argue for the disappearance of the order of nuns within Indian Buddhism by seventh century. The question than needs to be explored, then, is: was Śākyabhikṣuṇī Guṇamatī a local *bhikṣuṇī* or came from outside? Śākyabhikṣuṇī Guṇamatī has not stated anything to this effect in the dedicatory inscription on the image, which renders our task difficult. One may, however, recall that Kurkihar had a significant presence of monks from Kāñcī in Tamil Nadu and they were very careful in recording their Kāñcī origin in the dedicatory inscriptions on images donated by them to the Buddhist establishment of Kurkihar.[19] We do not see any effort of this kind in the dedicatory inscription on the image donated by Guṇamatī. We cannot rule out the possibility that she could have been a local *bhikṣuṇī*.

The dedicatory inscription, datable to late eighth or ninth century on palaeographic grounds, on a massive (almost 6 ft high) stone sculpture of Buddha in *bhūmisparśamudrā* that was discovered amidst the excavated ruins of the Nālandā Mahāvihāra, begins with the Buddhist Creed Formula and records the names of Ārya Śāriputra, Ārya Mahāmaudgalyāyana, Ārya Maitreyanātha and Ārya Vasumitra.[20] It also records that the image was the *deyadharma* of Paramopāsikā Gaṅgākā.[21] As indicated by the use of the term Paramopāsikā, Gaṅgākā was a woman with expressed Mahāyāna identity and she took care to get recorded the names of some famous

Mahāyāna *ācārya*s in the dedicatory inscription. Ārya Maitreyanātha was the founder of the Yogācāra or Vijñānavāda school of Mahāyāna and Ārya Vasumitra was the founder of the Vaibhāṣika school of Mahāyāna. Similarly, Ārya Śāriputra and Ārya Mahāmaudgalyāyana were the two chief disciples (*aggaśāvaka*s) of Śākyamuni Buddha.[22] Given the massive size of the donated image, its donation must have involved the mobilization of considerable resources on the part of the donor and it must have been a prominent object of public worship within the Nālandā Mahāvihāra.[23] The authorities of the Mahāvihāra were willing to accept patronage from a Mahāyāna *upāsikā* without any expressed aristocratic pedigree (no claim to this effect has been made by Gaṅgākā in the dedicatory inscription) and allow the installation of this image as a prominent object of public worship.[24]

The ninth century also witnessed donation by women who identified themselves as housewives. We have two reported examples of this kind: Umādukā, wife of Iddāka, who donated a sculpture of Tārā to the Buddhist establishment of Kurkihar[25]; and Vikhākā, who donated the bronze image of Pancika to the Nālandā Mahāvihāra. The dedicatory inscription on the bronze sculpture of Pancika (no. 2 in Table 3) records that 'in the third regnal year of Devapāla, Vikhākā (Viśākhā), the sole wife of the 'destroyer of the Kalchuris', and a resident of the village of Purikā in Rājagṛha Viṣaya, together with the people, set up this image at the famous Nālandā'.[26] No political epithet (*sāmanta, mahāsāmanta,* etc.) has been used for her husband. Even his name is not recorded. But the donation of this image to the Nālandā Mahāvihāra offered her an opportunity to announce that she was the sole wife of her husband.

All five reported examples of the donation of Buddhist sculptures by women donors during the tenth century have been reported from the Buddhist establishment of Kurkihar. Among the donors who have not recorded the names of their male relatives are Upāsakī Gopāli Sāuka[27] and Upāsakī Duvajha,[28] donors of the bronze images of Tārā (nos. 8 and 9 in Table 3), and Bhadevī, the donor of a bronze image of Avalokiteśvara[29] (no. 7 in Table 3). Dedicatory inscriptions donated by them come in a very short dedicatory format, just recording that these images were there *deyadharma*. Due to this factor, it is difficult to read much social history in them. It may be noted that Upāsakī Duvajha appears as the donor of the image of Avalokiteśvara (no. 13 in Table 3) in the eleventh century.[30] This indicates that she had longer association with the Buddhist establishment of Kurkihar, yet she remained an *upāsakī* and did not become a *bhikṣuṇī*. Nor do we have any example of donation of a sculpture to the monastic establishment of Kurkihar after Guṇamatī. All this indicates the decline of *bhikṣuṇīsaṅgha* at Kurkihar after the ninth century.

This decline was despite the presence of non-monastic non-aristocratic devotees who patronized the Buddhist establishment of Kurkihar for many years. We may infer this through an analysis of the dedicatory inscriptions on sculptures donated by a man named Gopālahino and his two wives. His two wives – Vāṭukā[31] and Gāukā[32] – donated images of Vasudhārā, the Buddhist goddess of wealth and prosperity (no. 10 and 11 in Table 3) to the Āpaṇaka Mahāvihāra as their *deyadharma*. In the dedicatory inscription on both sculptures, their husband Gopālahīno has been simply referred to by his name.[33] But in the eleventh century, at least 35 years after the donation of images by Vāṭukā and Gāukā, Gopālahīno donated an image of the Buddha in *vajraparyaṅkāsana*.[34] In the dedicatory inscription on that image, he referred to himself as *paramopāsaka* Gopālahīno.[35] That is to say, he was more emphatic in asserting his Buddhist identity now. Despite commanding the patronage of such committed devotees, *bhikṣuṇīsaṅgha* at Kurkihar declined after the ninth century.

Seven inscribed Buddhist sculptures donated by women have been reported so far for the eleventh century. They show one important trend. Unlike the reported examples of the previous centuries, which are confined to Magadha, this century witnessed the donation by women in the Aṅga area, north Bihar, and Varendra as well. In the previous centuries, images of the donated Buddhist deities were either of the Buddha Śākyamuni in different *mudrā*s or of those deities that were worshipped for different *laukika* needs: Tārā, Vasudhārā, Pancika and Avalokiteśvara. In this century, the donation of an image of Puṇḍeśvarī indicates the continuation of the trends of the previous centuries. However, the donation of an image of the Crowned Buddha and an image of a Tantric Siddhācārya indicates the patronage to Tantric Buddhism by women.

The reported examples from Kurkihar are miniature bronze sculptures. Only one donor (Yekhokā, wife of *mahattama* Dūlapa, donor of a sculpture of the Crowned Buddha – no. 12 in Table 3) has recorded the name of her husband.[36] Two other donors to Kurkihar – Upāsakī Duvajha, who donated an image of Avalokiteśvara[37] (no. 13 in Table 3) and Jākhyā, who donated an image of Mañjuśrī Kumārabhūta[38] (no. 14 in Table 3) – have not recorded any information regarding their social background or the names of their male relative, indicating their independent agency, initiative and access to wealth in the donation of Buddhist sculptures. They all appear to be from the non-monastic non-aristocratic section of society. Similarly, Apparikā, who donated a large and beautifully carved stone image of Avalokiteśvara to the Nālandā Mahāvihāra (no. 15 in Table 3), was most probably from the same section of society.[39] As she has recorded the name of her father and not of her husband, we have some reasons to believe that she was an unmarried woman at the time of the donation of this image.

Three reported examples of the eleventh century – a stone sculpture of Vasudhārā donated by Āśokā, wife of Dhāmmajī, to some Buddhist religious centre of Naulagarh in the Begusarai district of north Bihar (no. 16 in Table 3);[40] a stone sculpture of Puṇḍeśvarī donated by *pravara-mahāyāna-yāyinyā-paramopāsikā* Śoma in the Kiul-Lahisarai area (no. 17 in Table 3);[41] and the stone sculpture of Buddhist Tantric *siddhācārya* donated by a donor called

Ālasī in some part of Varendra (no. 18 in Table 3)[42] – indicate two different trends. In the dedicatory inscription on the image donated by Dhāmmajī, not only the name of her husband but also that of her father has been recorded. In contrast, Śoma and Ālasī did not record the name of any male relative. In fact, in the dedicatory inscription on the image donated by Ālasī, we have the earliest epigraphically recorded example of devotion to a Buddhist *siddhācārya* by any devotee in early medieval Bihar and Bengal. The *siddhācāryas*, it has been rightly argued by Ronald Davidson, represented the non-institutional form of Buddhist esoterism, having an ambivalent relationship with monastic Buddhism.[43] They were generally not mindful of the prevailing social norms on sexuality, *varṇa* and *jāti*. If a woman became a devotee of a *siddhācārya* and publicly acknowledged her association with him by inscribing her name on the image of the *siddhācārya*, it must have been an act of exceptional courage.

In the stone image donated by Ālasī, we see a central male figure, almost nude, surrounded by subsidiary figures, and a seated image of Tārā on top of the relief.[44] The dedicatory inscription on this image records that this image was the *deyadharma* of a woman called Ālasī.[45] It has been rightly argued by G. Bhattacharya that the central figure of this sculpture was a *Siddha* and he was the preceptor of the donor. This *siddhācārya*, as indicated by the depiction of Tārā in the upper portion of the sculpture, was a devotee of Tārā.[46] We may add that Ālasī too, like her preceptor, could have been a devotee of Tārā.

To sum up the patterns in the eleventh century, we see the donation of images by women donors of diverse social backgrounds. Even Tantric Buddhism was not without its women patrons.

This diversity probably explains the survival of a *bhikṣuṇīsaṅgha* in the Kiul-Lakhisarai area of Aṅga in the twelfth century. The inscription (datable to *c*.1150 CE) on an image of Siṁhanāda Avalokiteśvara that was discovered at Jainagar near Lakhisarai (no. 19 in Table 3), records that this image was the *deyadharma* of

Śākya-sthavirā Vijayaśrībhadrā belonging to the branch (*viṭapi*) of Mallikādevī (*mallikādevī-viṭovi-sthitā-śākya-sthavirā vijayaśrī-bhadrāya deyadharmmoyama*).[47] Though J. Kim takes the term *śākya-sthavirā* in the sense of 'elderly Buddhist nun', but on the analogy of the term *śākyabhikṣuṇī,* we infer that this term may have been used in the sense of a Mahāyāna nun. It has been rightly argued that the *viṭovi* mentioned in this inscription is the incorrect rendering of *viṭapi*.[48] Mallikādevī was the head of a *bhikṣuṇisaṅgha* and Vijayaśrībhadrā belonged to that *bhikṣuṇisaṅgha*. Like Guṇamati of Kurkihar, Vijayaśrībhadrā did not record if she was a local nun or came from outside. It has been noted elsewhere that those non- local monk-donors of sculptures, who came to Bihar on pilgrimage, were very careful in recording their place of origin.[49] We do not see any attempt of this kind in the dedicatory inscriptions on sculptures donated by nuns Guṇamatī and Vijayaśrībhadrā. This indicates that a *bhikṣuṇisaṅgha* existed in the late twelfth-century Kiul-Lakhisarai area.

Summing Up

The limited database of just 19 inscribed Buddhist sculptures donated by women in early medieval Bihar and Bengal, does not allow us to offer macro theorizations. Some broad patterns, though, stand out. Major Buddhist religious centres of Magadha – Bodh-Gayā, Nālandā, and Kurkihar – were willing to accept donations of inscribed Buddhist sculptures from women donors of diverse social backgrounds. Buddhist religious centres of the Kiul-Lakhisarai area of Aṅga too displayed a similar pattern. The pattern seems to change when we move to the areas east of Kiul-Lakhisarai. No example of an inscribed sculpture by a woman has been reported from Vikramaśilā or any monastic centre of Bengal. It has been noted elsewhere that monastic centres of early medieval Bengal were reluctant to enter into ritual engagement with their non-monastic non-aristocratic devotees.[50] One wonders if this reluctance was responsible for some women devotees like Ālasī finding spiritual solace in the *siddhācāryas*.

NOTES

1. This is a slightly modified version of my paper, originally published with the same title in the *Journal of the Oxford Centre for Buddhist Studies*, vol. 18, 2020, pp. 136-50.
2. Ronald Davidson, *Indian Esoteric Buddhism: A Social History of the Tantric Movement*, Columbia University Press, New York, 2002, pp. 91-8.
3. Excluding the dedicatory inscriptions on the sculptures of Kurkihar, the reported corpus of dedicatory inscriptions on Buddhist and Brahmanical sculptures of early medieval Bihar and Bengal have been analysed in Birendra Nath Prasad, *Archaeology of Religion in South Asia: Buddhist, Brahmanical and Jaina Religious Centres in Bihar and Bengal, c.* AD *600-1200,* Routledge, London and New York, 2021, pp. 231-381. Dedicatory inscriptions on sculptures donated to the Buddhist establishment of Kurkihar were analysed in Birendra Nath Prasad, 'The Socio-Religious Dimensions of Dedicatory Inscriptions on Sculptures Donated to a Buddhist Establishment in Early Medieval Magadha: Kurkihar, *c.*800-1200 CE', *Journal of the Oxford Centre for Buddhist Studies*, vol. 7, 2014, pp. 116-52. Most of the inscriptions discussed in the present research article were also discussed in the book and the research article referred to above, but without analysing the evolving pattern of feminine patronage to the donation of Buddhist images and its implications for the decline of Buddhism. The present research article hopes to fill that gap.
4. Birendra Nath Prasad, *Archaeology of Religion in South Asia: Buddhist, Brahmanical and Jaina Religious Centres in Bihar and Bengal, c.*AD *600-1200*, Routledge, London and New York, 2021, pp. 239-40.
5. Ronald Davidson, op. cit., p. 91.
6. Birendra Nath Prasad, *Archaeology of Religion in South Asia: Buddhist, Brahmanical and Jaina Religious Centres in Bihar and Bengal, c.* AD *600-1200*, Routledge, London and New York, 2021, pp. 83-230. Within this general pattern, some significant variations existed. In south Bihar, Buddhism was practically absent in the areas to the west of the Sone

River. In West Bengal, it was practically absent in the districts of Purulia and Bankura, where Jaina sculptures and temples dominated. On the whole, this period saw the proliferation of Brahmanical sculptures in all parts of Bihar and Bengal. Buddhism was an expanding religion, but Brahmanical expansion was more profound and its patronage base was more diversified (pp. 83-230.)

7. Ibid., pp. 231-361. See particularly p. 345.
8. For an analysis of the role of Tārā as a saviour deity, see N.N. Bhattacharyya, 'The Cult of Tara in Historical Perspective', in N.N. Bhattacharyya (ed.), *Tantric Buddhism: Centennial Tribute to Dr Benoytosh Bhattacharya*, Manohar, Delhi, 2005, pp. 190-207.
9. Jacob N. Kinnard, 'Reevaluating the 8th-9th Century Pāla Milieu: Icono-Conservatism and the Persistence of Śākyamuni', *Journal of the International Association of Buddhist Studies*, vol. 19, no. 2, 1996, pp. 290-2.
10. Birendra Nath Prasad, 'A Folk Tradition Integrated into Mahāyāna Buddhism: Some Observations on the Votive Inscriptions on Sculptures of Puṇḍeśvarī/Pūrṇeśvarī/Puṇyeśvarī Discovered in the Kiul-Lakhisarai Area, Bihar', in G. Mevissen (ed.), *Berlin Indological Studies*, vol. 21, 2013, p. 302.
11 Hiram W. Woodward Jr., 'The Life of the Buddha in the Pāla Monastic Environment', *Journal of Walters Art Gallery*, vol. 48, 1990, p. 20; Claudine Bautze-Picron, *The Bejewelled Buddha: From India to Burma*, Sanctum Books, New Delhi, 2010, p. 141.
12. Frederick Asher, 'The Bodh Gaya Image of the Year 64: A Reconsideration', *Journal of Bihar Research Society*, vol. LVIII, 1972, pp. 151-7.
13. S.L. Huntington, *The 'Pāla-Sena' Schools of Sculpture*, E.J. Brill, Leiden, 1984, p. 204.
14. Ibid.
15. Ibid.
16. G. Schopen, *Indian Monastic Buddhism: Collected Papers on Textual, Inscriptional and Archaeological Evidence*, Part I, Motilal Banarsidass, Delhi, 2010, p. 37.
17. G. Bhattacharya, *Essays on Buddhist Hindu Jaina Iconography and Epigraphy*, ICSBA, Dhaka, 2000, p. 464.
18. For the short dedicatory inscription on image donated by Paramopāsakī

Mañju, see P.L. Gupta, *Patna Museum Catalogue of Antiquities,* Patna Museum, Patna, 1965, p. 128, inscription no. 12. For the short dedicatory inscription on image donated by Śākyabhikṣuṇī Guṇamatī, see G. Bhattacharya, op. cit., p. 463.

19. Birendra Nath Prasad, 'The Socio-Religious Dimensions of Dedicatory Inscriptions on Sculptures Donated to a Buddhist Establishment in Early Medieval Magadha: Kurkihar, *c.*800-1200 CE', *Journal of the Oxford Centre for Buddhist Studies*, vol. 7, 2014, pp. 116-52.
20. B. Sahai, *The Inscriptions of Bihar (From Earliest Times to the Middle of the 13th century A.D.)*, Ramananda Vidya Bhavan, Delhi, 1983, p. 126.
21. C.S. Upasaka, *Nālandā: Past and Present*, Nava Nālandā Mahāvihāra, Nalanda, 1977, p. 180.
22 Birendra Nath Prasad, *Archaeology of Religion in South Asia: Buddhist, Brahmanical and Jaina Religious Centres in Bihar and Bengal, c.AD 600-1200,* Routledge, London and New York, 2021, p. 269.
23 Ibid., pp. 269-70.
24. At present, this image is locally known as Dhelvā Bābā. Some local villagers believe it to be a demon and throw stone on it to ward off evil and keep away calamity. This is one of the indications of the profound transformation Buddhism has undergone in Magadha.
25. G. Bhattacharya, *Essays on Hindu Buddhist and Jaina Iconography and Epigraphy*, ICSBA, Dhaka, 2000, p. 464. The dedicatory inscription on this image is very short, just recording that the image was the *deyadharma* of Umādukā, wife of Iddāka.
26. H. Sastri, *Nālandā and Its Epigraphic Material*, Memoirs of the Archaeological Survey of India, No. 66, Delhi, 1942, p. 87.
27. P.L. Gupta 1965, op. cit., p. 145, inscription no.107.
28. Ibid., p. 146, inscription no. 116.
29. Ibid., p. 137, inscription no. 64.
30. Ibid., p. 139, inscription no. 73.
31. P.L. Gupta, op. cit., p. 150, inscription no. 134.
32. Ibid., p. 150, inscription no. 135.
33. Birendra Nath Prasad, 'The Socio-Religious Dimensions of Dedicatory Inscriptions on Sculptures Donated to a Buddhist Establishment in Early Medieval Magadha: Kurkihar, *c.*800-1200 CE', *Journal of the Oxford Centre for Buddhist Studies*, vol. 7, 2014, p. 134.
34. P.L. Gupta, op. cit., pp. 130-1, inscription no. 25.

35. Ibid., pp. 130–1, inscription no. 25.
36. P.L. Gupta, op. cit., p. 133, inscription no. 33.
37. For the short dedicatory inscription on this image, see ibid., p. 146, inscription no. 116.
38. For the short dedicatory inscription on this image, see ibid., p. 143, inscription no. 95.
39. For the dedicatory inscription on this image, see J. Kim, 'Unheard Voices: Women's Roles in Medieval Buddhist Artistic Production and Religious Practices in South Asia', *Journal of the American Academy of Religion,* vol. 80, no. 1, 2012, pp. 218–19. We agree with her suggestion that the donation of this big and beautifully carved stone image must have involved the mobilization of considerable wealth on the part of the donor.
40. For the dedicatory inscription on this image, see D.C. Sircar, 'Some Inscriptions from Bihar', *Journal of Bihar Research Society*, vol. XXXVII, Parts 3–4, 1951, p. 4.
41. For the text of the dedicatory inscription on the image of this deity, see Frederick Asher, 'An Image at Lakhi Serai and its Implications', *Artibus Asiae*, vol. LIX/3–4, 2000, p. 301. For an analysis of this inscription, see Birendra Nath Prasad, 'A Folk Tradition Integrated into Mahāyāna Buddhism: Some Observations on the Votive Inscriptions on Sculptures of Puṇḍeśvarī/Pūrṇeśvarī/Puṇyeśvarī Discovered in the Kiul-Lakhisarai Area, Bihar', *Berlin Indological Studies*, vol. 21, 2013, p. 303.
42. For the text of the dedicatory inscription on this image, see G. Bhattacharya, op. cit., pp. 380–1.
43. Ronald Davidson, op. cit. pp. 293–335.
44. G. Bhattacharya, op. cit., p. 380.
45. Ibid.
46. Ibid.
47. J. Kim, 'Unheard Voices: Women's role in Medieval Buddhist Artistic Production and Religious Practice in South Asia', *Journal of the American Academy of Religion*, vol. 80, no. 1, 2012, p. 207.
48. J. Kim, op. cit., pp. 207–10.
49. Birendra Nath Prasad, *Archaeology of Religion in South Asia: Buddhist, Brahmanical and Jaina Religious Centres in Bihar and Bengal, c.AD 600–1200,* Routledge, London and New York, 2021, pp. 231–381.
50. Ibid., pp. 231–381; 493–533.

5

Monarchs, Monasteries and Trade on an 'Agrarian Frontier'

Early Medieval Samataṭa-Harikela, Bengal, *c.*400 CE–1250 CE[1]

Introduction

In this chapter, an attempt would be made to understand the decline of South Asian Buddhism through the vantage point of Samataṭa-Harikela, roughly corresponding to the Sylhet-Comilla-Noakhali-Chittagong tract of modern Bangladesh. We aim to have a micro understanding of the processes behind the decline of Buddhism within a sub-regional framework. We will also try to situate it within the larger theoretical debate regarding the decline of Buddhism in South Asia.

In a significant section of Indian historiography, it is generally believed that the survival and flourishing of Buddhism in India depended on the strength of its monasteries and not on a well-integrated community of lay worshippers.[2] This theory is not much different from earlier theories, which place emphasis on the social and ritual 'failure' of Buddhism in explaining the decline and disappearance of the faith from India.[3] A significant section of Indian Marxist scholarship attributes this decline to an alleged Buddhist failure on agrarian frontiers.[4] Andre Wink has added the dimensions of long distance overland and maritime trade in explaining this phenomenon: that by the eleventh century CE, Islam replaced

Buddhism as the 'greatest trading religion of Asia', while the agrarian world within India was gradually lost to the Brahmins by the Buddhist. It was this simultaneous loss of agrarian and mercantile space that precipitated a 'systemic crisis' within Indian Buddhism.[5] To what extent this is true for early medieval Bengal in general and Samataṭa–Harikela area in particular? Is there any inherent link between the Buddhist monastic patterns of socialization in the early medieval phase and the medieval Islamization of eastern Bengal in general and trans-Meghna Bengal in particular?

Introducing Trans-Meghna Bengal: Cultural Shifts in a 'Frontier' Society

Studies in the religious dynamics of pre-modern Bengal in general and east Bengal (today's Bangladesh) in particular, frequently flounder in explaining the cultural shift – mass conversion to Islam – in the medieval period. Medieval Islamization has been such a great success in Bengal that 'today the Bengalis constitute the second largest group in the rank of Islam after the Arabs'[6]; rendering Bangladesh to be 'an island of Muslim majority in a sea of Hinduism'.[7] Medieval Islamization is most pronounced in eastern Bengal in general and trans-Meghna Bengal in particular. Factors behind this cultural shift in eastern Bengal have been attributed to the 'frontier' character of the landscape and Islamic negotiations and resolutions of the same.[8] Such formulations expect us to believe that Islam wrote its script on a credulous *tabula rasa* by spreading its message of wet rice agriculture to a 'tribal' population.[9] However, early medieval Samataṭa – Harikela does not appear to be a blank space. Home to various 'minor' dynasties – Khaḍga (*c*.650–700 CE), Rāta (*c*.700–750 CE), Deva (*c*.750–800 CE), and Chandra (900–1040 CE) dynasties – nearly all of them being Buddhist in affiliation, it was also the area where Xuan Zang saw the highest number of Buddhist monasteries in the seventh century Bengal.[10] It is also the area of a massive Buddhist religious complex on the Lalmai-Mainamati ridge in Comilla district.[11] Besides, this is the only area in entire South Asia where Buddhism has survived as a living religion.[12] Yet Samataṭa-Harikela has offered the single biggest seat for medieval Islamization in the entire Indian subcontinent to the east of the Sutlej River. Buddhist monastic patterns of socialization in the early medieval phase and subsequent Islamization could not have been unrelated. Obviously, the issue is much more complex than what we are supposed to believe. In this chapter, an attempt will be made to understand some aspects of this complexity.

At this juncture, to have a better understanding of some particular features of trans-Meghna tracts within early medieval Bengal, it is important to underline the geographical and cultural heterogeneity of early medieval Bengal. In an interesting study of political geography of early medieval Bengal, Morrison has found that Bengal had at least four sub-regions:[13] (1) Varendra (covering the areas of north Bengal), (2) Dhaka-Faridpur area (roughly the historical Vaṅga), (3) areas to the west of the Bhagirathi-Hughli River (roughly corresponding to Rāḍha), and (4) Sylhet-Comilla-Chittagong tract (variously referred to as Samataṭa or Harikela). In the Varendra area, from the very beginning, land was transferred in favour of individuals and the extent of the transferred land was always small. The same pattern was more or less visible in Dhaka-Faridpur area as well as in Rāḍha.[14] But the pattern was fundamentally different in the Sylhet-Comilla-Chittagong sector. In this sector, land was always granted to institutions: Buddhist monasteries or Brahmanical temples or to a group of large number of Brahmins and the size of the land grant was very large compared to the same in other subregions of Bengal. Within this subregion too, there were important variations. Compared to Comilla or Chittagong area, size of land grants was larger in Sylhet area.[15] His conclusions are obvious: in central, northern and western sectors of Bengal, property relations were fully developed, and culturally they were more or less integrated with the same of the middle Ganga Valley. As per Morrison, they were the 'heartlands of Brahmanical culture in the Delta'.[16] Samataṭa-Harikela had different orientations: economically, politically and even culturally. It was a society of relatively sparse population, lacking a long history of individual property rights; hence the land grants to the institutions or large congregation of the Brahmins. Within the Delta, 'Buddhism had not attracted a major following anywhere except in the lands lying east of the Meghna where it continued to receive benefactions in the thirteenth century'.[17]

Early medieval Samataṭa also displays the evidence of continued minting of high quality metallic coinage and biggest concentration of brick built architecture in the Delta, i.e. the Mainamati-Lalmai monastic complex.[18] We should not have any problem agreeing with his observation that 'the land that now lies in the modern Sylhet-Comilla-Chittagong districts was the home of people with a culture different from those found elsewhere in the Delta'.[19] This Sylhet-Comilla-Chittagong sector, as per Eaton, was the ultimate 'frontier' won by Islam through agrarian expansion centering upon rural mosques made of thatch and wood and 'linked politically to the state and economically to the hinterland' and acting as the 'nucleus of integration in an expanding agrarian civilization whose cultural counterpart was the growth of the cult of Allah'.[20] If that is the case, what could have been the Buddhist monastic pattern of socialization in early medieval Samataṭa-Harikela? What was the role of the Buddhist monasteries on agrarian frontiers? What was their relationship with contemporary political and economic processes? It is with these questions in mind that we will begin our study by focusing upon the societal linkages of Buddhist monasteries in early medieval Samataṭa-Harikela. Much of our analysis will be based on the study of land grant inscriptions engraved on copper plates, recording the donation of land to Buddhist monasteries and Brahmanical institutions.

State Formation in Early Medieval Samataṭa-Harikela, its Legitimization and Consolidation Process, and the Role of Buddhist Monasteries in this Matrix

One of the characteristic features of early medieval India was the 'emergence of regions with their distinct cultural personalities'.[21] 'Indian Feudalism' school of historiography tends to see it as a 'feudal' imposition from above, but it appears to be a case of developments from below. It was inextricably linked with the process of local state formation. Kulke has aptly observed that:

> The overwhelming majority of the early medieval states of India emerged from a process of continuous agrarian expansion and political integration. This development took place in those areas of South Asian subcontinent that had lain at the periphery or even outside the core areas of ancient Indian state formations. This process started from local nuclei of early socio-economic and political developments and increasingly came to include their hinterlands.[22]

This paradigm is fundamentally important for us. In the early historic period, Samataṭa was, no doubt, a peripheral area. In the Prayāga *praśasti* of the Gupta emperor Samudragupta, it has been referred to as one of the *pratyānta* (frontier) kingdoms defeated by the emperor. We may infer that by this period, formation of a local state had already taken place in Samataṭa or it was in the offing. Later it could have become a part of the Gupta Empire but convincing proofs for this are lacking as most of the Gupta period copper-plate inscriptions are confined to Varendra area only. However, as attested by archaeology, Comilla district does not appear to be in cultural backwaters during the early historic period. It has been observed that in terms of number and concentration of early historic archaeological sites, modern Comilla district was second only to Bogra district, the early historical heartland of Bengal.[23] We may safely suggest that modern Comilla district was the 'local nuclei of early socio-economic and political developments' of Samataṭa. It was the core of various local polities of Samataṭa. From this base, these polities adopted different means to integrate their peripheral areas in the process of consolidation and expansion of their resource base. It has been proved beyond doubt that the core area of the Rāta dynasty and the Khaḍga dynasty was in the modern Comilla district only. The Candras, originally hailing from Rohitagiri (Rosangi in Arakan), had their earlier political centre in the modern Comilla district only; only later they moved to the more centrally located Vikrampur area from where they could have controlled larger parts of Bengal. For these dynasties, land grants to Brahmins and Brahmanical temples, and, of course, to Buddhist monasteries, appear to have been an important instrument for affecting economic and cultural integration of peripheral areas to the nuclear areas of their domain. This is a theme we will analyse later. Let us first consider another important variable of this complex matrix: trade.

For early medieval Samataṭa, the significance of trade may not be overlooked, as it is likely to have a fundamental impact on the political economy of various local dynasties as well as on the socialization patterns of Samataṭa monasteries. Seventh century CE onwards, port cities of Western Delta – Tāmralipti and Chandraketugarh – began to decline due to diverse factors. There is no evidence to prove that sea-faring merchants used it for maritime adventures eighth century CE onwards.[24] Decline of port activities at Tāmralipti was also reflected in the dwindling number of Buddhist monasteries in this area.[25]

An important consequence of these developments was the gradual shift of the maritime focus of the Delta towards the east, towards the Comilla-Chittagong coast.[26] Archeological or literary evidences for any port in Western Delta not forthcoming for the early medieval period, it may not be unreasonable to infer that Samataṭa could have provided the main opening to the sea for entire Bengal. It is important to mention that, compared to other parts of Bengal, early medieval Samataṭa offers a remarkable contrast in terms of continuation of high-quality metallic coinage. Excavations at the Mainamati monastic complex had resulted in the discovery of around 350 coins in gold, copper and silver.[27] This could have been due to the developed trading contacts of Samataṭa-Harikela area. Samataṭa-Harikela area was, no doubt, well-connected with neighbouring regions by overland and maritime routes. The political and cultural centre of Mainamati–Devaparvata too appears to have been well-connected with the hinterland by rivers. These riverine routes could have been useful in channelizing resources as well as merchandize. In fact, it has been suggested that Mainamati-Devaparvata complex was an important riverine port in Samataṭa from the second half of the seventh century to the first quarter of the tenth century CE.[28]

The discovery of the coins of Abbasid Caliphs at Kutila Mura in Mainamati monastic complex suggests that south-eastern Bengal was well-connected to the Arab maritime network stretching from Africa and Europe in the west to China in the east.[29] This is also reflected in the intimate knowledge of the south-eastern coast of Bengal in the Arab maritime literature[30] as well as in growing Arab presence at the Chittagong coast, eighth-ninth centuries CE onwards.[31] This is not to suggest that Buddhist network in the Bay of Bengal had collapsed by this time.[32] It is generally believed that Indian Ocean witnessed a 'trade revolution' in the eleventh century CE[33] and Samataṭa rulers could have benefited from this.[34] But the absence of indigenous currency in these centuries remains a puzzle.[35] A general absence of references to merchants in the copper-plate inscriptions of Samataṭa – a situation fundamentally different form Gupta period Varendra where merchants were accorded important place in *viṣaya* administration – renders this theory plausible that much of the Samataṭa maritime trade could have been in foreign hands. The overall impact of foreign trade on economy could not have been significant; nor could it have provided a stable resource base for Samataṭa monasteries. Tarafdar has pointed out that the kind of commercial activities, as evidenced in early medieval

Samataṭa, could hardly originate a process of urbanization that might bring into being a stable commercial middle class, for profits from trade were either appropriated by feudal lords or establishments. Capital formation under these conditions could have been impossible and the ruralization resulting from a predominantly agrarian economy perhaps remained unaffected by trade and money economy.[36]

That notwithstanding, Samataṭa monasteries benefited from this trade and a portion of wealth from this maritime trade, as indicated by the discovery of Abbasid and indigenous coins from Mainamati monastic complex, flown to the monasteries. The significant question, which one needs to ask in this context, is: how did these coins reach the Buddhist monasteries on the Mainamati-Lalmai ridge? Did they get them through mercantile patronage or through royal patronage? In this context, it must be pointed out that we do not have epigraphically recorded instances of mercantile patronage to Buddhist monastic centres on the Mainamati-Lalmai ridge. We do not have evidences for direct mercantile patronage to Samataṭa monasteries in the way we see in the cases of early medieval Kanheri,[37] Brahmanical *maṭha*s of Konkan,[38] and early medieval temples of Rajasthan.[39] Due to this factor, the dependence of Samataṭa monasteries on royal patronage appears to have been greater.

At this juncture, it must be emphasized that a mono-causal or unilinear approach may not be useful in understanding the Buddhist monastic survival strategies as they assume different forms across time and topography.[40] In the case of early historic western Deccan, it has been seen that in their earliest phase, Buddhist monasteries had greater involvement with the agrarian sector. It was much later that, with increasing trade and commerce, the monasteries could have got involved directly in trade and could have accumulated wealth.[41] Should we visualize a similar chronological evolution in the role of Samataṭa monasteries as well? Should we believe that initially they had greater involvement with the agrarian sector and it was only later that they depended more on wealth from foreign trade? Where do they stand vis-à-vis Brahmanical religious institutions in this regard? And why did they lose hegemony to the Brahmins in the long run? Any analysis of this issue will naturally entail an analysis of copper-plate inscriptions recording endowments of lands to Buddhist and Brahmanical religious institutions of early medieval Samataṭa. That will give us some idea about the milieu in which these monasteries were interacting with other social institutions. That will also be useful in comparing the role of Buddhist monasteries with the same of Brahmanical religious institutions on agrarian frontiers of this area.

Buddhist Monasteries on Agrarian Frontiers: The Samataṭa-Harikela Experience

The earliest dating copper-plate inscription discovered so far in Samataṭa-Harikela is the Gunaighar copper-plate inscription of Mahārāja Vainyagupta (507 CE), discovered at Gunaighar village (18 miles north-east of Comilla town). This inscription records the donation of 11 *pāṭaka*s of *khila* (uncultivated) land in Kānteḍadaka-grāma to a Buddhist monastery headed by Ācārya Śāntideva.[42] This monastery was dedicated to Ārya Avalokiteśvara. References to Guṇikāgrahāra (obviously modern Gunaighar) occur in this inscription.[43] Hence it may be inferred that the donated land was located in the vicinity of modern Gunaighar itself. A careful analysis of this inscription offers three important inferences: the poly-religious character of the locality (which appears to be well-settled) in which Buddhist monasteries had a privileged place; monastic alliance with the royalty; as well as evidences of evolution of hierarchy among Buddhist monasteries in this area. The significance of evolution of hierarchy among Buddhist monasteries in Samataṭa at such an early date is yet to be worked out.

The land granted to this monastery was low-lying, water logged and marshy.[44] Obviously, the monastery was expected to undertake agrarian expansion in the donated land. Landscape surrounding this donated land was poly-religious. Besides being bordered by cultivated fields belonging to various individuals, it was bordered by a Brahmanical *agrahāra* settlement in the east;[45] a *rājavihāra-kṣetra* (i.e. cultivated fields belonging to the 'royal monastery') in the south;[46] and also the cultivated fields belonging to the Buddhist monastery headed by Ācārya Jitsena in the south.[47] In the western side, it was bordered by cultivated fields belonging to the temple of Pradyumneśvara, a Brahmanical deity.[48] Frequent references to various water channels and boat parking stations in this inscription will naturally make us think that the locality in which land was granted bordered some river and it was low lying and marshy. Here religious institutions (Buddhist monasteries, Brahmanical temples and *agrahāras*) seem to have acted as agents of agrarian expansion and 'forging of linkages across space for social integration'. This could have been helpful in the consolidation and expansion of the material and ideological resource base of emerging local states in the trans-Meghna areas.

Another important inference is that at such an early date, hierarchy had developed among Samataṭa monasteries. This inscription attests to the presence of at least three monasteries in or around Gunaighar: the monastery headed by Ācārya Jitsena; the monastery headed by Ācārya Śāntideva (to which land was transferred by this inscription); and a 'royal monastery' (*rājavihāra*). Obviously the *rājavihāra* stood at the top of the hierarchy. Patronage to Buddhist monasteries, thus, seems to have played an important role in royal legitimation. It has been asserted that 'Buddhism was the dominant vehicle through which kingship and state formation was articulated in early Bengal'.[49] Gunaighar inscription indicates that this was largely true for sixth century CE Samataṭa as well.

The tendency of direct royal association with particular monasteries later culminated in the practice of naming monasteries on the names of individual kings, such as Bhavadeva Vihāra and Ānanda Vihāra in the Mainamati Complex. Clearly, patronage to such institutions constituted an important element in the articulation of royal sovereignty.

Political pattern in Samataṭa in the late sixth and seventh centuries CE is not very clear. This period is marked by the emergence of a powerful, semi-independent *sāmanta* stratum, owing nominal allegiance to the paramount ruler of Samataṭa (Samataṭeśvara). This stratum, out of sheer devotion, or for the consolidation and expansion of its resource base and legitimacy, patronized Buddhist monasteries or Brahmanical religious institutions. However, it is also from this period only that a differentiation emerged in the pattern of land grants to the Buddhist monasteries and Brahmanical institutions. Besides the Nidhanapur copper-plate inscription of Kāmarūpa king Bhāskaravarmana, which informs us the creation of Mayuraśālmala-agrahāra in the Chandrapuri-viṣaya (presumably in Sylhet district) for settling hundreds of Brahmins by granting them a large tract of uncultivated land as per the principle of *bhūmichidra-nyāya*; three more seventh century copper plates have come to light from trans-Meghna areas: (1) Kailan copper plate of *pañca-mahāśabdaprāpta* Śrīdharaṇa Rāta, (2) Tippera copper plate of *sāmanta* Lokanātha, and (3) Kalapur copper plate of sāmanta Maruṇḍanātha.

Any study of these copper-plate inscriptions will have to take into account the remarkable similarity in their seals. Seals attached to all the three copper-plate inscriptions refer to *kumārāmātyādhikaraṇa.* In the next line, they record the name of the individual donors: Śrī Śrīdharaṇa Rāta, Lokanātha and Maruṇḍanātha respectively. D.C. Sircar has rightly opined that these seals actually belonged to the *adhikaraṇa* (i.e. Office of the Board of Administrators) attached to the *kumārāmātya* (i.e. the administrative officer, who was enjoying the status of a prince of royal blood) who was usually the ruler of a *viṣaya* or its subdivision.[50] D.C. Sircar has rightly argued that the names of Lokanātha, Śrīdharaṇa Rāta, and Maruṇḍanātha were written on the seals, apparently to indicate that they had countersigned the original document, which was afterwards incised on the copper plates.[51] As per Sircar's assessment, the importance given to Lokanātha, Śrīdharaṇa Rāta, and Maruṇḍanātha suggests that they had risen to semi-independent status.[52]

We may begin with an analysis of the Tippera copper plate inscription (*c.*564 CE), discovered in the old Tippera district (modern Comilla district). In this copper plate, we are informed that at the request of *mahāsāmanta* Pradoṣaśarmana, an orthodox Brahmin, forested lands (*āṭavi bhūkhaṇḍa*) were granted in the Suvvuṅga-viṣaya for providing *bali-satra-caru* to the temple of the Brahmanical deity Ananta Nārāyaṇa; as well as for the support of a community of some two hundred Brahmins.[53] As the tract was granted without any reference to its boundaries, it appears to have been very large. The distinct non-Sanskritic name of the *viṣaya* (Suvvuṅga) in which land was granted might suggest that it was located on the remote frontiers, probably in a tribal area.[54] Obviously this is a case of attempted expansion of agrarian and cultural frontiers in which temple and *agrahāra*s acted as nuclei of integration.

A similar attempt is visible in the Kalapur copper plate of Sāmanta Maruṇḍanātha (second half of sixth century CE). This grant seems to have been made on the request of a Brahmin Jayaswāmina, who had earlier received one *pāṭaka* of land and built a *maṭha* and installed therein an image of Bhagavata Ananta Nārāyaṇa.[55] Kalapur copper-plate records the donation of one *pāṭaka* and two *droṇa*s of marshy and forested land (*jalāṭavi bhūkhaṇḍa*) for providing *bali*, *satra* and *caru* at this *maṭha,* as well as for the maintenance of Brahmins attached to the same.[56] The location of the donated land has satisfactorily been identified in the Srimangala Police Station area of Sylhet district, on the borders of hills of Tripura.[57] Tippera and Kalapur copper plates prove beyond doubt that Brahmanical institutions were pioneers in advancing agrarian and cultural frontiers in the forested tracts of Comilla and Sylhet districts as well as in the adjoining districts of Assam and Tripura.

This contrasts sharply with the Kailan copper-plate inscription of Śrīdharaṇa Rāta (*c.*575 CE), found at the village of Kailan, 18 miles south-west of Comilla town. This plate was issued from Devaparvata. It records the transfer of 25 *pāṭaka*s of land at the request of *mahāsandhivigrahika* Jayanātha. Part of this tract was donated to a congregation of 13 Brahmins; Jayanātha himself retained part of the land; whereas five *pāṭaka*s were granted to a Buddhist monastery.[58] The location of the donated tract of land could not be exactly identified so far, though it may be assumed that it could have been somewhere near the find spot of the copper-plate inscription.[59] A developed agrarian structure of the donated tract is discernible in this inscription, which indicates that this monastery functioned in a well-settled zone and subsisted on the agrarian resources drawn from the donated tract. This tendency of Buddhist monastic preference for concentration in the Comilla district, which was, arguably, the heartland of early medieval Samataṭa, becomes more pronounced in the coming centuries. That makes us think that royal legitimization and not agrarian expansion was the main motive behind grant of land to the monasteries in Comilla district.

This tendency of monastic concentration in the relatively well-settled Comilla district, and surviving mainly by appropriating agrarian resources of well-settled villages instead of attempting agrarian expansion in outlying areas, is discernible in the two Asharafpur copper-plate inscriptions (*c.*665 CE). They have been found at Asharafpur village (30 miles to the north-east of Dacca city) and the location of the donated land has satisfactorily been proved to be either in the eastern portion of Dhaka district or in the western portion of Comilla district.[60] In the first plate, king Devakhaḍga donated 9 *pāṭaka*s and 10 *droṇa*s of cultivated land to Ācārya Saṅghamitra, for the use of a Buddhist monastery.[61] In the second plate, Rājarāja, son of Devakhaḍga, donated 6 *pāṭaka*s and 10 *droṇa*s of cultivated land to the same monastery.[62]

These inscriptions suggest that some monasteries got deeply involved in the agrarian relations of contemporary society. They throw valuable light on the position of some peasants who cultivated the land granted to this monastery. The first copper plate speaks of some land 'enjoyed' by Sarvatantra and some other persons, but cultivated by a certain *mahattara* Śekhara and others.[63] In the second copper-plate inscription, mention is made of some land 'enjoyed' by Sulabdha and others, but cultivated by Durggata and Rājatasa.[64] But the plots mentioned in these copper-plates were actually owned by the king and the crown prince, who took them away from the 'enjoyers' of the same and donated the land to the monasteries. It appears that the peasants, who tilled the land under the previous landholders, continued to do so even after it became the property of the *vihāra*s. Obviously, when such a well-settled land was granted to the *vihāra*s, main motive could not have been agrarian expansion, but royal legitimization. Of course, it may be argued that in the western portions of Comilla district, concerted attempts of agrarian expansion of the type we see in the Sylhet district might not have been required. But that does not explain why the monasteries conceded space to Brahmanical institutions in Sylhet district.

In the Devaparvata copper-plate inscription of Bhavadeva (eighth century CE), we see the transfer of 7.5 *pāṭaka*s of cultivated land in favour of *vendamati vihārikā*. The donated land was scattered in four villages in Peranāṭaṇa-viṣaya.[65] The donated land was probably located in the modern Comilla or Noakhali district.[66] The same inference, as noted in the context of Asharafapur copper-plate inscriptions, is applicable here as well.

However, that should not be taken to mean that Buddhist monasteries were totally inactive on the tribal frontiers. In fact, in some of the copper plates, we see that patronage to Buddhist monasteries was the medium though which some of the tribes, which were undergoing the transition to state polity, sought their legitimacy and stability.[67] That is, Buddhist monasteries were having a catalytic role in the tribal state formations and their legitimizations. This aspect seems to be most marked in Chittagong area.

This process is, however, not discernible in the Sylhet area. In the Paschimabhag copper-plate inscription (*c.*930 CE), a process of the colonization of a huge, uncultivated area spread over three *viṣayas*, centering upon Brahmanical institutions, is visible.[68] A similar attempt of agrarian expansion, though on a much lesser scale, is visible in two Bhatera copper plates of eleventh century CE.

In the Mainamati plates of Laḍahacandra and Vīradharadeva, we see that idioms have turned more and more Brahmanical. That may indicate a gradual loss of Buddhist influence in Samataṭa.[69] Buddhist monasteries in the Comilla area received patronage from local rulers even after the foundation of the Muslim rule in Bengal.[70] That, however, does not negate a gradual erosion of Buddhist influence in Samataṭa in the previous centuries. Gradual erosion of Buddhist influence is reflected in some comparatively late sculptures of the Buddha, discovered in the Salban Vihara excavations, in which the Buddha is portrayed as wearing a sacred thread[71]; as well as in inscriptions. This erosion is despite continued trumpeting of *paramasaugata* appellation in their inscriptions by the rulers of Samataṭa.

Summing Up: Implications of Buddhist Monastic Reluctance to Enter into Institutional Collaboration with the State in Engaging Agrarian Frontiers

One important inference, which was highlighted in the previous pages, was the apparent heterogeneity in the trans-Meghna portions of Bengal. Elements of similarity could not have been absent in the swamps and forests of low-lying Sylhet plains, fertile Comilla-Noakhali districts and the plains of Chittagong coast, where maritime activities could have had a greater significance. Yet, elements of dissimilarity appear to have been more profound. Obviously spatial linkages of religious institutions – Buddhist monasteries and Brahmanical temples/*maṭhas* – had differentiations across this variegated space. It has been noted in the previous pages that the areas which constitute Comilla and Noakhali districts today, appear to be the 'local nuclei of early socio-economic and political developments. From this core, various dynasties attempted to integrate two 'frontiers' – Sylhet and Chittagong districts – by extending patronage to Buddhist monasteries and Brahmanical institutions. A portion of wealth accruing from maritime trade could have flown to the monasteries. But in the absence of epigraphically recorded instances of mercantile patronage to Buddhist monastic institutions, mercantile patronage, if any, does not seem to have been of much significance. The major resource base of Buddhist monasteries seems to have been agrarian.

However, as we have seen in the previous pages, most of the land grants to Buddhist monasteries took place in a very limited area: in the Sadar area of Comilla district. Land grant to Buddhist monasteries in this area was motivated primarily by the urge for royal legitimization. Of course, this is not to suggest that they were not present on the agrarian frontiers of Sylhet or Chittagong, but on the whole, this is a saga of gradual loss of space to the Brahmins and Brahmanical religious institutions. In a nutshell, Brahmanical institutions outsmarted Buddhist monasteries on the agrarian frontiers of early medieval Samataṭa-Harikela. That seems to be the unmaking of Buddhist influence in trans-Meghna Bengal in the long run. Yet we are not fully sure that the apparent matrix – 'Samataṭa rulers making money from maritime trade and patronizing Buddhist monasteries with a portion of this money and land grants for royal legitimacy; and relying primarily on Brahmanical institutions for advancing agrarian frontiers' – explains the dynamics of early medieval Samataṭa-Harikela in totality. Further researches are required to unveil aspects of this complexity.

NOTES

1. This is a slightly modified version of my paper, which was originally published with the same title in *South and Southeast Asia: Culture and Religion*, vol. 2, 2008, pp. 160-77.
2. Andre Wink, *Al-Hind: The Making of the Indo-Islamic World*, vol. II, Oxford University Press, Delhi, 1999, pp. 335-6.

3. P.S. Jaini, 'The Disappearance of Buddhism and the Survival of Jainism in India: A Study in Contrast', in his *Collected Papers on Buddhist Studies,* Motilal Banarsidass, Delhi 2001, p. 142.
4. D.D. Kosambi, 'The Decline of Buddhism in India' in his *Exasperating Essays: Exercises in the Dialectical Method*, Peoples' Publishing House, Pune, 1986, p. 66; R.S. Sharma, *Urban Decay,* Munshiram Manoharlal, Delhi, 1987, p. 131.
5. Andre Wink, op. cit., pp. 349-50.
6. Richard M. Eaton, 'Who are the Bengal Muslims? Conversions and Islamisation in Bengal', in R. Ahmed (ed.), *Understanding Bengal Muslims,* Oxford University Press, Delhi, 2001, p. 34.
7. Akabar Ali Khan, *Discovery of Bangladesh: Explorations in the Dynamics of a Hidden Nation*, University Press Limited, Dhaka, 2001, p. 18.
8. Richard M. Eaton, op. cit., p. 36; Ralph Nicholas, 'Vaisanavism and Islam in the Environs of Rural Bengal', in Rafiuddin Ahmed (ed.), *Understanding Bengal Muslims,* Oxford University Press, Delhi, 2000, pp. 52-70. Nicholas has analysed the sectarian affiliations of different castes and religious communities of deltaic portions of Bengal during the pre-1947 phase. He found that Bengal peasantry adhered either to Islam or Vaiṣṇavism. His explanation of this particular feature is: 'Bengal Delta was a kind of slowly opening frontier which was gradually settled agriculturally, in which Islam and Vaiṣṇavism are likely to have functioned to provide authority in an anarchic frontier society through their loosely constituted religious organizations, *millat* and *maṇḍalī* respectively' (p. 66).
9. See for example, Richard Eaton, who argues that 'in much of eastern Delta, rice agriculture and Islam were introduced simultaneously' (Richard M. Eaton, *Essays on Islam and Indian History*, Oxford University Press, Delhi, 2001, p. 264). As per Eaton, Eastern Bengal 'experienced a transition to settled agriculture at the time that Islam took hold among common folk' (Richard M. Eaton, 'Shrines, Cultivators, and Muslim "Conversion" in Punjab and Bengal, 1300-1700', *Medieval History Journal*, vol. 12, no. 2, 2009, p. 208).
10. In Puṇḍravardhana, Xuan Zang noted the presence of 'about twenty *saṅghārāma*s with some 3,000 priests'. In Samataṭa, he found 'thirty or so *saṅghārāma*s with about 2,000 priests'. In the 'country of Tāmralipti', he noted the presence of 'ten *saṅghārāma*s, with about 1,000 priests'.

In the 'country of Karṇasuvarṇa', he found 'ten *saṅghārāmas* or so with about 2,000 priests'. See S. Beal, *Si-Yu-Ki, Buddhist Records of the Western World: Translated from the Chinese of Hieun Tsiang*, vol. II, Trubner & Co., London, 1884, pp. 194-204.

11. In terms of extent, Mainamati Complex appears to be one of the largest Buddhist monastic complexes in South Asia. The entire area (approximately 18 km in length and at times 5-km in width) was studded with a large number of monasteries built over a period of six to seven hundred years, under the patronage of different Samataṭa dynasties. At least 55 archaeological sites have been identified so far, each representing the remains of some Buddhist religious centre (monastery/*stūpa*). Only exception is the site of Charapatra Mura, which appears is the ruin of a Brahmanical temple. In recent years, many monographs dealing with the art and architecture of Mainamati Complex have been published. See particularly F.A. Khan, *Mainamati: A Preliminary Report on the Recent Archaeological Excavations in East Pakistan,* Dept. of Archaeology, Govt. of Pakistan, Karachi, 1963; B.M. Morrison, *Lālmāi: A Cultural Centre in Early Bengal,* University of Washington Press, Seattle, 1974; A.K.M. Shamsul Alam, *Mainamati,* Dept. of Archaeology and Museums, Govt. of the Peoples' Republic of Bangladesh, Dacca,1982; A.B.M. Husain and M. Harunur Rashid, *Mainamati-Devaparvata: A Survey of Historical Monuments and Sites in Bangladesh,* Asiatic Society of Bangladesh, Dhaka,1997; Abu Imam, 'Samataṭa-Mainamati: Some Observations', in G. Sengupta and S. Panja (eds.), *Archaeology of Eastern India: New Perspectives,* Centre for Archaeological Studies and Training-Eastern India, Kolkata, 2002, pp. 613-29.
12. For the practices of living Buddhism in Southeastern Bengal, see Sukomal Chaudhury, *Contemporary Buddhism in Bangladesh,* Atisha Memorial Publishing Society, Calcutta,1982; A. M. Khan, *The Maghs: A Buddhist Community in Bangladesh,* University Press Limited, Dhaka, 1999. Also see N. Ahmed, *Discover the Monuments of Bangladesh,* University Press Limited, Dhaka, 1984. Ahmed has noted that contemporary Bangladesh has a Buddhist population of around half-a-million concentrated mainly in Chittagong, Comilla and Dhaka districts (p. 45).

13. B.M. Morrison, *Political Centres and Cultural Regions in Early Bengal*, Vikash, Jaipur, 1980 (Indian edition), p. 38.
14. Ibid., p. 38. However, important variations were noted within each subregion of early medieval Bengal in later studies. See Birendra Nath Prasad, *Archaeology of Religion in South Asia: Buddhist, Brahmanical and Jaina Religious Centres in Bihar and Bengal, c.AD 600–1200*, Routledge, London and New York, 2021. Also see my article on Purulia in the present book.
15. B.M. Morrison, op. cit., p. 38.
16. Ibid.
17. Ibid., p. 154.
18. Ibid., p. 153.
19. Ibid., p 119.
20. Richard M. Eaton, 'Who are the Bengal Muslims?: Conversions and Islamisation in Bengal', in R. Ahmed (ed.), *Understanding Bengal Muslims,* Oxford University Press, Delhi, 2001, p. 35.
21. B.D. Chattopadhyaya, *The Making of Early Medieval India,* Oxford University Press, Delhi, 1994, p. 35.
22. Hermann Kulke, 'The Early and Imperial Kingdom: A Processual Model for Integrative State Formation in Early Medieval India', in Hermann Kulke (ed.), *The State in India 1000–1700,* Oxford University Press, Delhi, 1995, p. 250.
23. M.M. Hoque and Seema Hoque, 'Ancient Human Settlement Pattern of Bangladesh: A Preliminary Study', *Journal of Bengal Art*, vol. 2, 1997, p. 289.
24. A. Bhattacharya, 'Trade Routes of Ancient Bengal', in A. Dutta (ed.), *History and Archaeology of Eastern India,* Books and Books, Delhi, 1998, p. 64.
25. At Tāmralipti, Faxian saw 22 monasteries but Xuan Zang could see only 10 monasteries (Chitaranjana Patra, 'Spread of Buddhism in Bengal', in A. Dutta (ed.), op. cit., p. 203), and later records (after Itsing) are silent about the presence of monasteries at Tāmralipti.
26. Ranabir Chakravarti, *Trade and Traders in Early Indian Society,* Manohar, Delhi, 2002, p. 135.
27. M.R. Tarafdar, 'Trade and Society in Early Medieval Bengal', in his *Trade, Technology and Society in Medieval Bengal,* University Press Limited, Dhaka, 1995, p. 13.

28. Ranabir Chakravarti, *Trade and Traders in Early Indian Society*, Manohar, Delhi, 2002, p. 152.
29. M.R. Tarafdar, op. cit., p. 15.
30. Ibid., p. 16.
31. Ibid., p. 18.
32. Rila Mukherjee, 'Rice Culture of Divine Right in a Celestially Ordered Zone: A Case Study of South Asian and South-East Asian Ideologies and Hegemonies from *c.*2000 BC to *c.*1800 AD with Specific Reference to Bengal', *Revista Lusofona de Ciencias Sociais*, 1, 2004, p. 56; idem, *Strange Riches: Bengal in the Mercantile Map of South Asia*, Foundation Books, Delhi, 2006, p. 25.
33. Hermann Kulke, 'Rivalry and Competition in the Bay of Bengal in the Eleventh Century and its Bearing on Indian Ocean Studies', in Om Prakash and Denys Lombard (eds.), *Commerce and Culture in the Bay of Bengal, 1500-1800,* Manohar, New Delhi, 1999, pp. 17-35.
34. Rila Mukherjee has taken this argument to another extreme. She asserts that there were two sectors in the Bengal delta: the western delta and the eastern delta. Western delta relied primarily on wet rice agriculture and its society was overwhelmingly agrarian. Despite having evidences for the expansion of agrarian frontiers, eastern delta was primarily maritime in orientation. After the tenth century CE, the eastern delta (Samataṭa) engaged more in trade and less in agriculture. She has related this phenomenon to the Indian Ocean 'trade revolution' of the eleventh-twelfth centuries CE (Rila Mukherjee, 'Rice Culture of Divine Right in a Celestially Ordered Zone: A Case Study of South Asian and South-East Asian Ideologies and Hegemonies from *c.*2000 BC to *c.*1800 AD with Specific Reference to Bengal', *Revista Lusofona de Ciencias Sociais*, 1, 2004, p. 60). However, she fails to explain the puzzling absence of indigenous coinage and meagre references to the native merchants or mercantile groups in Samataṭa-Harikela copper-plate inscriptions during these centuries.
35. M.R. Tarafdar, op. cit., p. 16.
36. Ibid., p. 26.
37. In fact, Kanheri may provide a good case for comparison with the Mainamati monastic Complex. Like Mainamati, it seems to have benefited from maritime trade. Unlike some other Buddhist monastic sites on the Maharashtra coast, which declined after 400 CE, Kanheri

displays the evidences of flourishing occupation till tenth-eleventh centuries CE. The presence of important port towns in the close vicinity of Kanheri (Chaul, Sopora, Kalyan, etc.), which made possible the continuous flow of mercantile patronage, and its widespread pilgrimage networks through which it attracted pilgrims from such far off places like Sindh and Gauḍa (north Bengal) ensured its survival and growth despite the apparent lack of royal patronage during these centuries. See H.P. Ray, 'Kanheri: The Archaeology of an Early Buddhist Pilgrimage Site in Western India', *World Archaeology,* vol. 26, no. 1, 1994, p. 37. Right now, we don't have anything to visualize the nature of mercantile patronage to the Mainamati Complex, if any. Similarly, we don't know why we don't have epigraphically recorded instances of local and supra-local pilgrimage to different Buddhist monastic centres on the Mainamati-Lalmai ridge.

38. For an interesting analysis of the impact of commercial rivalries between the local merchants of early medieval Konkan and the merchants coming from north India (Rajasthan, etc.) on the fortunes of a *maṭha*, see Ranabir Chakravarti, 'Monarchs, Merchants and a *Maṭha* in Northern Konkan, *c.*900-1053 AD', *Indian Economic and Social History Review*, vol. 27, no. 2, 1990, pp. 189-208.
39. For an analysis of the impact of royal and mercantile patronages on the fortunes of temples of early medieval Rajasthan, see Shanta Sharma, 'Rulers, Urban Milieu and Temple Patronage: Shifting Contours in Rajasthan, *c.*AD 700-1000', *History Today,* vol. 4, 2003, pp. 9-21.
40. For a historiographical review of the evolving functional roles of ancient Indian Buddhist monasteries, see Birendra Nath Prasad, 'Major Trends and Perspectives in Studies in the Functional Dimensions of Indian Monastic Buddhism in the Past One Hundred Years: A Historiographical Survey', *Buddhist Studies Review*, London, vol. 25, no. 1, 2008, pp. 54- 89.
41. H.P. Ray, *Monastery and Guild: Commerce under the Sātavāhanas,* Oxford University Press, Delhi, 1986, p. 208.
42. D.C. Bhattacharya, 'A Newly Discovered Copperplate from Tippera (The Gunaighar Grant of Vainyagupta: The Year 188 Current (Gupta Era), *The Indian Historical Quarterly*, vol. 6, no. 1, 1930, p. 54.
43. Ibid., p. 55.
44. Ibid., p. 49.

45. Ibid., p. 55.
46. Ibid., p. 56.
47. Ibid.
48. Ibid.
49. Rila Mukherjee, 'Rice Culture of Divine Right in a Celestially Ordered Zone', p. 55.
50. D.C. Sircar, *Epigraphic Discoveries in East Pakistan,* Sanskrit College, Calcutta, 1973, p. 15.
51. Ibid., p. 15.
52. Ibid.
53. D.C. Sircar, *Select Inscriptions Bearing on Indian History and Civilization*, vol. II: *From the Sixth to the Eighteenth Century*, Motilal Banarsidass, Delhi, 1983, p. 31-32.
54. Suvvuṅga viṣaya has been identified with the Cachar district of south Assam. See N.K. Bhattasali, 'New Light on the History of Assam', *Indian Historical Quarterly,* XXI, vol. 1945, p. 28.
55. D.C. Sircar, *Epigraphic Discoveries in East Pakistan*, Sanskrit College, Calcutta, 1973, p. 16.
56. K.K. Gupta, *Copper Plates of Sylhet*, vol. 1: *7th – 11th Centuries AD*, Lipika Enterprises, Sylhet, 1967, pp. 70-1.
57. Ibid., p. 80.
58. D.C. Sircar, 'The Kailan Copper-plate Inscription of King Śrīdhāraṇa Rāta of Samataṭa', *Indian Historical Quarterly*, vol. XXIII, 1947, pp. 221-40.
59. B.M. Morrison, *Political Centres and Cultural Regions in Early Bengal*, Vikash, Jaipur, 1980, p. 33.
60. Ibid., p. 37.
61. G.M. Lashkar, 'Ashrafpur Copper-Plate Grants of Devakhaḍga', *Memoirs of the Asiatic Society of Bengal*, vol. 1, no. 6, 1906, p. 85.
62. Ibid., p. 90.
63. Ibid.
64. Ibid., pp. 90-1.
65. D.C. Sircar, 'Copper-Plate Inscription of King Bhavadeva of Devaparvata', *Journal of Asiatic Society, Letters*, vol. XVII, 1951, pp. 83-94.
66. B.M. Morrison, op. cit., p. 39.

67. See G. Bhattacharya, 'A Preliminary Note on the Inscribed Metal Vase from the National Museum of Bangladesh', in D. Mitra (ed.), *Explorations in the Art and Archaeology of South Asia: Essays Dedicated to N.G. Majumdar,* Directorate of Archaeology and Museums, Govt. of West Bengal, Calcutta, 1996. This inscription records the donation of land to Buddhist monastery by one Devātideva Bhaṭṭāraka (eighth century CE), who belonged to the non-Aryan Khasa tribe. He had embraced Buddhism (p. 239). Also see G. Bhattacharya, 'An Inscribed Metal Vase, Most Probably from Chittagong', in A.J. Gail and G.J.R. Mevissen (eds.), *South Asian Archaeology*, 1991, pp. 323-38.
68. For an analysis of this inscription, see D.C. Sircar, op. cit., pp. 19-40.
69. For an analysis of these inscriptions, see D.C. Sircar, *Epigraphic Discoveries in Eastern Pakistan,* Sanskrit College, Calcutta, 1973, pp. 41-59.
70. See the Mainamati plate of Raṇavaṅkamalla Harikāladeva, *c.*1220 CE, which records the donation of 20 *pāṭaka*s of land in favour of a monastery dedicated to the Buddhist goddess Durgottārā (D.C. Bhattacharya, 'The Mainamati Copper Plate of Raṇavaṅkamalla Harikāladeva: 1141 Saka', *Varendra Research Society Monographs No. 5,* Rajshahi, 1934, pp. 11-12). This monastery was located in the 'city' of Paṭṭikera, somewhere on the Mainamati ridge or in its vicinity.
71. Harunur Rashid, *Early History of Southeast Bengal in the Light of Archaeological Material*, Itihas Academy, Dhaka, 2008, p. 110.

6

Jaina and Brahmanical Temples and Political Processes in a Forested Frontier of Early Medieval South-Western Bengal

A Study of Purulia[1]

Introduction

With an increasing realization of the need to study Brahmanical temples not merely as repositories of art and architecture but as social institutions in dynamic interaction with other social institutions,[2] studies in the social history of these temples have witnessed many paradigm shifts.[3] An important shift is the emphasis on the micro-study of the locale in which these temples emerged, functioned and declined.[4] Generally, scholarship has highlighted the catalytic roles of these temples in hastening the transition from *vana* to *kṣetra*[5] or *araṇya* to *janapada*,[6] and in the legitimation of the dynasty that patronized them. Probable similar roles of Jaina temples in some parts of India have not invited serious academic enquiry.

Through an analysis of the reported archaeological data, this chapter aims to understand the roles of Jaina and Brahmanical temples in the process of state formation and legitimation on a tribal and forested frontier of early medieval southwestern Bengal: Purulia, an area which remained under heavy tribal influence until the recent past.[7] Due to a great paucity of epigraphic records associated with the temples of this area, this chapter shall place emphasis on the relationships between temples and hero stones, and on the socio-political ramifications of those relationships.

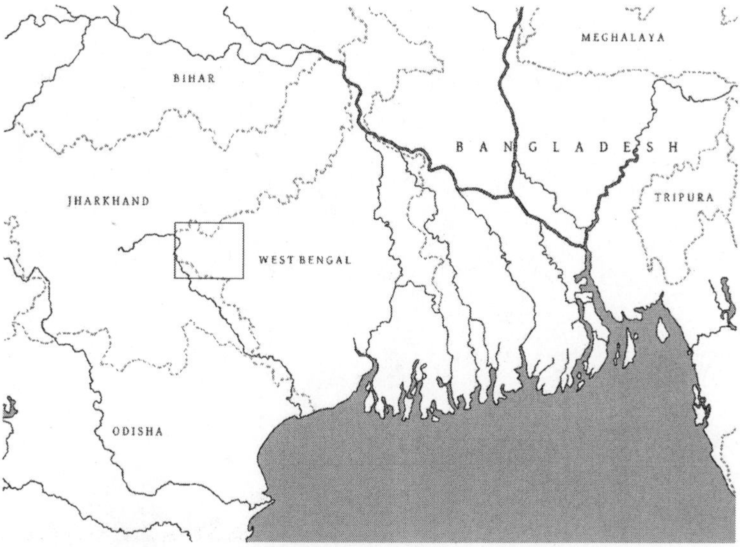

Figure 1: The location of Purulia district in West Bengal. The rectangle shows the approximate area covered by Fig. 2. Map not to scale. Map by the author.

Situating Purulia in Early Medieval Bengal

In some existing studies on ancient and early medieval Bengal, one may discern a peculiar tendency to generalize the perceived cultural experience of the valleys of the great rivers of Bengal to its other geographical zones.[8] Bengal being the world's largest delta, this tendency is quite understandable, but it obfuscates the historical dynamics of other areas. Thus, in a significant study of the political geography of early medieval Bengal, Morrison has found that Bengal had at least four sub-regions:[9]

(1) Varendra, covering the areas of north Bengal; more appropriately the tract of land bounded by the Mahananda River in the west, the Karatoya and Brahmaputra in the east, and the Padma in the south;

(2) Vaṅga, the tract of land to the south of the Padma River,

Figure 2: Administrative blocks in the district of Purulia, West Bengal. Map not to scale. Map by the author.

bounded by the rivers Hughli in the west and Meghna in the east;

(3) Rāḍha, covering the areas to the west of the Bhagirathi–Hughli River; and

(4) Samataṭa-Harikela, the area to the east of the Surma and Meghna rivers, roughly corresponding to Sylhet, Comilla and the Chittagong tract of Bangladesh.

In the Varendra sub-region, from the very beginning, land was transferred to individual owners, and the extent of the transferred land was always small. The same pattern was more or less visible in the Dhaka-Faridpur area of Vaṅga as well as in Rāḍha.[10] But the pattern was fundamentally different in the Sylhet-Comilla-Chittagong sector. In this sector, land was always granted to institutions – Buddhist monasteries or Brahmanical temples – or to a large group of Brahmins, and the size of the land grant was generally very large compared to that in other sectors of Bengal. Within this sector too, there were important variations. Compared to Comilla or the Chittagong area, the size of land grants was larger in the Sylhet area.[11] Morrison's conclusions are obvious: in the central, northern and western sectors of Bengal, property relations were fully developed, and culturally these sectors were more or less integrated with the middle Ganga Valley. In fact, they were the 'heartlands of Brahmanical culture in the Delta'.[12] Samataṭa-Harikela had different orientations – economically, politically and culturally. It was a society of relatively sparse population, lacking a long history of individual property rights; hence the land grants to institutions or to large congregations of Brahmins.

Morrison's study suffers from some limitations, mainly due to the fact that it over-generalizes the inferences from one particular kind of data source: royal copper-plate charters, which are not found in all parts of Bengal. Besides, this study overlooks spatial differentiations and their socio-economic and cultural ramifications within different sub-regions of Bengal. No sub-region of Bengal was homogeneous, and this heterogeneity was especially marked in Samataṭa-Harikela and Rāḍha. Thus, in the context of Samataṭa-Harikela, fundamental differences have been noted between Comilla (which was the core area of various polities of Samataṭa) and Sylhet.[13] In the context of Rāḍha, a fundamental difference has been noted as we move from its alluvial parts in the east to the plateau parts in the west.[14] Even in the case of a single district of Rāḍha-Vardhaman for example, which has flat alluvial topography in the east and undulating hilly topography in the west –

fundamental differences have been noted as one moves from east to west.[15] Similarly, in the case of the Bankura district, its eastern part experienced an early historic state formation with its nucleus in the Pakhanna area, but its western part could witness regular human occupation only during the early medieval period, from around the eighth and ninth centuries CE onward.[16]

Compared to Bankura, Purulia offers an altogether different experience during the early historic period. This district was under greater influence from the tribal cultures of Jharkhand, and was bound to have a different kind of historical personality from that seen in the alluvial portions of West Bengal. This is reflected in the evolution of the archaeological sequence of the district. Not a single Neolithic, Chalcolithic or early historic site has yet been reported there.[17] The Palaeolithic–Mesolithic phase is followed directly by the early medieval archaeological material from the eighth and ninth centuries onwards.[18]

The district of Purulia abounds in early medieval materials dating, more specifically, from the eighth and ninth centuries onwards: Jaina and Brahmanical temple ruins and associated structural presence, hero and *satī* stones, and loose sculptures, which also indicate the past existence of temples in the district.[19] A largely coeval phenomenon was the evolution of a local polity in the area. It is apparent that the evolution of a local polity was related to two related features of this district during this period: large-scale construction of Jaina and Brahmanical temples, and the erection of hero stones. What was the nature of the relationship between these three developments? How were the construction of Jaina and Brahmanical temples and the erection of hero stones related to the political processes in the area? Did Brahmanical and Jaina temples have similar kinds of engagements with these political processes? These are some of the issues that will be explored in the present article on the basis of an analysis of published archaeological and epigraphic data. But before looking into these issues in some detail, we would like to outline the nature of polity formation in the area.

State Formation in the Purulia Area

In some peripheral areas of Bengal – Sylhet, for example – a common mechanism of state formation was through the process of agrarian expansion, which often involved land grants to religious donees (individual Brahmins or groups of Brahmins, Brahmanical temples, and, in some cases, Buddhist monasteries as well). Immigrant Brahmins often brought some extra-local influences, ideologies and institutional changes, which, coupled with local developments, paved the way for the evolution of local polities in areas that were hitherto untouched by this process.[20] Patronage towards Brahmanical temples was an important matrix of this whole process. In the Sylhet area of Bengal, it was through the state-sponsored establishment of Brahmanical temples and the settlement of a huge congregation of non-local Brahmins by the political powers based in the Comilla-Dhaka area of Bengal during the tenth century that conditions were created for the emergence of a local state in the Sylhet area in the eleventh century.[21]

The process of state formation in the Purulia area was unlikely to have been similar to that in the alluvial areas of Bengal, basically due to its undulating landscape, heavily forested nature and proximity to the cultures based in the Jharkhand plateau. The landscape was different. In fact, in this area in the period under study, there is a singular absence of copper-plate charters recording donation of land in favour of religious donees (Brahmins or Brahmanical or Jaina temples) by any political power based in deltaic Bengal.[22] The local political formation that emerged in this area does not seem to have adopted the policy of donation of land grants in favour of religious donees. This is probably due to the geography of the area, most of which was plateau-like and heavily forested.

What could have been the mechanism of state formation in this area? In our view, it was most probably related to trade passing through it. It has been noted elsewhere that the Purulia area covered a vital segment of trade route that connected Vārāṇasī to coastal portions of West Bengal and Odisha.[23] The trade passing through this area brought many non-local influences, which in the long run paved the way for state formation. The penetration of Jainism into the area was also most probably a by-product of the trade passing through it. Once Jainism penetrated into this area, it localized itself by entering into a complex relation with political and social processes.

Some available epigraphic records of early medieval Purulia throw interesting light on the political formation that emerged in this area. Thus, in the recently deciphered Dhuluri rock inscription, datable to the seventh or eighth century, we are informed of an illustrious prince (*śrīyuvarāja*) and [his?] illustrious preceptor (*ācārya*) whose name ends with *deva*.[24] As this inscription is fragmented at vital spots, no other detail (the name of the *yuvarāja* or the *ācārya*) is available. We do not know the sectarian affiliation (Brahmanical or Jaina) of the *ācārya* either. For this reason, it is difficult to determine which religion (Brahmanism or Jainism) provided the initial push for state formation in the area. The short, fragmentary nature of the inscription does not allow us to infer much regarding the nature of the polity that was in operation in this area in the seventh and eighth centuries. One inference, though, stands out: the *ācārya* was important enough to have figured in the inscription.

Some interesting information regarding the nature of polity in the Purulia area is provided in the *Rāmacaritam* of Sandhyākara Nandī, an eleventh-century text. In this text, we are informed that the Pāla ruler Rāmapāla (latter half of the eleventh century) had to seek help from his circle of *sāmanta*s (*sāmantacakra*) to recover Varendri from Kaivartta occupation. The Pāla state theoretically claimed suzerainty over these *sāmanta*s, but in practice it did not have the power to impose its writ over the areas controlled by them. This inability on the part of the Pāla state was more pronounced in this moment of crisis when the ruling Pāla king was in exile and one of the heartlands of his empire, Varendra, was under the occupation of the Kaivarttas. Thus, we are informed that Rāmapāla, 'by a lavish offer of land and enormous wealth, gained over to his side a number of powerful chiefs, who possessed well-equipped forces'.[25]

It may be noted that the same text describes 13 *sāmanta*s who were approached by the Pāla king for fighting the Kaivarttas. Out of these 13 *sāmanta*s, nine were from the western fringes of Rāḍha and Daṇḍabhukti, and four from Puṇḍra (in north Bengal). In the group of *sāmanta*s from Rāḍha and Daṇḍabhukti, we are informed of the following:[26]

1. Vīraguṇa, 'king' of Koṭāṭavī.[27]
2. Jayasiṁha, 'king' of Daṇḍabhukti.
3. Vikramarāja, 'ruler' of Bāla-Balabhī.[28]
4. Lakṣmīśūra, 'lord' of Aparamandāra.[29] Lakṣmīśūra has been described as *samastāṭavika-sāmantacakracūḍāmaṇī*.[30]
5. Śūrapāla, 'ruler' of Kujavaṭī.[31]
6. Rudraśikhara, 'ruler' of Tailakampī.[32]
7. Bhāṣkara, 'king' of Ucchāla.[33]
8. Pratāpasiṁha, 'king' of Dhekkarīya.[34]
9. Narasiṁhārjuna, 'king' of Kayaṅgalamaṇḍala.[35]

Sandhyākara Nandī, being more concerned with the heroics of his patron King Rāmapāla, has not left much detail regarding the nature of the polities headed by these *sāmanta*s, but a contextual analysis of this text has made R.C. Majumdar, one of the editors of the *Rāmacaritam*, conclude that a differentiation existed within this *sāmantacakra*: 'royal' epithets have been used for some *sāmanta*s only, not for all.[36] Majumdar has used the word 'king' only for those *sāmanta*s who have been referred to with 'royal' epithets by Sandhyākara Nandī. For Rudraśikhara, who ruled from the Telkupi area of Purulia, no royal epithet was used by Sandhyākara Nandī.

It is pertinent that Lakṣmīśūra has been mentioned as *samastāṭavika-sāmantacakracūḍāmaṇī* (the crest jewel of all the *sāmanta*s in the *āṭavika* zone, i.e. the forested zone), indicating that many of the *sāmantas* referred to by Sandhyākara Nandī were *āṭavika-sāmantas*. In fact, the use of the suffix *āṭavī* in the place-name Koṭāṭavī may indicate that Vīraguṇa too ruled in a forested zone (in the Bankura district) and that he too was an *āṭavika-sāmanta*. The status of Rudraśikhara of Purulia was, arguably, that of an *āṭavika-sāmanta*. Vīraguṇa has been referred to as a 'king', but no such epithet has been used for Rudraśikhara. It is apparent that, for Sandhyākara Nandī, the polity headed by Rudraśikhara, was considered to be less complex and powerful than the one headed by Vīraguṇa of the Vishnupur area of Bankura.

This was most probably the result of the differential history and geography of these two areas (eastern Bankura and Purulia). Elsewhere I have noted the emergence of the state of Puṣkaraṇa in the Pakhanna area of Bankura in the fourth century.[37] Besides, the Vishnupur area of Bankura was in closer proximity to the polities based in the Ganga Valley of Bengal than Purulia was. In short, the Vishnupur area of Bankura had greater interaction with the polities based in the Ganga Valley of Bengal. That ensured that the Vishnupur area of Bankura had a more complex polity than the Purulia area.

That notwithstanding, the family of Rudraśikhara seems to have enjoyed a long sway in Purulia. A twelfth- or thirteenth-century short inscription engraved on the lintel of a temple at the site of Para refers to the *vijaya-rājya-saṁvata* 2 (victorious regnal year 2) of Śikharadeva.[38] Similarly, a thirteenth- or fourteenth-century short inscription on a boundary pillar at the site of Boram refers to one *siṁhāsanacakravartī* Rudraśikhara-Yuvarāja.[39] It is apparent that these characters were all related to the family of Rudraśikhara.[40] The prolonged rule by the rulers of a single family in the Purulia area may indicate that their rule had some sustained source of legitimacy. Did temples serve as fountains of legitimacy for the rulers of this area? And what kind of relationship did they have with another important element of the political matrix of this area: those warrior heroes who died in battle but were immortalized in hero stones? This is something we will try to explore now.

Early Medieval Temples and their Support Systems in Purulia

No inscription records the construction of any temple, Brahmanical or Jaina, by any political elite in the Purulia area. Nor does any inscription record an endowment to an existing temple. The aforementioned twelfth- or thirteenth-century short inscription engraved on the lintel of a temple at the site of Para refers to the 'victorious regnal year 2' (*vijaya-rājya-saṁvata* 2) of a ruler named Śikharadeva which may indicate the patronage of this temple by Śikharadeva.[41] It is, though, difficult to determine whether an existing temple was patronized by Śikharadeva or whether he caused the construction of this temple. This is the only such example; no other inscription of this kind has yet been discovered. Such evidence, however, should not be taken as indicating that Brahmanical and Jaina temples were totally aloof from the political processes of this area. We may explore some aspects of the complex pattern of interactions by analysing two issues: location of the temples vis-à-vis important political centres, and location of these temples vis-à-vis hero stones.

With regard to the first issue (location of these temples vis-à-vis political centres), our sources provide contextual inferences only. We may analyse the situation at Tailakampī (i.e. Telkupi), the seat of power of Rudraśikhara. Since 16 out of the 26 temples documented at the site of Telkupi had Śaiva sculptures in their sanctum, it has reasonably been inferred that this site was primarily a Śaiva temple cluster, though with the sporadic presence of Vaiṣṇava and Jaina sculptures.[42] In other words, the administrative headquarters of this *āṭavika-sāmanta* had a major concentration of Śaiva temples. These temples could have been patronized by the political elites of the administrative headquarters. But we have no means of ascertaining whether these temples were actually caused to be constructed by the political elites of Tailakampī.

Even if it is assumed that the Śaiva temples at Telkupi were constructed by the political elites of the administrative headquarters of a local state in the area, we need to look into another related issue: did this result in the similar state-sponsored planting of Śaiva temples in other parts of the state? We are putting this question especially in view of the fact that the medieval Malla state that emerged in the neighbouring Bankura area followed a policy of patronizing the construction of temples in the areas beyond their capital in an attempt at 'geographical extension of the political control'.[43] The foundation of temples was 'one of the methods through which the ruling power tried to extend its control in a forested area that was rich in mineral and forest resources'.[44] We do not have any direct (epigraphic) evidence to undertake this kind of analysis.

One method of understanding the nature of the relationship between temples (Brahmanical and Jaina) and political processes in this area may be to analyse the nature of the relationship between these temples and hero stones. Hero stones abound in the district of Purulia. They have also been found in Bankura and in the western parts of Vardhaman district, and in western parts of the West Medinipur district.[45] We will examine their distribution pattern vis-à-vis temple sites, and try to arrive at some generalizations on the nature of the relationship between temples and this cult. We will try to see this against the background of some macro-studies on other parts of India.

Hero Stones and their Spatial Distribution Pattern vis-à-vis Jaina and Brahmanical Temples in Early Medieval Purulia

Broadly speaking, hero stones are memorial stones.[46] They were 'raised in memory or honour of the dead and did not form part of the actual practice of the disposal of the dead'.[47] These hero stones commemorated the 'death of those men who died in an act of heroism such as defending a village against raiders by land or sea, or defending cattle against cattle-lifters, or those who have died on the battlefield'.[48] The practice of erecting stones in memory of dead heroes is the product of the material ambience of the post-Gupta phase when daring adventurers attempted to establish 'little kingdoms'; or when new states or state-like structures emerged in arid zones which had pastoralism as their basic subsistence economy; or when some river-valley-based powers tried to expand in areas that generally did not have settled, intensive, agriculture as their basic subsistence economy.[49] It is probably for these reasons that hero stones are found in large numbers in the less fertile and arid zones of western India (Rajasthan, Gujarat and Maharashtra), central India (Madhya Pradesh and the southern edges of the Ganga Valley) and south India (Andhra, Karnataka, Kerala and Tamil Nadu).[50] They are generally absent in the Ganga valley. It has been noted that they were generally concentrated in what have acted as 'frontier zones' at some stage: the peripheral areas of kingdoms and the intersections of ecological zones, particularly where pastoralism separated areas of intensive cultivation or lay close to forested areas; areas where political security was transient and where royal armies did not necessarily guarantee protection to the local inhabitants. In such areas, the local population had to make its own arrangements for protection, in which the village hero or the local chief played a major role.[51] If the hero died in a heroic act of defending the local population, a memorial stone, often depicting the heroic action of the dead hero, was erected and his memory was thus immortalized.

These hero stones often provide important data to understand the cultic affiliation of the hero. Thus, the depiction of the *liṅgam* and *yoni* on such stones indicated that the hero was a Śaiva devotee, and the standing or seated figure of Mahāvīra indicated that he was a Jaina devotee.[52] Particularly in the context of early medieval Gujarat, but elsewhere too, it has been noted that those linked to the local ruling family had their stones in the courtyard of the temple.[53] But this entailed a different kind of negotiation between the temple authorities and the relatives of the dead hero: funerary rituals were restricted to the polluting space of the cremation ground, but the memorial stone of the hero was given space in the sanctified precincts of the temple, sharing space with gods – if not in the inner *sanctum sanctorum* of the temple, then at least within the temple compound. This entailed some give and take from both sides. The temple authorities had to accommodate the memorial of the local hero in the precincts of the temple. For the community that immortalized its dead heroes within the precincts of the temple, this process entailed discontinuing or modifying those aspects of rituals that were not acceptable to the priests: bloody sacrifices, offerings of alcohol, etc.[54] In short, the temple provided an avenue for the enhancement of the social status of the hero even after his death, but it came at a cost of considerable adoption of the value system of the priest(s) who controlled the temple. If the memorial stone of the hero was placed in the compound, or in the close vicinity of a Brahmanical temple, that entailed a considerable Sanskritization of the (cult of the dead) hero and his relatives. In the case of Jaina temples, this could have resulted in the dissemination and perpetuation of Jaina values, presumably of *ahiṁsā*. What was the pattern in Purulia?

I present the available religious context of hero stones of this district in Table 4, by collating data from earlier reported explorations.[55]

TABLE 4: SITES OF HERO STONES IN PURULIA DISTRICT AND THEIR RELIGIOUS AFFILIATIONS

Type of sites having hero stones	*Names of sites*	*No. of such sites*
Sites which appear to be Jaina mono-religious extant temple sites of earlier origin		0
Sites which appear to be Jaina mono-religious abandoned or ruined temple sites, or where the	Chharra, Anai Jambad, Palma, Karcha, Pabrapahari, Barumeshvara Dhama,	16

past presence of a temple is indicated by the presence of big stone sculptures	North Bandwan, Mahara, Basudevapur, Bhangra, Laulara, Chandanpur, Pichasi, Kushtarah, Mudidih, Dhadki	
Sites with a ruined or abandoned Jaina temple and Brahmanical presence, but with predominance of Jainism[56]	Bhabanipur, Ladhurka, Boram, Tuisuma, Lakhra	5
Sites which appear to be Brahmanical mono-religious standing temple sites of earlier origin		0
Sites which appear to be Brahmanical mono-religious abandoned or ruined temple sites	Ralibera, Ranipukur, Sasandihi, Budhpur	4
Sites with both Jaina and Brahmanical presence, but with predominance of Brahmanism	Kroshjuri, Para	2
Sites with hero stones but without any religious structure or sculpture, or where the religious affiliation of the site is difficult to determine	Pabanpur, Bargora, Bhagabandh, Garhpanchakot, Bero	5
Sites with temple ruins, *āmalaka*s, doorjambs etc., but where the cultic affiliation is difficult to determine	Raibaghini, Borrha, Choto Balrampur	3
Total		35

Source: Table prepared by the author by collating data from earlier publications.

Out of the 80 reported sites in the district, hero stones have been reported from 35 sites. Twenty-one out of 35 hero-stone-bearing sites (i.e. 60 per cent of hero-stone-bearing sites) appear to be either Jaina mono-religious sites or sites with a predominant presence of Jainism. Sites which appear to be Brahmanical mono-religious abandoned or ruined temple sites account for 11.42 per cent of hero-stone-bearing sites. Sites with both Brahmanical and Jaina presence, but with a clear-cut dominance of Brahmanism, account for 5.7 per cent of hero-stone-bearing sites. Only five hero-stone-bearing sites (i.e. 14.25 per cent) do not have any religious structure or sculpture. But in this category, at the site of Bhagabandh, the carving of Śiva's *liṅgam* in the central portions of the hero stones indicates the Śaiva affiliation of the hero.[57] On the whole, it is quite apparent that Jaina temples provided the primary, and preferred, avenue for accommodating the cult of hero stones in the district of Purulia.

The hero stones of Purulia district display a peculiar feature. At the major Śaiva temple-cluster site of Telkupi, there are none: only a small stone tablet containing the depiction of a hero, rather than a sculpted stone containing the depiction of the hero, has been found there.[58] Telkupi was, arguably, the political centre of Rudraśikhara. Similarly, there are no hero stones at major Jaina temple clusters such as Pakbira.[59] But we get them frequently at less monumental Brahmanical and Jaina temple sites. That remains true for the hero stones found at the sites which have rightly been believed to be the satellite sites of Pakbira: Lakhra[60] and Dhadki.[61] Both sites – Lakhra and Dhadki – appear to be Jaina mono-religious sites.

What were the social backgrounds of the heroes who were immortalized in stones? Much of this question will remain unanswered, as inscriptions are available only on three hero and *satī* stones. All three have been found at the site of Budhpur, which appears to be a Brahmanical mono-religious site. The remains of a *pañcāyatana* temple have been found here.[62] Here a cluster of hero stones has been reported, and all but one of the hero stones in this area is found inside the temple complex.[63] This Brahmanical temple acted as a legitimizing place for these dead heroes.

A considerable diversity is seen in the social background of heroes in the available corpus of inscribed hero stones and *satī* stones at the site of Budhpur. The earliest dated *satī* stone (*c*.700 CE) reads *rāja-mātāe vadhadhuga*, 'of the king's mother Vadhadhuga'.[64] One inscribed hero stone, datable to *c*.900–1000 CE, has the legend *rājaputra śrī Vadadhuga*.[65] As a considerable span of time (minimum 200 years) separates 'Vadhadhuga' mentioned in both inscriptions, we cannot be sure if they referred to the same person. Another *satī* stone, datable to *c*.1000 CE, carries the legend *gharavatī dhruvakasya* (wife of Dhruvaka). An inscribed boundary pillar or mark, datable to *c*.1050–1100 CE, showing a cow in an act of coitus with an ass, has also been reported from this site. It carries the legend 'the boundary flag of the lord of five mountains (viz. Panchet), which one should not curtail or decrease'.[66]

This last inscription in particular indicates that a local political formation with territorial claims was in operation in this area in the eleventh or early twelfth century. But the beginning of this process may be found in the seventh or eighth century. The inscription at Dhuluri shows that a local polity emerged in this area in the pre-Pāla period. The inscribed *satī* stone referring to Rājamātā Vadhadhuga (*c*.700 CE) and the inscribed hero stone datable to *c*.900–1000 CE with the legend *rājaputra śrī vadadhuga* both also indicate the existence of a local polity in the Purulia area. We do not know if we should take *rājaputra* in its literal meaning 'son of a king', or in the sense of an extended lineage of the ruling family. Again, the wife of Dhruvaka is simply referred to the name of her husband; no epithet such as *rājaputra* has been used for him. Even the honorific *śrī* has not been used for him. Even if he was a hero dying in some battle, his social position was not so distinct as to be recorded in the inscription. Hero stones of Purulia thus immortalized the memory not only of different *rājaputra*s but also of persons like Dhruvaka from indistinct backgrounds. This society was differentiated, and a Brahmanical temple provided an avenue for securing legitimacy even for as not-so-privileged a hero as Dhruvaka.

At a broader level, we may infer that many of the uninscribed hero stones found either within temple precincts or in their close neighbourhood could have belonged to dead heroes less privileged than the *rājaputras*. By placing the memorial hero stones of the dead warriors either in or near the precincts of the temple, the institutional roles of temples were utilized to enhance the prestige of the dead heroes and their surviving relatives. Both Jaina and Brahmanical temples provided institutional avenues for this process, but the role of Jaina temples seems to have been more prominent.

We need to look into one more issue: were the hero stones erected by the persons associated with the Sena state, as postulated by G. Sengupta?[67] He has argued that the Sena and Karṇāṭa adventurers, hailing from south India, were familiar with the practice of erecting hero stones in the memory of their dead warriors. The Senas imposed a rudimentary form of Hinduized polity in those areas of Bengal where hero stones are found.[68] This, according to Sengupta's analysis, created a conflict with the local tribal society: 'hero stones and sati stones of South-western Bengal commemorate the conflict between 'emergent political elite' of the region and autochthonous population'.[69] For him, elements (soldiers, priests, etc.) encouraged and probably sponsored by the Sena state ventured into this area and were resisted by the local tribal population. Many persons associated with the Sena state were killed in the process, and their hero stones were installed within the temple precincts. In other words, the temple was not the result of local dynamics but an institution somehow sponsored by the powers based in the Bengal delta (i.e. the Senas).

This argument is difficult to accept for many reasons. First of all, many hero stones antedate the Sena rule by many centuries – the Budhpur *satī* stone has been dated to *c*.700 CE, and the inscribed hero stone with the legend *rājaputra śrī vadadhuga* to *c*.900–1000 CE – and none of them had any association with the powers based in the Ganga Valley. The four hero stones in the precincts of the

Begunia temple in Barakar (in the western part of Vardhaman district) have been dated to the earliest phase of the temple, around the ninth or tenth century.[70] It may also be added that 'a rudimentary form of Hinduized polity' was not something to be 'imposed' in the Purulia area by the Senas: long before the foundation of the Sena rule in alluvial Bengal, a local polity had already evolved in the Telkupi area, and the administrative headquarters of this polity had a cluster of Śaiva temples, indicating that the patronage of Śaiva temples was one of the mechanisms through which the political elites of this local state sought their legitimacy. Besides, at least in the case of Purulia, Jaina temples, not Brahmanical temples, provided the preferred location for hero stones, and there was hardly any reason why the Senas, who were ardent Śaivites, would sponsor Jaina temples. It may also be added that we have no direct evidence of a (Sena) state-sponsored socio-economic and religious restructuring of the Purulia-Bankura area, of the kind that we see in the case of the Sylhet area by the Chandra state in the tenth century, as indicated by the Pashchimbhag copper-plate inscription.[71] We do not even know if any political power of alluvial Bengal had any effective control over the Purulia area.

In this kind of situation, we may logically infer that with the penetration of Jaina influence in the area in the wake of expanding trade, a section of the local tribal population became influenced by Jainism. Brahmanical influence also spread to the area. The section of the local population that was influenced by Jainism and Brahmanism patronized Jaina and Brahmanical temples. The conflict between this section and the tribal section was immortalized in hero stones.

Before we conclude our analysis of Purulia, I would like to highlight the almost total failure of Buddhism on this tribal frontier. Barring some stone sculptures discovered at Kroshjuri, Buddhist architectural or sculptural remains have not been reported from this district. We cannot rule out the possibility that some Buddhist monks from Magadha might have travelled to Odisha through Purulia, but they failed to connect with the local population and could not find any significant foothold in the district.

Conclusion

What has been presented above is certainly not a comprehensive account of the socio-political and religious dynamics of early medieval Purulia. The lack of dedicatory inscriptions on temples or on the stone sculptures that were enshrined therein does not allow us to attempt a fuller study of the interface between temples and the socio-political processes of this area.

Some inferences, however, stand out. The patterns we observed in early medieval Purulia force us to question many generally held notions. For a major part of India, the general character of Jainism has been largely perceived to have been 'as exclusive, or perhaps more, a merchant religion as was Judaism in the Occident'.[72] In Purulia it could have penetrated as a 'merchant religion', but after this penetration, Jainism and Jaina temples found other sources of patronage. They became an essential part of the lives of many sections of population, and the primary and preferred avenue for the legitimation of those heroes who died in the protection of the cattle or wealth of their community or family. At the available stage of our database, the Jaina temples of Purulia seem to have functioned without any kind of state patronage. Many Brahmanical temples, too, functioned without state patronage, but many of them also became an essential element of the legitimacy of the political elites of an important political centre of this area.

Instead of attempting macro-theorizations for the cultic dynamics of the whole of Bengal, a more pertinent approach may be to undertake micro-studies of select zones. In the context of purely textual studies on the cultic dynamics of early medieval Bengal, which neglect inferences from archaeological data and overlook spatial and geographical variations in the cultic dynamics, the general penchant has been on building macro-theorizations: the supposed evolution of Bengal into a 'cult region' converging on the cult of Durgā.[73] Methodological discrepancies and factual errors associated with this approach have been highlighted elsewhere.[74] It has been noted that early medieval Bengal offers a picture of cultic plurality marked with a simultaneous expansion of all major religions, not its supposed transformation into a 'cult region'.[75] As indicated by the data from Purulia, Bankura and the western portion of Vardhaman district, future studies in the cultic dynamics of early medieval Bengal will benefit immensely by analysing the role of Jainism in this complex dynamic.[76]

NOTES

1. This research article was originally published with the same title in *Religions of South Asia*, vol. 14, no. 3, 2020, pp. 188-214.
2. This approach is discernible in Arjun Appadurai and Carol Breckenridge, 'The South Indian Temple: Authority Honour and Redistribution', *Contributions To Indian Sociology*, vol. 10, no. 2, 1976, pp. 191-3; Arjun Appadurai, 'Kings, Sects and Temples in South India, 1350- 1700 AD', *Indian Economic and Social History Review,* vol. XIV, no. 1, 1977, pp. 47-73; B.D. Chattopadhyaya, 'Historiography, History and Religious Centres: Early Medieval North India, circa AD 700-1200', in Visakha N. Desai and D. Mason (eds.), *Gods, Guardians and Lovers: Temple Sculptures from North India, AD 700-1200,* Mapin Publishing Company, Ahmedabad, 1993, pp. 33-47; Sudarshan Gupta, 'Temples in Their Wider Context: A Study of Temples of Early Medieval Assam', in Birendra Nath Prasad (ed.), *Monasteries, Shrines and Society: Buddhist and Brahmanical Religious Institutions in India in their Socio-Economic Context,* Manak Publications, Delhi, 2011, pp. 181-219; R.N. Misra, 'Beginning of Śaiva-Siddhānta and its Expanding Space in Central India', in Sadananda Das and Ernst Furlinger (eds.), *Sāmarasya: Studies in Indian Arts, Philosophy, and Interreligious Dialogue,* D.K. Printworld, Delhi, 2005, pp. 275-306; Birendra Nath Prasad, 'Brahmanical Temples, *Maṭhas, Agrahāra*s and a Buddhist Establishment in a Marshy and Forested Periphery of Two

"Frontier" States: Early Mediaeval Surma Valley (Sylhet and Cachar), *c*.600 CE–1100 CE', *Religions of South Asia*, London, vol. 6, no. 1, 2012, pp. 33-60; Burton Stein, 'Introduction' to the special issue on South Indian Temples, *Indian Economic and Social History Review,* vol. 14 (1), 1977, pp. 1-9; Elizabeth A. Cecil, *Mapping the Pāśupata Landscape: Narrative, Place, and the Śaiva Imaginary in Early Medieval North India,* E. J. Brill, Leiden, 2020, pp. 246-48.

3. For a brief historiographical survey of studies in the social history of Brahmanical temples, see Birendra Nath Prasad (ed.), *Monasteries, Shrines and Society: Buddhist and Brahmanical Religious Institutions in India in their Socio-Economic Context,* Manak Publications, Delhi, 2011, pp. 1-24.
4. Cynthia Talbot, 'Temples, Donors and Gifts: Patterns of Patronage in Thirteenth-Century South India', *The Journal of Asian Studies*, vol. 50, no. 2, 1991, pp. 308-40; idem, *Precolonial India in Practice: Society, Religion and Identity in Medieval Andhra*, Oxford University Press, Delhi, 2001; Birendra Nath Prasad, 'Brahmanical Temples, *Maṭhas*, *Agrahāras* and a Buddhist Establishment in a Marshy and Forested Periphery of Two "Frontier" States: Early Mediaeval Surma Valley (Sylhet and Cachar), *c*.600 CE–1100 CE', pp. 33-60; idem, 'A Viṣṇu Temple and Its Social Linkages in 11th–12th Century AD, Comilla, Bangladesh: A Study in Some Copper-Plate Inscriptions', in D.P. Dubey (ed.), *Sanskrit Epigraphy in South Asia: Proceedings of the Epigraphy Section of the 16th World Sanskrit Conference, Bangkok, 2015*, D.K. Publisher, Delhi, 2019, pp. 139-48.
5. G.D. Sontheimer, 'The *Vana* and the *Kṣetra*: The Tribal Background of Some Famous Cults', in G.C. Tripathy and H. Kulke (eds.), *Religion and Society in Eastern India,* Manohar, Delhi, 1994, pp. 117-64.
6. B.D. Chattopadhyaya, 'State Perception of the "Forest" and the "Forest" as State in Early Medieval India' in B.B. Chaudhury and Arun Bandopadhyaya (eds.), *Tribes, Forests and Social Formations in Indian History*, Manohar, Delhi, 2004, pp. 23-37.
7. In the 1920s, as observed by Arthur Geddes, the entire Manbhum was 'a debatable land, much of it jungle, half Bengali and half primitive in settlement and life' (Arthur Geddes, *Man and Land in South Asia*, edited with an Introduction by A.T.A. Learmonth et al., Concept Publishing Company, Delhi, 1982, p. 191).

8. One of the best examples of this approach is Kunal Chakrabarti's work (*Religious Process: The Purāṇas and the Making of a Regional Tradition*, Oxford University Press, Delhi, 2001) on the religious dynamics of early medieval Bengal, which does not include a single word on the role of Jainism in the complex religious matrix of early medieval Bengal.
9. B.M. Morrison, *Political Centres and Cultural Regions in Early Bengal*, Vikash, Jaipur, 1980, p. 38.
10. Ibid.
11. Ibid.
12. Ibid.
13. Birendra Nath Prasad, 'Monarchs, Monasteries and Trade on an "Agrarian Frontier": Early Medieval Samataṭa-Harikela Region, Bengal', *South and Southeast Asia: Culture and Religion,* vol. 2, 2008, pp. 160-77; idem, 'Brahmanical Temples, *Maṭhas*, *Agrahāras* and a Buddhist Establishment in a Marshy and Forested Periphery of Two "Frontier" States: Early Medieval Surma Valley (Sylhet and Cachar), *c.*600 CE -1100 CE', pp. 39-40; idem, 'A Viṣṇu Temple and Its Social Linkages in 11th-12th Century AD. Comilla, Bangladesh: A Study in Some Copper-Plate Inscriptions', in D.P. Dubey (ed.), *Sanskrit Epigraphy in South Asia* (*Proceedings of the Epigraphy Section of the 16th World Sanskrit Conference*, Bangkok, 2015), D.K. Publisher, Delhi, 2019, pp. 139-48.
14. Birendra Nath Prasad, *Archaeology of Religion in South Asia: Buddhist, Brahmanical and Jaina Religious Centres in Bihar and Bengal, c.AD 600-1200,* Routledge, London and New York, 2021, pp. 162-80.
15. Ibid., pp. 165-72.
16. D.K. Chakrabarti, *Archaeology of Eastern India: Chhotanagpur Plateau and West Bengal*, Munshiram Manoharlal, Delhi, 1993, p. 209; R.K. Chattopadhyay, *Bankura: A Study of its Archaeological Sources,* Platinum Publishers, Kolkata, 2010, p. 155.
17. R.K. Chattopadhyay and D. Acharya, 'Contexts of Early Medieval Remains of Purulia: Researching Ideologies', *Pratnatattva*, vol. 16, 2010, pp. 9-10.
18. D.K. Chakrabarti, 'Pakbira: A Jain Site in Purulia District, West Bengal', in B.M. Pande and B.D. Chattopadhyaya (eds.), *Archaeology and History: Essays in Memory of Shri A. Ghosh*, vol. II, Agam Kala

Prakashan, New Delhi, 1987, pp. 351-7; idem, *Archaeology of Eastern India: Chhotanagpur Plateau and West Bengal,* Munshiram Manoharlal, New Delhi, 1993, p. 122; R.K. Chattopadhyay and D. Acharya, 'Contexts of Early Medieval Remains of Purulia: Researching Ideologies', *Pratnatattva*, vol. 16, 2010, pp. 9-10. More or less the same feature has been observed in the cases of the western portions of the districts of Bankura, Vardhaman and Birbhum. That has made one scholar conclude that 'these regions could go on housing their hunter–gatherers' until the advent of Brahmanical and Jaina temples in the area (D.K. Chakrabarti, *Archaeology of Eastern India: Chhotanagpur Plateau and West Bengal,* Munshiram Manoharlal, New Delhi, 1993, p. 208).

19. In some existing studies, these ruins have been mostly studied from art-historical perspectives. See, for example, D. McCutchion, 'Notes on the Temples of Purulia District', in B. Roy (ed.), *Census 1961, West Bengal, District Census Handbook: Purulia*, Government Printing Press, Calcutta, 1961, pp. 33-43; P.C. Dasgupta, 'The Early Medieval Art and Architecture of Purulia', in Asok Datta (ed.), *Studies in Archaeology: Essays in Memory of P.C. Dasgupta*, Books and Books, New Delhi, 1991, pp. 203-7; Debajani Mitra, *A Survey of Jainism and Jaina Art of Eastern India with Special Emphasis on Bengal from the Earliest Period to the Thirteenth Century*, R.N. Bhattacharya, Kolkata, 2004; Shubha Majumder, 'Newly Discovered Jaina Antiquities from Cheliyama, District Purulia, West Bengal: An Archaeological Perspective', *Proceedings of the Indian History Congress*, vol. 73, 2012, pp. 1250-60; idem, 'Understating the Archaeological Contexts and Iconic Details of Jaina Antiquities from Rakṣatpura and Śaṅkā, District Puruliā, West Bengal', *International Journal of Jaina Studies*, vol. 10, no. 1, 2014, pp. 1-32; idem, 'Recent Explorations at Balarampur (Purulia District, West Bengal)', *Purātattva*, vol. 46, 2016, pp. 236-41; idem, 'A Rare Icon of Tīrthaṅkara Mallinātha from Purulia, West Bengal: An Analytic Approach', *Pratnatattva*, vol. 23, 2017, pp. 1-6; idem, 'Some Newly Documented Tīrthaṅkara Ṛṣabhanātha Sculptures from Pakbirra, Purulia District of West Bengal', *Heritage: Journal of Multidisciplinary Studies in Archaeology*, vol. 5, 2017, pp. 419-32; Shubha Majumder et al., 'An Iconographic Study of Jaina *Chaumukhas* from the Eastern Fringe Areas of the Chhotanagpur Plateau', *Kosala*,

vol. 10, 2017, pp. 98-110; Swati Ray et al., 'Exploring the Jaina Sculptural Remains in Ancient Manbhum', *Berlin Indological Studies*, vol. 22, 2015, pp. 205-36.

20. For an analysis of this process in the Sylhet area, see Birendra Nath Prasad, 'Brahmanical Temples, *Maṭhas*, *Agrahāras* and a Buddhist Establishment in a Marshy and Forested Periphery of Two "Frontier" States: Early Medieval Surma Valley (Sylhet and Cachar), *c.*600 CE-1100 CE', *Religions of South Asia,* London, vol. 6, no. 1, pp. 33-60.
21. Ibid.
22. A similar absence of land grants through royal copper-plate charters is discernible in the whole of Bankura and West Medinipur districts. In the Vardhaman district, instances of land grants through royal copper-plate charters have been noted only in the alluvial eastern parts of the district, not in the plateau-like western parts. For an analysis of this feature with particular reference to the western parts of Vardhaman district, see Chitrarekha Gupta, 'Bengal Art and Bengal Inscriptions: An Approach Towards Co-relation – A Case Study with Punchra, A Village in the Vardhaman District, West Bengal', *Journal of Bengal Art*, vol. 7, pp. 83-100.
23. R.K. Chattopadhyay and D. Acharya, 'Contexts of Early Medieval Remains of Purulia: Researching Ideologies', p. 10; R.K. Chattopadhyay et al., 'In Search of the Jaina Identity: A Study of the Sculptural Remains of the Vishnupur Region', *Journal of the Indian Society for Oriental Art*, vol. XXVIII, 2012, p. 144.
24. Rajat Sanyal, 'Dhuluri (Puruliya, West Bengal) Rock Inscription', *Pratna Samiksha*, New Series, vol. 7, 2016, p. 59. The site of Dhuluri is in the Santuri block of the district. For the location of this block within the district of Purulia, see Fig. 2.

    In the Indian province of West Bengal, a block is an administrative unit consisting of many villages.
25. R.C. Majumdar (ed.), *The History of Bengal,* vol. 1*: Hindu Period*, University of Dacca, Dacca, 1943, p. 156.
26. Ibid., p. 157.
27. This site has been identified with Koteshvar to the east of Vishnupur in the Bankura district (R.C. Majumdar, op. cit., p. 156; R.K. Chattopadhyay, *Bankura: A Study of its Archaeological Sources,* Platinum Publishers, Kolkata, 2010, p. 196).

28. Bāla-Balabhī was on the boundaries of the district of Midnapur in Bengal and Balasore in Odisha, most probably on the mouth of the Suvarnarekha river (R.C. Majumdar, op. cit., p. 157).
29. Aparamandāra has been identified with the area of Bhatargarh near Arambagh in the Hoogly district (R.C. Majumdar, op. cit., p. 157).
30. Ibid.
31. Kujavaṭī is supposed to be located 14 miles north of Dumka in Jharkhand (ibid.).
32. Tailakampī has been identified with the site of Telkupi in Purulia district (R.C. Majumdar, op. cit., p. 157; A. Bhattacharya, *Historical Geography of Ancient and Early Medieval Bengal*, Sanskrit Pustak Bhandar, Calcutta, 1970, p. 101; Debala Mitra, *Telkupi: A Submerged Temple-Site in West Bengal*, Memoirs of the Archaeological Survey of India, No. 76, Delhi, 1969, p. 1).
33. This site was located somewhere in Birbhum district (R.C. Majumdar, op. cit., p. 157).
34. This site has been identified with Dhekuri near Katwa in the Vardhaman district (R.C. Majumdar, op. cit., p. 157).
35. This site has been identified with the Kankajol area, south of the Rajmahal district in the Santhal Parganas (R.C. Majumdar, op. cit., p. 157; A. Bhattacharya, op. cit., p. 101).
36. R.C. Majumdar, op. cit., pp. 156-7.
37. Birendra Nath Prasad, *Archaeology of Religion in South Asia: Buddhist, Brahmanical and Jaina Religious Centres in Bihar and Bengal, c. AD 600-1200,* Routledge, London and New York, 2021, p. 175.
38. Rajat Sanyal, op. cit., p. 62.
39. Ibid., p. 62; D. McCutchion, op. cit., p. 35.
40. Even in the medieval period, this area was known as Śikharabhūm, indicating its lasting association with the family of Rudraśikhara.
41. D. McCutchion, op. cit., p. 35.
42. Debala Mitra, op. cit., pp. 51-2; R.K. Chattopadhyay and D. Acharya, op. cit., p. 13.
43 Sharmila Saha and Rajat Sanyal, 'Templescape and Culture under the Mallas of Medieval Bengal: A Case Study', in Ratnabali Chatterjee (ed.), *Urbanity and Economy: The Pre-Modern Dynamics in Eastern India*, Setu Prakashani, Kolkata, 2013, p. 174.
44. Ibid.

45. G. Sengupta, 'Hero Stones of West Bengal: A Preliminary Study', *Journal of Bengal Art*, vol. 4, 1999, p. 80.
46. Hans T. Bakker, 'Monuments to the Dead in Ancient North India', *Indo-Iranian Journal,* vol. 50, no. 1, 2007, p. 19.
47. D.R. Patil, 'The Origin of Memorial Stones', in S. Settar and Gunther D. Sontheimer (eds.), *Memorial Stones: A Study of Their Origin, Significance and Variety*, Institute of Indian Art History, Karnataka University, Dharwad, 1982, p. 48.
48. Romila Thapar, *Cultural Pasts: Essays in Early Indian History*, Oxford University Press, Delhi, 2005, p. 681; see also S. Settar and F.A. Ganihar, 'Artists of Memorial Stones: Cāḷukya-Hoysaḷa', in S. Settar and Gunther D. Sontheimer (eds.), op. cit., p. 326.
49. Romila Thapar, op. cit., p. 704.
50. Ibid., p. 681.
51. Ibid., pp. 690–1.
52. Ibid., p. 682.
53. Ibid., p. 685.
54. Ibid., p. 704.
55. For a catalogue of the data discovered at the sites referred to in this table, see Appendix 1.
56. This category also includes those sites where Brahmanism penetrated later than Jainism, and the site gradually lost its Jaina character, becoming a predominantly Brahmanical site in the course of time.
57. For the description of the hero stone of this site, see R.K. Chattopadhyay and D. Acharya, op. cit., p. 18.
58. Ibid., pp. 12–13.
59. This site has also been spelt as Pakbirra or Pakbirrah in some other publications. See, for example, Benoy Ghose, 'Cultural Profile of Purulia', in B. Roy (ed.), *Census 1961, West Bengal, District Census Handbook: Purulia*, Government Printing Press, Calcutta, 1961, pp. 3–14.
60. Swati Ray et al., 'Exploring the Jaina Sculptural Remains in Ancient Manbhum', *Berlin Indological Studies*, vol. 22, 2015, pp. 213–14.
61. Ibid., pp. 214–16.
62. R.K. Chattopadhyay and D. Acharya, op. cit., p. 17.
63. Ibid.
64. Ibid.

65. Ibid.
66. Ibid.
67. G. Sengupta, 'Hero Stones of West Bengal: A Preliminary Study', *Journal of Bengal Art*, vol. 4, 1999, p. 95.
68. Ibid.
69. Ibid., pp. 94-5.
70. G. Sengupta and Shambhu Chakraborty, 'Locale, Material and Monuments: Begunia Group of Temples, Barakar, West Bengal', in G. Sengupta and Sheena Panja (eds.), *Archaeology of Eastern India, New Perspectives*, Centre for Archaeological Studies and Training: Eastern India, Kolkata, 2002, pp. 398-9.
71. For an analysis of this pattern in the Sylhet area, see Birendra Nath Prasad, 'Brahmanical Temples, *Maṭha*s, *Agrahāra*s and a Buddhist Establishment in a Marshy and Forested Periphery of Two "Frontier" States: Early Mediaeval Surma Valley (Sylhet and Cachar), *c.*600 CE–1100 CE', *Religions of South Asia,* London, vol. 6, no. 1, pp. 33-60.
72. Max Weber, *The Religion of India: The Sociology of Hinduism and Buddhism,* ed. and tr. H.H. Gerth and D. Martindale, Munshiram Manoharlal, Delhi, 1992 (reprint), p. 193.
73. Kunal Chakrabarti, *Religious Process: The Purāṇas and the Making of a Regional Tradition*, Oxford University Press, Delhi, 2001; idem, 'Cult Region: The Purāṇas and the Making of Cultural Territory of Bengal', in Upinder Singh (ed.), *Rethinking Early Medieval India: A Reader*, Oxford University Press, Delhi, 2011, pp. 233-51.
74. Birendra Nath Prasad, *Archaeology of Religion in South Asia: Buddhist, Brahmanical and Jaina Religious Centres in Bihar and Bengal, c.AD 600-1200,* Routledge, London and New York, 2021, pp. 229-30.
75. Ibid., p. 230.
76. The socio-economic roles of Jaina religious institutions in Bankura and western portions of Vardhaman district have been analysed in Birendra Nath Prasad, *Archaeology of Religion in South Asia: Buddhist, Brahmanical and Jaina Religious Centres in Bihar and Bengal, c.AD 600-1200,* Routledge, London and New York, 2021, pp. 162-78.

Appendix 1

Block-wise Catalogue of Reported Early Medieval Sites of the District of Purulia[1]

Block: Puncha

1. *Pakbira*. This site is located 1 mile east of Puncha, in the jurisdiction of Puncha Police Station. A cluster of eight or nine stone and brick temples in utter ruin, seen by Beglar in 1873; all of them disappeared by 1976-9, barring two renovated temples. Stone sculptures: numerous Jaina sculptures are kept in the modern village temple.[2] Two intact images of two *tīrthaṅkaras* from this site are kept in the State Archaeological Museum, Kolkata.[3]
2. *Laulara*. This site is near Pakbira and located 4 km north of Puncha, in the jurisdiction of Puncha Police Station. This site may be considered as a satellite site of Pakbira. Reported antiquities: ruins of Jaina temples; miscellaneous fragmented Jaina sculptures; five hero stones in different parts of the village.[4]
3. *Mudidih*, a neighbouring village of Laulara. Ruins of an abandoned Jaina temple complex; many hero stones from the temple ruins. Stone sculptures: several Jaina sculptural fragments.[5]
4. *Dhadki*, in Puncha Police Station, may be considered as a satellite site of Pakbira. Ruined temple. Jaina stone sculptures: Mahāvīra, Śāntinātha; a miniature *tīrthaṅkara* icon; two hero stones in front of the modern Śiva temple of the village.[6]

5. *Paruda*, in Puncha Police Station. This village belongs to the cluster of satellite sites associated with the Pakbira temple complex. Reported antiquities: fragments of *tīrthaṅkara* icons; several architectural members including a huge *āmalaka* strewn over the fairly high mound of the modern temple complex itself; a well-preserved specimen of Tīrthaṅkara Ādinātha.[7]
6. *Baramoshya*. This site is located near Pakbira and may be considered as a satellite site. Reported antiquities: Jaina votive *stūpa*s and sculptural fragments.[8]
7. *Lakhra*. An important satellite site of Pakbira. Reported antiquities: several mounds in the village; temple ruins strewn with architectural members, doorjambs, pillars; stone sculptures of Mahāvīra, Pārśvanātha; fragmented Umāmaheśvara; broken pieces of hero stones scattered in the village and temple ruins.[9]
8. *Tatari*, in Puncha Police Station. May be a satellite site to the great Jaina centre of Pakbira. Reported antiquities: two separate ruined temple complexes in this village; a fair number of architectural members and fragmentary sculptural remains; an outstanding eleventh-century stone sculpture of Mahāvīra.[10]
9. *Budhpur*, in Puncha Police Station. Reported antiquities: a *pañcāyatana* temple, now in utter ruin; stone sculptures of Viṣṇu and Gaṇeśa; cluster of hero stones, all but one of them found inside the temple complex.[11]
10. *Paruldiha*, near Budhpur, in Puncha Police Station. Reported antiquities: stone sculpture of Ādinātha, *circa* tenth to twelfth centuries; an exquisite specimen of *chaumukha*.[12]
11. *Tuisuma*, in Puncha Police Station. This site is about 4 km away from Pakbira. Reported antiquities: a small extant temple standing over the ruins of an older temple; many hero stones.[13]
12. *Nangtir Than*, 1 km upstream from the cremation ground of Puncha. Reported antiquities: a modern temple standing on the ruins of an earlier one; three large stone sculptures of Ādinātha.[14]
13. *Bargora Barapol*, approx. 2 km south of Puncha. A single hero stone at the entry-point to a sparse forest.[15]

14. *Bhagabandh*, in Puncha Police Station. A memorial hero stone with a Śivaliṅgam in its central part, found embedded in the walls of a modern temple.[16]

Block: Manbazar

15. *Manbazar*. Reported antiquities: stone sculptures of Ādinātha, Ṛṣabhanātha, Śāntinātha; scattered architectural remains including a broken *āmalaka*.[17]
16. *Palma*, in the jurisdiction of Kendra Police Station. Reported antiquities: a large mound covered with stone and bricks and many Jaina stone sculptures; a ruined Jaina temple; broken *tīrthaṅkara* sculptures; architectural pieces; many hero stones.[18] Many miniature *chaumukha* shrines are also reported from this site.[19]
17. *Mahara*, in Manbazar-1 Block. An abandoned Jaina temple complex with doorframes, doorjambs, *āmalaka*. An extant temple undergoing several layers of modification also present. An image of Tīrthaṅkara Ṛṣabhanātha. Numerous hero stones scattered over entire area.[20]
18. *Kurmasol*, in the jurisdiction of Kenda Police Station. Reported antiquities: a modern temple standing on the ruins of an older temple, probably Jaina; stone sculptures of Jaina tutelary couple.[21]
19. *Dakakendu*, in the jurisdiction of Kenda Police Station. Reported antiquities: architectural fragments of dilapidated temples (*āmalaka*s, etc.); two fragmented Jaina stone sculptures.[22]
20. *Chakolta,* a neighbouring site of Dakakendu, in the jurisdiction of Kenda Police Station. Reported antiquities: architectural fragments of dilapidated temples (*āmalaka*s, etc.).[23]

Block: Bandoan

21. *North Bandwan.* Site is in the midst of a forested tract. Stone sculptures: two big *tīrthaṅkara* images; a hero stone.[24]

22. *Ranipukur*. Reported antiquities: an abandoned Brahmanical temple site with doorframes, doorjambs, *āmalaka*; ruined *garbhagṛha* of a temple; a stone sculpture of Sūrya; a hero stone found *in situ* in the abandoned temple, two more hero stones near the same temple.[25]

Block: Barabazar

23. *Basudevapur*, in the jurisdiction of Barabazar Police Station. Reported antiquities: an abandoned Jaina temple complex with broken stone sculptures and architectural fragments; a stone sculpture of a *tīrthaṅkara*; a hero stone in the village excavated out of a nearby pond.[26]
24. *Chandanpur*, a neighbouring site of Basudevapur, in the jurisdiction of Barabazar Police Station. Reported antiquities: fragmented Jaina *tīrthaṅkara* stone sculptures beneath a tree; a single piece of hero stone.[27]
25. *Bansgarh*, 1 km south-west of Balrampur, on the Barabazar–Balarampur road. Reported antiquities: a low structural mound with brickbats, which is probably the ruins of a temple; stone sculptures of Tīrthaṅkara Ṛṣabhanātha; Tīrthaṅkara Chandraprabha; Viṣṇu.[28]
26. *Sonadaha*, in Barabazar Police Station. Reported antiquities: a stone sculpture of Ādinātha icon, tenth to twelfth century; two *chaumukha*s.[29]
27. *Pabanpur*, in Barabazar Police Station. Archaeological context of the site is disturbed by modern habitation. Reported antiquities: some fragmentary sculptures, unknown cultic affiliation; cluster of hero stones in the village.[30]
28. *Herbona*, in Barabazar Police Station. Reported antiquities: seven pieces of Jaina stone sculptures, including an image of Ambikā and Pārśvanātha; architectural fragments including *āmalaka*s and *kalaśa*s.[31]

29. *Borrha*, in Barabazar Police Station. Reported antiquities: many sculptural and architectural fragments; a single piece of hero stone in the village.[32]
30. *Sasandihi*, in Barabazar Police Station. Site is on the banks of the Kumari River, 'may be recognized as a burial ground having an *in-situ* cluster of many hero stones/menhirs. Reported antiquities: ruins of a Brahmanical temple located around 200 m east of the burial complex; a stone sculpture of Viṣṇu, tenth or eleventh century.[33]
31. *Sirgi*, 3 km west of Sasandihi, in Barabazar Police Station. Reported antiquities: many fragmented Jaina stone sculptures and a miniature *chaumukha*.[34]

Block: Baghmundi

32. *Deuli*, around 3 km from Suisa, in Baghmundi Police Station. Reported antiquities: a ruined *pañcāyatana* temple with sanctum, *antarāla*, *mahāmaṇḍapa*, *ardhamaṇḍapa*, a portico containing Ādinātha *in situ* in the sanctum.[35]
33. *Suisa*, in Baghmundi Police Station. Abandoned Jaina temple complex, with a few architectural fragments. Stone sculptures: Viṣṇu 1; Ṛṣabhanātha 1; Pārśvanātha 1; Jaina female deity 2; Śāntinātha 1; Jaina votive shrine 1; unidentified *tīrthaṅkara*s 2; Mallinātha 1; *liṅgam* 1; decorated doorjamb 1; *āmalaka* 1.[36] Many *chaumukha*s.[37]
34. *Harup*, a neighbouring site of Suisa, in Baghmundi Police Station. Reported antiquity: a stone image of a four-armed man riding an elephant, unknown cultic affiliation.[38]

Block: Jhalda

35. *Jhalda*, in the Jhalda Police Station. Reported antiquity: a stone sculpture of Ṛṣabhanātha, *circa* eleventh to tenth century.[39]

Block: Arsha

36. *Arsha*. Reported antiquities: ruins of two abandoned temple complexes along with Jaina *chaumukha* shrines and a stone image of Pārśvanātha.[40]
37. *Tumba*, a neighbouring site of Arsha. Stone sculptures: Neminātha, Pārśvanātha.[41]

Block: Jaypur

38. *Garh Jaypur*, in Jaypur Police Station. Stone image of Ṛṣabhanātha.[42]
39. *Boram/Deulghata*, around 7 km south of Jaypur town. Low mounds strewn with habitational ruins, two extant temples; many hero stones.[43] Stone sculptures: Mahiṣāsuramardinī[44]; Umāmaheśvara.[45]

Block: Purulia

40. *Gholmara/Golamara*, around 14 km north of Purulia town, in Purulia-2 Block. Abandoned Jaina temple site. Stone sculptures: Tīrthaṅkara Vāsupūjya, Mahāvīra.[46]
41. *Raibaghini*, 3 km from Purulia town along the Purulia–Ranchi Road. An older structural complex badly disturbed due to modern habitation; many hero stones.[47]
42. *Khelaichandirthan*, on the outskirts of Purulia town. Stone image of Tīrthaṅkara Ṛṣabhanātha.[48]
43. *Choto Balrampur*, about 3 km from Purulia town. Ruins of an abandoned temple complex with architectural and sculptural fragments; some hero stone fragments.[49]
44. *Pichasi*, a neighbouring site of Choto Balarampur. Stone sculptures: several Jaina and Brahmanical sculptural fragments. One hero stone in the village, five along the riverbank.[50]
45. *Dunrku*, about 4 km from Purulia town. Several Jaina stone sculptural fragments.[51]

46. *Gangagerah*, 4 km east of Purulia town. Ruins of a temple and scattered architectural fragments like *āmalaka*. A fragmented hero stone.[52]
47. *Kushtarah*, 20 km north of Purulia on the Purulia–Barakar road near Gajpur. A structural mound presumably containing Jaina remains. Stone sculptures: several Jaina sculptural fragments. A few hero stones from different parts of the village.[53]
48. *Podlara*, about 6 km from Purulia town, on the Purulia–Barakar road. Architectural and sculptural fragments suggestive of the presence of a Jaina temple at the site; a stone image of Pārśvanātha; three big Ādinātha images along with some architectural remains including a *kalaśa*.[54]
49. *Chharra*, around 7 km north-east of Purulia town. Ruins of several Jaina temples, Jaina votive *stūpa*s, many Jaina *chaumukha*s, very large stone image of Tīrthaṅkara Ṛṣabhanātha, many hero stones in the vicinity of the main site.[55]
50. *Hatuyara*, a neighbouring site of Chharra. Stone sculpture of Pārśvanātha.[56]
51. *Sitalpur*, about 9 km north-east of Purulia town. Architectural and sculptural fragments spread over the whole village. Stone sculptures: many Jaina sculptural fragments, an intact Ṛṣabhanātha.[57]
52. *Karcha*, a neighbouring site of Sitalpur. Jaina temple ruins, *āmalaka* and architectural fragments, broken *tīrthaṅkara* sculptures. A hero stone in the village, away from the temple site.[58]
53. *Bhangra*, 8 km east of Purulia town. An ancient Jaina temple that underwent several modifications. Hero stone from within the temple.[59] Stone sculpture of Tīrthaṅkara Ṛṣabhanātha; a miniature *chaumukha* shrine.[60]
54. *Bhabanipur*, 10 km east of Purulia town. Ruined Jaina temple site, along with a ruined Śaiva temple site, many *āmalaka*s, doorjambs. Stone sculptures: an inscribed image of Ṛṣabhanātha; Gaurīpaṭṭa. A hero stone affixed to the wall of a modern Śiva temple.[61]

55. *Nangti*, in the jurisdiction of Purulia Mufussil Police Station. Stone sculptures: three images of Ṛṣabhanātha.[62]
56. *Anai Jambad*, in the jurisdiction of Purulia Mufussil Police Station. Abandoned Jaina temple complex marked by structural ruins, *āmalaka*s, doorjambs, etc. Stone sculptures: six fragmented Jaina sculptures; two each of Pārśvanātha, Ṛṣabhanātha, Chandraprabha. Many hero stones, not inside the temple precincts.[63]
57. *Ralibera*, a neighbouring site of Anai Jambad; in the jurisdiction of Purulia Mufussil Police Station. Abandoned Brahmanical temple complex marked by structural ruins, *āmalaka*, doorjambs, etc. Stone sculptures: Umāmaheśvara, Gaṇeśa, etc. Many (9) hero stones about 2 km from the main temple; a shrine probably existed near the hero stones.[64]

Block: Para

58. *Para*. A stone and a brick temple standing on the same structural mound side by side; Lakṣmī in the stone temple and ten-armed Durgā in the brick temple. These two temples probably underwent several courses of modifications. Stone sculptures: many fragmented Jaina sculptures including a broken *tīrthaṅkara* and many *chaumukha* shrines; *liṅgam*, Naṭarāja; Umāmaheśvara and many much-mutilated Brahmanical sculptural fragments inside the brick temple. One hero stone.[65]
59. *Deulbhira*, a neighbouring site of Para. Structural mound strewn with architectural pieces and potsherds; abandoned temples marked by doorjambs and lintels; existence of a sizeable Sarak community in and around the village.[66]

Block: Kashipur and Hura

60. *Pabrapahari*, in Kashipur Police Station; 3 km from Hura. This site is in the neighbourhood of Kroshjuri. Abandoned Jaina

temple complex on a structural mound; a stone sculpture of Ādinātha; a hero stone.[67]

61. *Kroshjuri*, in Kashipur Police Station; 5 km from Hura. An extant temple site, either the original temple with several stages of renovation, or a modern temple surviving on the ruins of an older temple site. Several pieces of *āmalaka*s, doorjambs, etc. at the site. Stone sculptures: many old Brahmanical sculptures carved on the walls of a modern temple: Naṭarāja, Śivaliṅgam, etc. Stone sculptures of Buddha and Bodhisattva. Two hero stones: one on the southern wall of the modern temple, another on its eastern gateway.[68]
62. *Bauridi*, in Hura Police Station. A structural mound with many Jaina stone sculptures including Ṛṣabhanātha, Chandraprabha, Ambikā.[69]
63. *Ladhurka*, in Hura Police Station. A modern temple on the ruins of an earlier temple. Stone sculptures: fragmented Jaina sculptures; a fragmented Brahmanical sculpture. Four hero stones *in situ*, possibly from parts of the earlier temple.[70]

Block: Raghunathpur

64. *Telkupi*, in the jurisdiction of Raghunathpur Police Station. A site with a cluster of 26 temples (Chattopadhyay et al. 2010: 332); Śaiva sculptures in the sanctum of 16 temples. Stone sculptures: Umāmaheśvara, Lakulīśa, Viṣṇu, Sūrya, Narasiṁha; a few pieces of Ambikā. A hero tablet: the deceased hero is portrayed with a sword in his hand.[71]
65. *Gurudi*, in the jurisdiction of Raghunathpur Police Station. 'The site may be identified as a satellite site of Telkupi.' Stone sculptures: three Ṛṣabhanātha sculptures.[72]
66. *Lalpur*, a neighbouring site of Gurudi, in the jurisdiction of Raghunathpur Police Station. Stone sculptures: Ambikā; unidentified *tīrthaṅkara*.[73]
67. *Cheliyama*, a neighbouring site of Telkupi. Reported antiquities: a *śikhara* temple similar to many temples of Telkupi; a ruined

temple; three sculptures of Tīrthaṅkara Ṛṣabhanātha; a cluster of unidentified *tīrthaṅkara* images; a pillar with a carved image of a *tīrthaṅkara*.[74]

68. *Banda*, 1.5 km east of Cheliyama. Reported antiquities: a mound; an extant *śikhara*-type Jaina temple with pillared *maṇḍapa*, *circa* tenth century; fragmented and unidentified Jaina temples in the neighbourhood of the temple.[75]
69. *Shanka*, around 6 km east of Cheliyama. An abandoned Jaina religious complex; habitational remains (brickbats, iron slags); two big stone sculptures of the first two *tīrthaṅkaras*.[76]
70. *Badra*, a neighbouring site of Cheliyama. Jaina votive *chaumukha* shrine.[77] Fragmentary images including Chandraprabha and Ādinātha.[78]
71. *Mangaldiha*, 4 km east of Cheliyama. Reported antiquities: an abandoned Jaina temple complex; stone sculpture of Tīrthaṅkara Ṛṣabhanātha, *circa* eleventh–twelfth century; many unidentified fragmented Jaina sculptures.[79]
72. *Raghunathpur*. A fragmented *chaumukha*.[80]
73. *Bero*, in Raghunathpur-1 Block. Many hero stones.[81]
74. *Simra*, in Raghunathpur Police Station. Stone sculptures: many fragmented Jaina images.[82]
75. *Sagarka*, in Raghunathpur Police Station. Stone sculptures: many fragmented Jaina images.[83]

Block: Santuri

76. *Dhuluri*, in the Santuri Police Station. The find spot of a seventh- or eighth-century rock inscription. Stone sculptures: Devī in her Siṁhavāhinī form, second half of the seventh century; Viṣṇu, seventh century.[84]

Block: Neturia

77. *Naudiha*, in Neturia Police Station. A fragmented Jaina stone image.[85]

NOTES

1. In recent years, old Raghunathpur Block has been divided into two blocks: Raghunathpur-1 and Raghunathpur-2. Similarly, Jhalda, Purulia and Manbazar Blocks have also been divided into Jhalda-1, Jhalda-2; Purulia-1, Purulia-2; and Manbazar-1, Manbazar-2 Blocks, respectively. Here I use the old demarcation of these blocks because the publications which report the sites, as mentioned in the present article, have mostly followed the old administrative demarcations of these blocks. Besides the sites described in this Appendix, the following sites have also been reported from the district of Purulia:
    1. *Kantabera.* A ruined brick temple, *circa* eleventh century; cultic affiliation (Jaina or Brahmanical) difficult to determine (D.R. Das, 'An Early Brick Temple at Kantabera', *Pratna Samiksha,* vol. 1, 1992, pp. 191-3).
    2. *Delmi.* Stone sculptures: Matsya and Kūrma avatars of Viṣṇu; Sūrya; Devī (Enamul Haque, *Bengal Sculptures: Hindu Iconography up to c.1250 AD*, Bangladesh National Museum, Dhaka, 1992, pp. 357, 369, 371).
    3. *Harihar.* Stone sculpture of Viṣṇu (Ibid., p. 341).

    As I have not been able to ascertain the block-wise locations of these sites, I have not included them in Appendix 1.
2. R.K. Chattopadhyay and D. Acharya, 'Contexts of Early Medieval Remains of Purulia: Researching Ideologies', p. 18; D. McCutchion, op. cit., pp. 38-9.
3. G. Sengupta and Sharmila Saha, *Vibrant Rock*, Directorate of Archaeology and Museums, Govt of West Bengal, Kolkata, 2014, p. 221.
4. R.K. Chattopadhyay and D. Acharya, op. cit., p. 19; Swati Ray et al., 'Exploring the Jaina Sculptural Remains in Ancient Manbhum', *Berlin Indological Studies*, vol. 22, 2015, pp. 218-19.
5. R.K. Chattopadhyay and D. Acharya, op. cit., p. 19.
6. R.K. Chattopadhyay and D. Acharya, op. cit., p. 18; D. McCutchion, op. cit., p. 39; Swati Ray et al., op. cit., pp. 214-16.
7. Swati Ray et al., op. cit., pp. 212-13.
8. R.K. Chattopadhyay and D. Acharya, op. cit., p. 21.

9. R.K. Chattopadhyay and D. Acharya, op. cit., p. 18; Swati Ray et al., op. cit., pp. 213–14.
10. Swati Ray et al., op. cit., pp. 216–18; R.K. Chattopadhyay and D. Acharya, op. cit., p. 21.
11. R.K. Chattopadhyay and D. Acharya, op. cit., p. 17; D. McCutchion, op. cit., p. 39.
12. Swati Ray et al., op. cit., pp. 219–20.
13. R.K. Chattopadhyay and D. Acharya, op. cit., pp. 16–17; D. McCutchion, op. cit., p. 39.
14. Swati Ray et al., op. cit., pp. 220–2.
15. R.K. Chattopadhyay and D. Acharya, op. cit., p. 16.
16. Ibid., p. 18.
17. R.K. Chattopadhyay and D. Acharya, op. cit., p. 21; Swati Ray et al., op. cit., pp. 222–3.
18. R.K. Chattopadhyay and D. Acharya, op. cit., p. 11.
19. Shubha Majumder et al., 'An Iconographic Study of Jaina *Chaumukha*s from the Eastern Fringe Areas of the Chhotanagpur Plateau', *Kosala*, vol. 10, 2017, p. 106; D. McCutchion, op. cit., p. 40.
20. R.K. Chattopadhyay and D. Acharya, op. cit., pp. 15–16.
21. Ibid., p. 22.
22. Ibid.
23. Ibid.
24. Ibid., p. 15.
25. Ibid., pp. 15–16.
26. Ibid., p. 16.
27. Ibid., p. 19.
28. Shubha Majumder, 'Recent Explorations at Balarampur (Purulia District, West Bengal)', *Purātattva*, vol. 46, 2016, pp. 236–8.
29. Swati Ray et al., op. cit., pp. 226–8.
30. R.K. Chattopadhyay and D. Acharya, op. cit., p. 15.
31. Swati Ray et al., op. cit., 229–30.
32. R.K. Chattopadhyay and D. Acharya, op. cit., p. 19.
33. Ibid., p. 16.
34. Shubha Majumder et al., 'An Iconographic Study of Jaina *Chaumukha*s from the Eastern Fringe Areas of the Chhotanagpur Plateau', *Kosala*, vol. 10, p. 107.

35. R.K. Chattopadhyay and D. Acharya, op. cit., p. 15; D. McCutchion, op. cit., p. 39–40.
36. D. McCutchion, op. cit., p. 40.
37. Shubha Majumder et al., op. cit., p. 103.
38. R.K. Chattopadhyay and D. Acharya, op. cit., p. 15.
39. G. Sengupta and Sharmila Saha, op. cit., p. 226.
40. R.K. Chattopadhyay and D. Acharya, op. cit., p. 21.
41. Ibid., p. 21.
42. Ibid., pp. 20–1.
43. Ibid., p. 14; D. McCutchion, op. cit., pp. 34–5.
44. Enamul Haque, op. cit., p. 374.
45. Ibid., p. 391.
46. Atul Chandra Bhowmick, 'Jaina Sculptures from Bhavanipur, Hatuyara and Golamara', *Jain Journal: A Quarterly on Jainology,* vol. 18, no. 4, 1984, pp. 165–70; R.K. Chattopadhyay and D. Acharya, op. cit., p. 21.
47. R.K. Chattopadhyay and D. Acharya, op. cit., p. 10.
48. Ibid., p. 19.
49. R.K. Chattopadhyay and D. Acharya, op. cit., p. 19; D. McCutchion, op. cit., pp. 40–1.
50. R.K. Chattopadhyay and D. Acharya, op. cit., p. 19.
51. Ibid., p. 20.
52. Ibid., p. 18.
53. Ibid., p. 19.
54. Ibid., pp. 18–19; Swati Ray et al., op. cit., pp. 224–6.
55. R.K. Chattopadhyay and D. Acharya, op. cit., p. 10; D. McCutchion, op. cit., p. 40.
56. R.K. Chattopadhyay and D. Acharya, op. cit., p. 21.
57. Atul Chandra Bhowmick, 'A Note on Jaina Sculptural Remains at Sitalpur, Bhangra, Harup and Deoli Villages in Purulia District', *Jain Journal: A Quarterly on Jainology,* vol. 18, no. 1, 1983, pp. 38–42; R.K. Chattopadhyay and D. Acharya, op. cit., p. 20.
58. R.K. Chattopadhyay and D. Acharya, op. cit., p. 11.
59. Ibid., p. 18.
60. Shubha Majumder et al., op. cit., p. 105.
61. R.K. Chattopadhyay and D. Acharya, op. cit., pp. 11–12.
62. Ibid., p. 22.

63. Ibid., p. 10.
64. Ibid., p. 11.
65. Ibid., p. 13.
66. Ibid., p. 14.
67. Ibid., p. 12.
68. Ibid.; D. McCutchion, op. cit., pp. 35-6; G. Sengupta and Sharmila Saha, op. cit., p. 238.
69. R.K. Chattopadhyay and D. Acharya, op. cit., p. 20.
70. Ibid., p. 12.
71. Ibid., pp. 12-13; D. McCutchion, op. cit., pp. 37-8.
72. R.K. Chattopadhyay and D. Acharya, op. cit., p. 20.
73. Ibid., p. 22.
74. Ibid., p. 21; Shubha Majumder, 'Newly Discovered Jaina Antiquities from Cheliyama, District Purulia, West Bengal: An Archaeological Perspective', *Proceedings of the Indian History Congress*, vol. 73, 2012, pp. 1250-4.
75. Shubha Majumder, op. cit., pp. 1256-7.
76. R.K. Chattopadhyay and D. Acharya, op. cit., p. 20; Shubha Majumder 'Understating the Archaeological Contexts and Iconic Details of Jaina Antiquities from Rakṣatpura and Śaṅkā, District Puruliā, West Bengal', *International Journal of Jaina Studies,* vol. 10, no.1, 2014, pp. 7-9; Swati Ray et al., op. cit., pp. 207-8.
77. R.K. Chattopadhyay and D. Acharya, op. cit., p. 21.
78. Swati Ray et al., op. cit., p. 216.
79. Shubha Majumder, 'Newly Discovered Jaina Antiquities from Cheliyama, District Purulia, West Bengal: An Archaeological Perspective', *Proceedings of the Indian History Congress*, vol. 73, 2012, p. 1255.
80. Shubha Majumder 'An Iconographic Study of Jaina *Chaumukha*s from the Eastern Fringe Areas of the Chhotanagpur Plateau', p. 107.
81. R.K. Chattopadhyay and D. Acharya, op. cit., p. 20.
82. Ibid., p. 22.
83. Ibid.
84. Rajat Sanyal, 'Dhuluri (Puruliya, West Bengal) Rock Inscription', *Pratna Samiksha*, New Series, vol.7, 2016, pp. 59-61.
85. R.K. Chattopadhyay and D. Acharya, op. cit., p. 22.

7

Buddhist Revival in Contemporary Uttar Pradesh, *c.*2005 CE–2011 CE

Some Aspects of Ambedkarite and Ājīvika Discourses on Buddhism and Hinduism in Hindi Print Media[1]

Introduction

The Indian province of Uttar Pradesh, having a significant concentration of Dalit population, has witnessed some significant socio-religious churnings in the post-2000 CE period. An important aspect of this churning has been socio-political mobilization of a section of the Dalits and OBCs. A related phenomenon of this socio-political mobilization is the concerted efforts of revival of Buddhism. In this chapter, an attempt is being made to understand some aspects of this revival, as glimpsed in the Hindi print media, from *c.*2005 to 2011 CE.

The Long-term Context of Buddhist Revival in Uttar Pradesh

With an increasing realization of the need to see the multiple local mutations of Buddhism as a part of the process of its 'appropriation from below' – a phenomenon in which various local forms of Buddhism work within the normative framework of the Great Tradition of Buddhism, yet they retain the distinctively local forms to negotiate local needs – a framework has gradually evolved to analyse the pattern of interactions between the normative Great Tradition of Buddhism and its interactions with various local mutations of Buddhism.[2] That has forced us to rethink some of the generally accepted notions regarding the decline of ancient Indian Buddhism. Elsewhere, I had tried to show that instead of approaching the decline of Indian Buddhism through a monochromic subcontinental prism, a more prudent approach may be to see the local dynamics as the decline of Indian Buddhism had variations across time and space.[3]

If the decline of Buddhism was such a heterogeneous process, it is but natural that its attempted revival in colonial and post-colonial India display considerable variations in terms of the social groups who took part in its revival or became officially Buddhist.[4] Trevor Ling postulates that there were two types of Buddhism in modern India: one is a comprehensive religious and cultural package; the other is personal and has a strong philosophical and meditational element.[5] One may also add that the post-colonial Indian state, in its quest for cultural pride, also adopted some aspects of Buddhist symbolism, and Indians, generally irrespective of their caste and creed, took pride in India's rich Buddhist heritage.[6] Buddha – 'a great man respected by all sections of Indian population' – was treated as one of India's greatest gifts to the world.

Broadly agreeing with Trevor Ling, one may argue that, for some sections of the Dalits, even before Dr Ambedkar, Buddhism, due to its perceived emancipatory potential, was perceived as a 'comprehensive religious and cultural package', not just as another set of religious philosophy.[7] Under Dr Ambedkar, we see a renewed emphasis on this aspect of Buddhism. For him, the Dhamma was a tool for social reconstruction, with the basic aim of '*Sukhāvatī* now'.[8] His conception and propagation of Buddhism was so fundamentally different from all earlier forms of Indian Buddhism that he himself had to coin a new term – Navayāna – for this Buddhism. This was but natural as Dr Ambedkar has provided a new interpretation of some of the very fundamental concepts of Buddhism: *karma*, rebirth and *nirvāṇa*. Navayāna rapidly established itself as the only from of Buddhism acceptable to an important section of the population of Indian Dalits after the death of Dr Ambedkar.

One of the major concerns of Dr Ambedkar was to seal the rather porous boundaries between Buddhism and Hinduism. Some Ambedkarite intellectuals attribute this effort of Dr Ambedkar to a perceived desire of Dr Ambedkar to guard the ritual, social and philosophical autonomy of the neo-Buddhist convert by making 22 *pratijñā*s (twenty-two pledges/oaths/vows) mandatory for those who wanted to embrace Buddhism.[9] As per G. Omvedt, these *pratijñā*s were:[10]

1. I will not regard Brahmā, Viṣṇu or Mahādeva as gods and I will not worship them.
2. I will not regard Rāma or Kṛṣṇa as gods and I will not worship them.
3. I will not honour Gaurī, Gaṇapati or any god of Hinduism and I will not worship them.
4. I do not believe that god has taken any avatar.
5. I agree that the propaganda that the Buddha was the avatar of Viṣṇu is false and mischievous.
6. I will not do the ceremony of *śrāddhapakṣa* (for the departed) or *piṇḍadāna* (gifts in honour of the deceased).
7. I will do no action that is inconsistent with the Dhamma of Buddhism.
8. I will have no rituals done by Brāhmaṇas.
9. I regard all human beings as equal.
10. I will strive for the establishment of equality.
11. I will depend on the Eightfold Path declared by the Buddha.
12. I will follow the 10 vows declared by the Buddha.
13. I will have compassion for all creatures and will care for them.
14. I will not steal.
15. I will not lie.
16. I will not follow any addiction.
17. I will not drink alcohol.

18. I will carry on my life based on the three principles in the Buddhist Dhamma of *dhyāna, śīla* and *karuṇā.*
19. I renounce the Hindu religion which has obstructed the evolution of my former humanity and considered humans unequal and inferior.
20. I have understood that this is the true Dhamma.
21. I consider that I have taken a new birth.
22. From this time forward I vow that I will behave according to the Buddha's teachings.

After the death of Dr Ambedkar, Navayāna could establish some foothold in Maharashtra where the Mahāras embraced Buddhism in significant numbers, but other Dalit castes, partly in reaction to a perceived Mahāra hegemony in this Buddhism, largely kept aloof.[11] In Uttar Pradesh, the spread of Navayāna was less successful than even what was observed in Maharashtra. This was despite some interesting efforts by early pioneers such as Acharya Motiram Shastri, who anticipated most of the trends we see in Dalit Buddhist movements in Uttar Pradesh, 2005–11 CE.[12] Similar trends were discernible in the Buddhist revival movements in and around the city of Kanpur, which had a significant concentration of workers of Chamāra/Jāṭava caste in the leather mills of the city.[13] Yet, despite these early efforts, Buddhism could not witness any mass revival.

The situation changed fundamentally with the emergence of the Bahujana Samaja Party (BSP) as a significant political player in Uttar Pradesh. The BSP generally refrained from getting directly associated with Buddhist revival movements in Uttar Pradesh or elsewhere. This was due to electoral compulsions. The indirect repercussions of the rise of the BSP as a significant political player were, however, seems to be substantial. It seems to have created a fertile milieu for the revival of Buddhism among a certain section of the Dalits and OBCs.[14]

This process got a new spurt with the capture of political power by the BSP in Uttar Pradesh – the most populous and politically the most significant province of India – in 2007. On the whole, one may witness vigorous attempts to revive Buddhism from below by some Dalits and OBCs.[15] This has resulted into the many interesting developments: construction of Buddhist temples, open-air shrines, and *vihāras*, mostly through individual initiative and patronage; and a great spurt in the publication of popular literary journals, books and magazines.

Issues Probed in the Present Chapter

In this chapter; we shall be concentrating on the discourses on Buddhism propagated through these journals, books and magazines.[16] Most of them were the result of individual initiative and they reflect interesting perspectives from below. An avowed aim of these journals and books was the propagation of a new kind of Buddhism. The protagonists of this Buddhism also sought to consolidate the Dalits and OBCs as a coherent group having similar religious, political and social goals. These journals and books, published and sold at low price, were meant for mass dissemination and they have created ripples in a significant section of the Dalit and OBC population. These journals and books were the flag bearers of a new kind of Buddhism. Buddhism is being revived, but in a form that doesn't seem to have much parallel in the past. Survival strategies of this Buddhism also seem to be different from the earlier forms of Buddhism in India.

In this chapter, an attempt has been made to understand:

1. The methods of 'othering' through which a revival of Buddhism was attempted. As the process of 'othering' generally serves as the precondition for the creation of any 'imagined self', Ambedkarite discourses on creating the 'other' are as important as the discourse on Buddhism. This section will largely explain 'why to leave Hinduism' and 'why to adopt Buddhism'.
2. When a 'self' is created/attempted to be created by defining itself as the polar opposite to the 'other',[17] how the 'self' is to be

preserved and consolidated? That is, if the previous section was more concerned with 'why to become a Buddhist', this section is more concerned with 'how to become a good Buddhist', 'what kind of Buddhism we should follow' and 'how to follow that kind of Buddhism'.

3. How to woo the non-Dalits and tribals to Buddhism? Similar to the missionary character of early Indian Buddhism, this Buddhism is missionary to the core and it has devised some interesting discourses to attract other communities to Buddhism. It will be interesting to see how Buddhism is used as a cementing factor in integrating some non-OBC, non-Dalit castes and communities within the fold of Buddhism.
4. Challenges before, and dilemmas faced by, this Buddhism. In this section, we will also try to analyse the neo-Ājīvika critique of this Buddhist movement and its possible impacts on this Buddhist movement.

Some clarifications are necessary at the very outset. The processes mentioned above are not mutually exclusive: they, rather, frequently overlap. One may discern the operation of all of them simultaneously. Most of the issues of such journals contain some papers on 'why we should adopt Buddhism by renouncing Hinduism', some papers on 'how to become a good Buddhist', and 'what kind of Buddhism we should follow'; and some papers on how to spread 'our Buddhism to other social groups and castes'. Besides, these journals and books, largely being the results of individual efforts, do not present a coherent and homogeneous discourse on Buddhism. The only thing which unites various journals, books, their authors and editors, and readers, is the shared reverence to the Buddha and Dr Ambedkar. That notwithstanding, a considerable diversity is seen in various writings.

As this Buddhist revival was being attempted, a section of Dalit intellectuals developed some basic differences. They propagated that Buddhism – founded by a Kṣatriya (Siddhārtha, who later became Buddha) – could not be a religion of the Dalit-Bahujanas due to various reasons. They too developed their own arguments against the Buddha and Buddhism, and started to propagate that the Ājīvika-dharma is more endogenous to the Dalit-Bahujanas. To have a fuller understanding of the process of Buddhist revival in contemporary Uttar Pradesh, we will also briefly discuss the Ājīvika criticism of Buddhism in the latter section of the present chapter.

The Unfolding *telos*: 'Buddhism was the Moment of Our Glory; Hinduism is the Result of Our Defeat and Humiliation' – and the Process of 'Othering' to Create a Buddhist Self

Probably no other movement in India has used a perceived history to the extent and to the effect to ensure a sustained mobilization of its cadre and other supporters as we see in the Ambedkarite movements in Uttar Pradesh. Contemporary Ambedkarite discourses on their own past follow a rather straight unfolding of a perceived historical *telos*.

A perceived historical *telos* unfolds in a straight way: 'a glorious past of the *mūlanivāsī*s of India, which was overrun by the 'Aryan invaders'; 'enslavement' of the *mūlanivāsī* population and the imposition of the *varṇa/jāti* divisions on them so that they become unable to offer any united resistance to the invaders; resurfacing of the *mūlanivāsī* resistance under the Buddha; 'extermination' of Buddhism under Puṣyamitra Śuṅga; refusal of the *mūlanivāsī*s to renounce Buddhism; hence the imposition of untouchable status on them by the conquerors'. Hence, a 're-embracing of Buddhism by the Dalits will not be 'conversion' as such but rather a homecoming, as Buddhism was our original religion, only in the moments of humiliation and defeat, Hinduism was imposed on us'. This view, originally propounded by Dr Ambedkar,[18] surfaces again and again with persuasive exhortations of the need to 'come back to the original home' by renouncing Hinduism.[19]

Thus, some Ambedkarite intellectuals portray that the Harappan civilization was the result of the genius of the *mūlanivāsīs*; it was totally egalitarian in nature; *varṇa-jāti* system was not there; people were enterprising and industrious and they traded with distant lands; they had splendid traditions of arts and crafts; and their civilization was one of the most accomplished and prosperous civilizations of the ancient world.

We may discern a lively debate regarding the religious identity of this civilization. Dr Ambedkar's hints were indirect: 'even the early Pāli canon suggests that 27 Buddhas of previous eons existed before Śākyamuni Buddha, so the religion of the Harappan civilization could well be Buddhist, but it was certainly Śramaṇa in nature'.[20] The Śramaṇa tradition is, as per his claims, much older than the Brāhmaṇa tradition.[21] Barring some exceptions,[22] later writings are more emphatic in attributing a Buddhist identity to this civilization now.[23] This is one of the reflections of the extent to which this belief has been internalized by a section of the Ambedkarite intelligentsia of northern India.

Regarding the social identity of the persons who were the creators of the Harappan civilization, one may witness an important shift: if a significant section of writings in some Ambedkarite journals and books propagate the notion of an undifferentiated and homogeneous *mūlanivāsī* population defeated by the Aryans, some intellectuals are more forthcoming in attribution of the creation of this civilization to some particular castes. One of them claims that this civilization was the product of the Śūdra and Vaṇika castes.[24] Some intellectuals also claim that this civilization was the creation of the Chamāras.[25] In some writings, it is claimed that the last king of this civilization was Chamurī, who was killed fighting the invading Aryans and the Chamāras are the descendants of this brave ruler.[26]

The Aryan invasion, some Ambedkarite intellectuals argue, came as a 'great catastrophe to the *mūlanivāsī* followers of the Buddha or some Śramaṇic religion': 'the conquering Aryans enslaved the *mūlanivāsī*s, divided them in various castes and *varṇa* so as to prevent the chances of the emergence of any united *mūlanivāsī* front against the Aryans'.[27] Some Ambedkarite intellectuals also claim that the next one millennium was 'the period of untold miseries for the *mūlanivāsī* population, and the succor of relief came with the emergence of Buddhism'. The Buddha, as stated in many writings, was not a Kṣatriya: he was born in the family of the *mūlanivāsī* Nāgavaṁśa. It has been argued by some that the 'Nāgas were a brave race that has offered a stubborn resistance to the invading Aryans'.[28] Some intellectuals claim that the Buddha was born in *Chamaravaṁśa*, and the Chamāra caste originated from *Chamaravaṁśa*.[29]

One impression must be put on record here only. When Dr Ambedkar embraced Buddhism, he had no problem with the Kṣatriya identity of the Buddha: the Buddha was born in a Kṣatriya family and he was brought up as a Kṣatriya prince, but his heart was compassionate enough to contemplate on the problems of the lower rungs of the society and suggest a way out. Much water has flown down the Ganges in the last fifty years in the sense that, with an increasing assertion of Dalit identity, a significant section is not willing to accept even the symbolic leadership of a Kṣatriya spiritual leader.

One may gauge the seriousness of the issue by analysing some recent debates regarding the Kṣatriya lineage of the Buddha. The most fundamental point of contention is: 'why should the Dalits worship and follow a spiritual leader (the Buddha), who was neither a Dalit nor a Bahujana'?[30] It has also been asserted that 'if the Dalit-Bahujanas have to accomplish social, economic and spiritual emancipation, their spiritual leaders must be from within them only'.[31] It has also been argued that the religion of the *kamerī*[32] castes like the Dalits could not be Buddhism, which was 'a religion of the escapist monks who ran away from accepting any kind of social responsibility', and a 'religion which broke families'.[33] The Dalit-Bahujans must follow a spiritual leader who is from their own social background, and one of such leaders may be Makkhali Gosāla, the founder of the Ājivika Dharma, who was from the Kumhāra (potters) caste: so, 'Buddhism is not an appropriate religion for the Dalit-Bahujanas, but Ājivika Dharma is'. This argument, originally made by Dr Dharmavira, indicates a significant criticism of Buddhism coming from within the Dalits.

One may discern a certain degree of unease among the Ambedkarite protagonists of Buddhism vis-à-vis this tricky question. This question has created so much concern that a book containing the writings of some of the best-known Ambedkarite intellectuals, with the specific aim of demolishing the arguments of Dr Dharmavira, was brought out. This question was countered not by proudly accepting that the Buddha was a Kṣatriya (as done by Dr Ambedkar), but by claiming that the Buddha was a *mūlanivāsī*, belonging to the *nāgavaṁśa*.[34] It has also been claimed elsewhere that 'the Buddha was born in the *Chamaravaṁśa*, from which the Chamāra caste originated'.[35]

It must also be stated here that some OBC castes are also claiming that the Buddha was born in their castes. Leaving aside the more emphatic claims of some sections of Maurya, Kuśavāhā, Śākya and Saini castes to this effect,[36] we see this claim by an intellectual of one more OBC caste: Nāī (the barber caste). It has been claimed that not only the Buddha, but also Samrāṭa Mahāpadmananda of the Nanda dynasty of ancient Magadha, the Śiśunāga dynasty of the same, as well as the Maurya dynasty, belonged to this caste.[37] These competing claims over the 'ownership' of the Buddha by different castes have, rather than creating any rift or confrontation among such castes, seem to have cemented bonds of solidarity among them. Among the OBC castes, the Maurya, Kuśavāhā, Śākya and Saini castes have emerged as one of the main support bases for the BSP.

Despite these minor differences, a fundamental unity exists in the different interpretations of Buddhism by contemporary Ambedkarite intellectuals in the sense that Dr Ambedkar's book *The Buddha and his Dhamma* forms the only authoritative source to understand and interpret Buddhism.[38] Particular care is taken to disseminate the image of this Buddha (the one visualized by Dr Ambedkar) among the children of the Dalit Buddhist families. Two types of methods are adopted for this: short stories,[39] and pictorial comics.[40] In such writings, the Buddha is shown leaving his family, in broad daylight after taking proper permission from his wife and family members, in compliance of the decision of the executive council of the Śākya *gaṇasaṅgha*.[41] It is claimed that a conflict had emerged between the Śākyas of Kapilavastu and the Koliyas of the neighbouring state regarding the division of water of the Rohini river. A war was about to take place, but the Buddha advised against this. That enraged the executive council of the Śākya *gaṇasaṅgha*, which gave him three options: exile from the state; the confiscation of all agricultural lands belonging to his family; or joining the war against the Koliyas. The young prince, to avoid bloodshed, opted for the first option and he left home to find a way to end the conflicts of human society.[42]

Re-reading Popular Myths and Mobilizing a Buddhist Self

In the Dalit discourses on Buddhism, it is frequently claimed that the *mūlanivāsīs* had a golden time, first under the Buddha and then under Aśoka Maurya.[43] But the 'assassination of the last ruler of the Maurya dynasty marked the beginning of a new era of atrocities on the *mūlanivāsī* population'. We may see, for example:

> Bṛhadattha was the grandson of the great Buddhist emperor Aśoka. This tenth king of the Mauryan dynasty was deceitfully killed by Puṣyamitra Śuṅga in 184 BC. After usurping the throne, Puṣyamitra Śuṅga promulgated the order: whoever brings the severed head of a *chīvaradhārī bhikṣu*, he would be rewarded with one hundred gold coins. A great massacre of the *chīvaradhārī* Buddhist monks took place and thousands of such *chīvaradhārī* monks were eliminated. Many fled to the neighbouring countries. Some *chīvaradhārī* survived and their descendants were given the contemptuous appellation of Chamāra. The word Chamāra is a corrupt form of *cīvara*. The Chamāra people are found all over India. In some areas,

they are called Jāṭava. In some other areas, they are called Mahāra, Raidāsī, etc.[44]

That the '*mūlanivāsī*s were Buddhists in the time of their glory and it was only during the period of their defeat and "enslavement" that they were made untouchables due to their refusal to budge an inch from their commitment to Buddhism' has been one of the core beliefs in the Dalit appropriation of Buddhism even before Dr Ambedkar.[45] If we see the revival of these arguments in contemporary Uttar Pradesh, that may not come as any surprise. But the thing which may surprise many observers is that this appropriation is often associated with a wholesale rejection of Hindu festivals and other visible markers of Hindu identity.

Sometime, it involves the creation of an alternate sacred geography, even in those areas which are considered to be important places in Hindu sacred geography. One may see, for example, the attempted creation of a *mūlanivāsī* sacred geography in the Lucknow-Haradoi[46] area, which is a part of Avadha, the original land of Rāma in Hindu religion, in an article published in *Ambedkar Today*. This article states that 'in the olden times, a very pious and justice-loving Anārya king Hiraṇyakaśyapu ruled in the areas of Lucknow and its neighborhood'.[47] Being an Anārya king, 'he was a stubborn enemy of the Aryan heroes: Viṣṇu, Rāma, Hari, etc.' 'Hence the name of his kingdom was Haridrohī, which is now famous as Haradoi'.[48]

Hindu festivals are another target for criticism, which are, as per some writings, the 'celebration of the conquest by the "invading Aryans" or the followers of Puṣyamitra Śuṅga over the *mūlanivāsī* population'.[49] An article in *Ambedkar Today* claims that Holī is a '*bālaparva*'.[50] Similarly, in many writings, Dīpāvalī is portrayed as another 'celebration of defeat of Buddhism by Brahmanism'.[51]

In some other writings, we see another claim: when Emperor Aśoka formally embraced Buddhism, he undertook pilgrimage to important Buddhist pilgrimage centres. He, then, dug open the relics of the Buddha, which were buried in some *stūpa*s. To distribute the relics of the Buddha allover Jambūdvīpa, he got constructed 8,400 *stūpa*s all over Jambūdvīpa and enshrined the relics of the Buddha in the same. After the completion of the construction of these *stūpa*s, an inauguration ceremony was celebrated at Pāṭaliputra by lighting lamps and donations of lamps to inaugurate the great *stūpa*. Other *stūpa*s were also inaugurated by lighting lamps in other parts of India. The dark night of Kārttika *amāvasyā* got brightened with the lights of *dhammadīpa*s. This offering of lamps was also dedicated to the memory of Mahāmaudgalyāyana. This festival was celebrated in India for a long time: 'later it was Brahamanised and became Dīpāvalī'.[52]

We see a similar methodology in operation in attributing some new meanings to old myths. Thus, Rāvaṇa is depicted as an 'honest, pious, just and peace loving Buddhist ruler of the *mūlanivāsī*s', whose 'kingdom was so prosperous that people used to live in the golden houses'.[53] It is claimed in a paper that 'this brave king fought an invading Aryan hero to safeguard the honour of his sister and his *prajā*; and even when he was "deceitfully" killed by Rāma, the idea of *mūlanivāsī* honour, valour, and resistance could not be eliminated'.[54] In this kind of discourse, Vijayādaśamī, which is traditionally celebrated to mark the victory of Rāma over Rāvaṇa, is portrayed as 'another celebration of the defeat of Buddhism in India': 'it was originally Aśoka Dhammavijayadaśamī festival to celebrate the acceptance of Buddhism by Aśoka'.[55] This festival was 'celebrated every year for five days in the month of Kārttika, and it involved the gift of *cīvara* and other essentials to Buddhist monks by the king and other lay believers'.[56] This day was 'deliberately chosen by Puṣyamitra Śuṅga to assassinate the tenth ruler of the Maurya dynasty'. And, 'after the establishment of Brahmin rule, the nature of Aśoka Dhammavijayadaśamī was changed to Daśaharā or Vijayādaśamī to celebrate the defeat of Buddhism in India'.[57] But, 'unfortunately, Dalits celebrate this festival with great fanfare now a days due to their ignorance of their own history'.[58]

Professional historians may have their own set of reservations regarding such writings. These writings, however, may also be taken as an attempt by an emerging socio-religious identity to carve out an autonomous space by inventing myths and creating a counter sacred geography to claim that Uttar Pradesh was also the land of brave Anārya heroes. It is also claimed in many writings that Uttar Pradesh is also the land which was blessed with the visits of the Buddha, who visited not only the famous sites like Śrāvastī, Sārnāth or Kuśīnagar, but also lesser-known ones. These 'lesser-known sites need to be brought to the tourist map and pilgrimage to such sites should be encouraged'.

So, we see one more trend: the glorification of pilgrimage to Buddhist pilgrimage centres and the discouragement of visits to Hindu pilgrimage centres. Thus, an article in *Ambedkar Today* introduces us to a young boy, who, after his Board examinations, makes a telephonic call to seek his father's permission to visit Haridwar with his friends. His father replies that he should rather go to Ambedkar Udyāna in Lucknow.[59] Or, he may go to Bodh-Gayā, 'which is our most important religious centre'.[60] 'Bairanjā, Kuśīnagar, Śrāvastī and Kauśāmbī are also good places to visit'.[61]

Reconstructing a Perceived History: 'Ancient India was Not Hindu India but Buddhist India'

This urge to claim the Dalit share in ancient Indian history results into a re-assessing of some historical personalities and their patronage to Buddhism. One may see, for example, the case of Jayachandra, the last ruler of the Gahaḍavāla dynasty of Uttar Pradesh, who was defeated by Muhammad Ghori, leading to the foundation of the Turkic rule in northern India. In a significant section of popular memory, Jayachandra is treated as a traitor who invited Muhammad Ghori to teach a lesson to Pṛthvirāja Chauhāna, with whom his (Jayachandra's) daughter Sanyogitā has eloped. A paper published in an Ambedkarite journal claims that 'Jayachandra was a great patriot, a very just and upright ruler, who was also a great *upāsaka* of Buddhism'. His mother, 'a great *upāsikā*, appointed a Buddhist monk Jagatamitrānanda as his (Jayachandra's) personal tutor during his childhood'. Jagatamitrānanda was the '*saṅghanāyaka* of Buddhism that time'. Jayachandra's 'relationship with Jagatamitrānanda continued even after he became king and their relationship is attested to in an inscription of Bodh-Gayā'.[62] This paper claims that 'it was due to Jayachandra's unwavering support to Buddhism that he was attacked by Brahmanical rulers from all sides'.[63]

We see another important strategy in creating a 'Buddhist self' in 'continuous conflict' with the 'Hindu other' through the domain of history, which involves claiming the ownership of 'ancient Buddhist sites now under illegal Hindu occupation'.[64] Bodh-Gayā is often cited as the prime example and the efforts of Bhante Anāgarika Dharmapāla to 'liberate' this site are glorified.[65] At another level, this involves claiming those sites which have high symbolic value in the mobilization of Hindu identity. We may cite the example of Rāmajanmabhūmi-Bābarī Masjid dispute, which has played a significant role in catapulting the Bharatiya Janata Party (BJP) to be the most dominant political party of India. This dispute had a twofold impact on the political and social mobilization of the Dalits and the OBCs in Uttar Pradesh. At one level, it somehow contained the Mandal upsurge.[66] At another level, it created conditions for some leaders from OBC and Dalit background to occupy important posts within the BJP.[67]

Both situations posed some long-term challenges to the Ambedkarite socio-political mobilization. Some Ambedkarite intellectuals felt the need to counter this development. We discern a two-pronged effort towards this. The first involved the legal front: some Ambedkarite Buddhists filed legal cases in the courts of law to claim that the Buddhists should also be made a party in the dispute as the 'Rāmajanmabhūmi-Bābarī Masjid site was originally a Buddhist site'.[68] At another level, the strategy was to create maximum awareness regarding this among the Dalit population. We will not look into the legal merits of such claims.[69] We are more interested in the evolving polemic regarding the Buddhist 'ownership' of the site and its rather 'sure ramifications for the survival of Hinduism as an institutional religion'. In a paper, it has been claimed that 'the disputed site in Ayodhyā is not Rāmajanmabhūmi but Bāvarī Mahāvihāra, built by King Prasenjit in honour of Bāvarī, a Buddhist monk of great repute, the one who finds mention in the Pāli canon'.[70] It has been claimed by some Ambedkarites that Bāvarī was the *rājapurohita* of King Prasenjit. After many years in the service of the king, Bāvarī expressed his desire to go to the forests for higher meditations, which the king allowed, and constructed a *mahāvihāra* in his honour. As the *mahāvihāra* was named in his honour so it was named Bāvarī Mahāvihāra.[71] As per this paper, 'Ayodhyā, being part of the state of Kosala, was studded with one hundred Buddhist monasteries, which disappeared either due to natural decay or were destroyed by the Brahmins'.[72] The Bāvarī Mahāvihāra was also demolished and a temple was constructed on the very same place, but 'the public memory associated with Bāvarī could not be wiped out, so when a mosque was constructed by demolishing the temple at the site, it came to be known by the name of Bābarī Masjid, which is a corrupt form of Bāvarī'.[73] It is claimed that 'the ruins of one hundred *mahāvihāra*s could not vanish completely from the area': 'if proper archaeological excavations are conducted, many archaeological evidences will come to support the previous existence of these *mahāvihāra*s'.[74] But the acceptance of this 'fact' will have, it is claimed in this paper, severe implications for Hinduism as an institutional religion.[75] The perceived crux, which is propagated in such writings, is: Buddhism and Hinduism cannot coexist in harmony, one can be either a Buddhist or a Hindu.

But a complete rejection of the past may have its own dangers, especially in a situation in which a great majority of the Dalit population in Uttar Pradesh is not officially Buddhists but the follower of one *Bhakti santa* or another. During the medieval period, the *Bhakti* movement provided an important channel to vent the

Dalit dissent with the existing social order.[76] Practically every Dalit caste has its own patron *santa*, more so in the case of the Jāṭava caste, the backbone of Dalit mobilization in contemporary Uttar Pradesh. A great majority of this caste still follows Guru Ravidāsa. Guru Ravidāsa was a contemporary of Kabīr. Despite voicing his anger against contemporary ritualism and hierarchical social order, he did not walk out of Hinduism. Given his popularity among the Jāṭava caste, any castigation of this great *santa* for his refusal to decisively walk out of the Hindu socio-religious order may be counterproductive. So, a considerable energy is devoted to prove that Guru Ravidāsa, like Dr Ambedkar, was a great follower of the Buddha: 'he was in fact a Bodhisattva'[77] and 'he followed the *pañcaśīla* propagated by the Buddha'.[78] The subtext is: the acceptance of Ambedkarite Buddhism by the Dalits will not be a decisive break with the past, but its logical culmination.

Why Dalits must 'Readopt' Buddhism: The Evolving Discourse

Besides the sustained attempts of creating a Buddhist self by a process of othering, we see a considerable emphasis on explaining 'why we must readopt Buddhism'. In this pursuit, one may notice four broad trends:

(a) The social push: a perceived escape from the *varṇa-jāti* system.

(b) The economic pull: 'Buddhism promotes a superior economic system and we have greater chances of economic betterment by becoming a Buddhist'.

(c) The pride of being the 'original creators' and propagators of a 'world-conquering religion'.

(d) The stamp of legitimacy from Dr Ambedkar the Great: 'a Dalit is not a true follower of Dr Ambedkar until he starts following (Ambedkarite) Buddhism'.

The language of such writings is generally persuasive. In the same piece of writing, we may often see all the four trends mentioned above.

The biggest complaint against Hinduism is that it is 'caste-ridden' and 'a result of our slavery': 'till the *varṇa-jāti* system exists, every Dalit has every right to convert'.[79] So, the basic argument is: 'Buddhism must be re-adopted as it offers not only an escape from the *varṇa-jāti* ridden Brahmanical Hinduism, but it also offers a superior economic system': 'Buddhism promotes an open society, entrepreneurship, long distance trade, commerce and urbanization'. To give it a more contemporary colour, the example of the economic success of 'Buddhist Japan' is frequently cited.[80]

But the biggest pull to Buddhism comes through the towering example of Dr Ambedkar: 'a Dalit is not a true follower of Dr Ambedkar until he starts following (Ambedkarite) Buddhism'. In some writings, it is often argued that no improvement in the social situation of any Dalit is possible within the Hindu social order, and any attempt of Sanskritization is futile.[81]

In fact, the gratitude to, and the awe of the stature of, Bābāsāheb Dr Ambedkar is so much that we see a straightforward argument: 'if you are not (an Ambedkarite) Buddhist, and still claim to be a follower of Dr Ambedkar, then you are a 'pseudo-Ambedkarite', a traitor to the cause of Dalit emancipation, the greatest threat to Dalit empowerment'. This is a perspective shared and promoted by both the emerging clergy[82] and the laity.[83] Ambedkarite intellectuals, activists and Buddhist monks display great anger towards those Dalits who display tendencies towards Sanskritization. It has been stated that these 'pseudo-Ambedkarites' – those persons who claim to be a follower of Dr Ambedkar; get into government jobs due to reservation provided to them through the Constitution drafted by Dr Ambedkar; yet they worship Hindu gods and goddesses and celebrate Hindu festivals; marry Hindu girls from upper caste background; corner most of the benefits which are meant for the Dalits; and 'behave like neo-feudal lords'[84] – are the single-most important factor hampering the revival of Buddhism in India today':[85] 'had these pseudo-Ambedkarites truly followed the teachings of Dr Ambedkar, there would not have been less than 50 crore Buddhists in India by now'.[86] This reflects the extent to which contemporary Ambedkarite discourses on Buddhism expect the Dalits to reject any kind of association with Hinduism. This kind of 'either you reject Hinduism completely or you are a traitor' syndrome has its own limitations in a popular democracy. This is something we shall analyse in the last section of the present chapter.

But despite all this, a great majority of the Dalits in Uttar Pradesh are, in fact, not Buddhist, and the use of an aggressive language may push them more firmly into the folds of Hinduism. In this kind of situation, a more fruitful approach may be to avoid vehement criticism of Hinduism, but to appeal to the stature of Dr Ambedkar in a very persuasive language: 'if you feel that Dr Ambedkar was more educated than you and he had more wisdom than you, then you should follow his words, that is, you should convert to Buddhism by renouncing Hinduism'.[87] Given the impressive educational qualifications of Dr Ambedkar, not many Dalits would be more educated than him, so this is a subtle call to all Dalits to accept Buddhism. Not only this, it is exhorted that every Dalit household must have at least one photograph or statue of Dr Ambedkar, and below that, his educational qualifications (PhD, DSc, Bar At Law, etc.) must be written in bold letters to inspire children to get as educated as Dr Ambedkar was.[88]

In fact, one may gauge the extent of the centrality of Dr Ambedkar in the Buddhist revival movements in contemporary Uttar Pradesh by the fact that he or his writings serve as the reference point not only in the matter of doctrinal aspects of this religion, but also in solemnizing many *rites de passage*. His *The Buddha and His Dhamma* commands the place of the most sacrosanct (and often the only) scripture of this Buddhism; marriages are supposed to be solemnized before the statues or the photographs of the Buddha and Dr Ambedkar; one of the essential commitments both the bride and the groom are supposed to make at the time of solemnization of their marriage is that they will fully comply with the '22 *pratijñās*' prescribed by Dr Ambedkar; and the father of the bride is supposed to gift a copy of *The Buddha and His Dhamma* to the bride and the groom after the solemnization of the Buddhist marriages. Sometimes, Dr Ambedkar is also depicted at par with the Buddha, which causes concern among the older generation of clergy.[89] These are, undoubtedly, some of the steps an emerging Buddhist community is taking to ensure the consolidation of its Buddhist identity, a theme we shall try to explore in the next section.

Preserving and Consolidating an Emerging Buddhist Self: Reviving the Monastic Tradition in a Largely Lay Buddhism, and Formulating *Rites de Passage* and Code of Conduct for the Laity

Side by side with an attempt of winning more converts to this form of Buddhism, we see attempts of preserving and consolidating this emerging Buddhist identity. This works at two levels simultaneously: revival of the monastic tradition, but with a changed nature and orientation of the Saṅgha, and formulating *rites de passage* and a code of conduct for the laity. The latter is probably intended to take care of the what has been referred to as the 'chronic social anemia of Indian Buddhism'.[90] Many writings associated with these concerns also claim to derive their legitimacy from Dr Ambedkar. Thus, a paper[91] in the October 2006 issue of *Ambedkar Today* states that Dr Ambedkar, in his paper entitled 'The Buddha and the Future of His Dhamma', which was published in *Mahābodhi* journal in 1950, emphasized three things for the mass revival and expansion of Buddhism in India:

1. 'Creation of the Buddhist Bible': the author claims that Dr Ambedkar intended to make his *The Buddha and His Dhamma* the Bible of this Buddhism, and this book should be accepted by every Dalit-Bahujana Buddhist as such.[92]

2. Modifying the nature, structure and the orientations of the Bhikṣu Saṅgha.[93]
3. Foundation of the World Buddhist Council.[94]

But one of the most important concerns of Dr Ambedkar, as claimed by the author of the above-mentioned paper, was to keep the neo-Buddhist community free from any kind of Hindu influence, so he formulated his '22 *pratijñā*'. The author of the above-mentioned paper states that:

In his *dīkṣā* ceremony speech in 1956, Dr Ambedkar exhorted his followers not to involve any Brahmin in any ritual. He wanted that the twentieth century Buddhists of India should have an independent identity. Besides, he did not want to repeat the same mistake which many *upāsaka*s had been committing since the period of the Buddha. Impressed by the Buddha, many persons entered the *Saṅgha* as monks, but the common persons, even when fully following the teachings of the Buddha, had to get their rites and rituals performed by the Brahmins. Living examples of this practice are still found in many Buddhist countries such as Laos, Cambodia, Thailand, etc. Among the Indian neo-Buddhists too, this practice is quite evident. Even when they have accepted a new religion, they continue to stick to their old customs, traditions, rites and rituals.[95]

In view of its quest to actualize a complete rupture with Hinduism, it should not come as any surprise if se see a great emphasis on the formulation of *rites de passage* for an emerging Buddhist identity: attracting a section of Dalits to Buddhism may not be that difficult, but retaining them in Buddhism may be a problem; many of them may end up being 'pseudo-Ambedkarite'. One may witness a recurring concern: If a 'code of conduct' for the Buddhist laity and *rites de passage* are not formulated, this fragile community may well end up getting assimilated into Hinduism, especially in a situation when its own Buddhist monastic Great Tradition is very weak. Reviving the Buddhist monastic tradition, of course with new orientations, naturally appears as a strong priority. Let's see this aspect of Ambedkarite discourses on Buddhism in contemporary Uttar Pradesh.

'To Become a Good Buddhist, You Must Undertake *Putradāna* to the Saṅgha'

It is a well-known fact that when Dr Ambedkar decided to formally embrace Buddhism, he was reluctant to take the third vow ('I take refuge in the Saṅgha').[96] This was due to his reservations regarding the prevailing state of affairs in the monastic orders of many Buddhist countries he visited. The non-sustainability of the Saṅgha–centred Buddhism, given the precondition of the mobilization of considerable resources to run the monasteries, among the Dalit Buddhists from not-so-strong economic background could have been another factor. Even after Dr Ambedkar, Navayāna in Maharashtra largely remained a religion run by lay initiative.[97] To sum up, Navayāna had a sustained reluctance to a Saṅgha-centred Buddhism.

In this kind of background, it is interesting to see a considerable emphasis on the revival of monastic Buddhism in contemporary Uttar Pradesh. We see at least an individual publishing his desire to build a *vihāra* in the memory of his mother.[98] We may also discern a systematic attempt to involve the Saṅgha in most of the *rites de passage* for the laity.[99] We may see, for example, the normative format of wedding invitation cards for Buddhist marriages. Wedding invitation cards of Hindu families generally begin with a verse in praise of either Gaṇeśa or Viṣṇu. But when a person becomes a Buddhist; he is supposed to give up not only these old habits, but also to make these cards as effective instruments of propagating the complementariness of the Saṅgha and the laity. It has been recommended that the following verse should be printed on this card:

Buddha kī śobhā dhamma se, dhamma kī śobhā saṅgha
saṅgha kī śobhā āpase, saṅgha āpake saṅga[100]

(The Buddha is adorned by the Dhamma, the Dhamma is adorned by the Saṅgha. The Saṅgha is adorned by you, the Saṅgha is always with you.)

It is more than apparent that Navayāna has shed its initial reservations regarding monastic Buddhism and contemporary Ambedkarite discourses on Buddhism in Uttar Pradesh are trying to revive the monastic tradition.

But the real problem is to find well-trained monks[101] and ensure the survival of the monastic tradition by attracting new entrants to the same. Buddhist families are encouraged to 'donate' their sons to the Saṅgha, that is, inspire their sons to become monks. In this aspect, who can be more instrumental in inspiring the *upāsakas* than the perceived example of Aśoka Maurya?

When Emperor Aśoka embraced Buddhism, he undertook pilgrimage to important Buddhist pilgrimage centers. He, then, decided to erect 84,0000 *stūpas* all over Jambūdvīpa. For that, he dug open the nine original *stūpas* containing the body-relics of the Buddha. 84,0000 *stūpas*, containing the portions of the body-relics of the Buddha, were erected all over Jambūdvīpa. He also got constructed 84,000 pillars and 84,000 *vihāras*. He also got engraved 84,000 inscriptions on the pillars exhorting the common population to follow the teachings of the Buddha. He also made arrangements for the lodging, feeding, study and other expenses of the monks in the 84,000 *vihāras*. He, then, asked his Guru Mogaliputta Tiṣya: am I a promoter of Buddhism now? Mogaliputta Tiṣya tersely replied: leave aside your claim of being a promoter of Buddhism, you have not even entered into the fold of Buddhism. Getting shocked, Aśoka said: 'I have done so much to spread Buddhism. I have erected 84,000 *vihāras* and *stūpas*, I have made full arrangements for the lodging, feeding, study and other expenses of the monks residing in these *vihāras*. I have erected 84,000 pillar-inscriptions to exhort my subjects to follow the Buddha. Due to my efforts, entire Jambūdvīpa is praising the glory of the Buddha. Even then I am not a promoter of Buddhism! What should I do to become a promoter of the Dhamma'? Hearing this, Mogaliputta replied: 'you will not be a *pūrṇa* Buddhist unless at least one member of your family becomes a monk'. Listening to this, his son Mahendra decided to become a monk, which Aśoka proudly allowed. His daughter Saṅghamitrā too decided to become a nun, and both Mahendra and Saṅghamitrā proceeded to Sri Lanka. Nowadays, people do become Buddhist, but nobody undertakes *putradāna*.

Unless *putradāna* is done, we will not have good monks. For every Buddhist *upāsaka*, donating at least one son to the *Saṅgha* is essential.[102]

The subtle message is: if Emperor Aśoka could not become a complete Buddhist, even after his proverbial efforts for the propagation of Buddhism, ordinary *upāsaka*s should not feel proud of their acceptance of Buddhism unless they donate their sons to the Saṅgha to revive the monastic tradition of Buddhism. In fact, it has been claimed that the dream of Dr Ambedkar to make India a Buddhist country remains unfulfilled due to the reluctance of the *upāsaka*s to perform *putradāna*: 'if the dream of Dr Ambedkar is to be actualized, you should not only embrace Buddhism, but also inspire at least one of your sons to become a monk'.[103]

But this kind of commitment to the Saṅgha may be difficult for a community which has yet to embrace Buddhism fully.[104] Some intellectuals try to provide a way out: if 'donating' your son to the Saṅgha to become a fully-ordained monk is difficult, at least send him to some *vihāra* as a *śramaṇera*. Let him live and study there for some time. After sometime, he may decide to come back to the society to live as an *upāsaka*; or he may decide to become a fully-ordained monk.[105]

In exhorting the lay believers to send their sons to the *vihāra*s as a *śramaṇera*, we see the use of the legend of Aśoka.[106] But the exhortations of the need to revive the monastic tradition comes with a renewed assurance to the laity that the *upāsaka*s always had an honoured place in Buddhism and they will continue to enjoy the same.[107] And, from the monks, the lay expectation is: 'to initiate new *śramaṇera* into Dhamma through *pravajjā-upasampadā* and propel the *upāsaka*s towards *nirvāṇa* is the first and last duty of the monk'.[108]

Formulating a Code of Conduct for the Laity and Monks and *Rites de Passage* for the Laity

If reviving the monastic Buddhism and attracting and retaining *śīlavāna* monks is an important concern, formulating a code of conduct and a set of *rites de passage* for the laity is another important concern. Formulating a set of *rites de passage* involves formulating specific rituals for important occasions, from the time of conception of a child in mother's womb to rituals for funerary rites. Generally, the recital of a particular *Sutta* from the Pāli Canon is prescribed for a particular occasion. Most of the rites are expected to be performed in front of the photographs or statues of the Buddha and Dr Ambedkar. On most of the occasions, the vow of fully following the 22 *pratijña*s prescribed by Dr Ambedkar is expected to be repeated. Another important exhortation is to make the maximum social display of practiced Buddhism, both by monks and the laity. That involves formulating a set of code of conduct for both.

Expanding the Self: Integrating other Castes and Communities into Buddhism

In the previous pages, we have seen that this Buddhism is missionary in its very nature: it is a religion in which even converts from Christianity[109] and Islam[110] are welcome. Given this kind of missionary zeal, it should not come as any surprise if we see a determined effort to bring new castes and communities to the fold of Buddhism. We see this attempt with reference to the Jāṭas of western U.P., Haryana and Punjab, and the Muṇḍā tribe of Jharkhand. In both cases, the attempt is to appropriate some existing religious and social practices, attribute 'originally Buddhist' nature to them, and then claim that these practices are the reflection of their 'Buddhist' past. The underlying message is: get back to your original faith by 're-adopting' Buddhism. Thus in the case of the Jāṭas, it has been claimed by an Ambedkarite intellectual that they are the descendants of the 'Buddhist Śakas'.[111] Thus, it has been claimed that 'barring the examples of Samrāṭa Aśoka and Samrāṭa Milinda, every Buddhist ruler in the Indian subcontinent, including Kaniṣka, was related to the Śakas', that is, 'all such rulers were the ancestors of the Jāṭas'.[112] It is also claimed that 'even today, their social and ritual behaviour displays a considerable "Buddhist influence": they don't practice idolatry; they are hardworking, they generally don't consume wine; they earn their livelihood through hard and honest labour; they don't believe in casteism and they believe in social equality and fraternity; these virtues are basically "Buddhist virtues", which indicate that they were Buddhist in the past'.[113] Ārya Samāja had a sustained influence among this caste in the past and an Ārya Samājī activist may attribute these virtues to the Ārya Samāja influence on them. But in a changed political and social landscape of Uttar Pradesh, these features are attributed a Buddhist colour.

We see similar attempts to woo the Muṇḍā tribe of Jharkhand. It has been claimed by an Ambedkarite intellectual that 'the word "Muṇḍā" is a corrupt form of *Muṇḍaka* or *Muṇḍa*': '*Muṇḍaka* or *Muṇḍa* were used in a derogatory sense for Buddhist monks'.[114] It has been claimed that when Puṣyamitra Śuṅga, and later, Śaśāṅka (the ruler of Gauḍa in Bengal, who later occupied parts of Bihar also) committed great atrocities on the Buddhist population of the Gangetic plains of Bihar and adjoining portions of Bengal, they moved to the inaccessible forests of Jharkhand.[115] So, it has been claimed that 'even today, the religious practices and beliefs of the Muṇḍā population show a considerable Buddhist influence': 'even today, they practice Saraṇā Dharma, which is nothing but a survival of *Triśaraṇa* of Buddhism'.[116]

These efforts are, apparently, reflections of the missionary zeal of a neo-convert to Buddhism. With the increasing political and social confidence of Ambedkarite Dalits, we may expect a more sustained propaganda of this kind in future.

Challenges before this Buddhism

As we approach the last section of this chapter, we may discuss some challenges these Buddhist movements seem to be facing in their quest for the revival of Buddhism among the Dalits and OBCs of Uttar Pradesh. One may, in this context, mention the closing down of *Ambedkar Today*, one of the most important flagbearers of this movement, in the latter part of 2010. In 2009 and 2010, many articles were published in this journal 'exposing' the 'corruption' and 'superstition' within Hinduism, which resulted into the filing of many legal cases against the journal for 'hurting the religious sentiments of Hindus', and the journal was closed abruptly. Its publication has not yet resumed. The BSP too has moved into the *sarvajana* phase and has tried to enter into an electoral alliance with the Brahmins of Uttar Pradesh. That also seems to have put a restraint on a sustained propaganda. Dalits cannot be persuaded to embrace Buddhism without a sustained propaganda, which is difficult in a representative democracy in which 79 per cent of the population of Uttar Pradesh is non-Dalit. That is one of the external challenges this movement is facing.

But its inner contradictions are likely to have a more fundamental impact in determining its trajectory. In the previous pages, we have seen that this movement is intricately linked to the political and social mobilization of some Dalit and OBC castes. The initial attraction to Buddhism among some Dalit and OBC castes was due to its perceived advocacy of a casteless society. Among the Dalits, its primary success has been in the Jāṭava caste. Other Dalit castes have their own folk memory, which renders the ideology of the RSS (Rāṣṭrīya Swayamasevaka Saṅgha) quite attractive to them.[117] In the previous section, we have seen the claim that the Buddha was born in Nāgavaṁśa/Chamaravaṁśa. Similarly, one of the most important factors behind the Maurya caste and Śākya caste enthusiasm for Buddhism is due to the claim that the Buddha was born in their castes. This may induce a counter-mobilization.

Contrasting the pattern with the Buddhist revival movements in post-Ambedkar Maharashtra may provide some interesting inferences. In Maharashtra, Buddhism had its primary success among the Mahāras, and increasing Mahāra hegemony in Buddhist revival movements in Maharashtra led to the shift of non-Mahāra Dalits away from Buddhism.[118] Perhaps Mr. Kanshiram was the first person to realize the mistakes of caste-based pattern of Buddhist revival movements: 'if you have to revive and advance Buddhism in India, keep *jāti* away from it'.[119] Though a Maharashtra-like situation has not developed in Uttar Pradesh during the period of our study (2005–11 CE), this possibility cannot be ruled out.

Many Buddhists see some other causes of concern in contemporary Buddhist movements. One of the important grudges against Brahmanism in the Ambedkarite discourses on Buddhism has been the alleged priestly pretensions and ritualism of Brahmanism. With the formulation of a specific set of *rites de passage* for the laity, and exhortation of the need to get them performed by Buddhist monks, a similar situation may emerge. In fact, it has been noted that:

> In a city, a conference of *bhikṣu mahāsaṅgha* was taking place. Famous monks from different provinces of India were participating in the same. Social activists were also allowed to express their opinions. One *upāsaka* opined that Buddhist monks should not get involved in performing rituals of marriage, etc. for the laity, otherwise, there would not be any difference between Buddhist monks and *paṇḍā-pujārī* and *pādarī*. He claimed that this was the belief of Dr Ambedkar. Immediately after that, a monk came to the dais and said: 'If you so desire, you may kick us on back, but why are you depriving us of our livelihood'? If this is not an emerging Brāhmaṇavāda in the *bhikṣusaṅgha* then what else is it?[120]

These developments give an *upāsaka* enough reasons to feel concerned about the current state of affairs in Buddhist revival movements:

> Our problem is that we call ourselves Ambedkaravādī, but, in reality, we have become Āḍambaravādī. One of my friends has rightly said that our monks do not practice the *vinaya*, our *upāsaka*s do not believe and practice *sutta*; and our intellectuals are not willing to believe in *abhidhamma*. Probably these people want to mould Buddhism as per their desires. But they do not know that Brahmanism is getting strengthened by this. 22 *pratijñā*s of Dr Ambedkar should have been the basis of our lives, but we are keeping a distance of 22 miles from them.[121]

These issues bring us face to face with some of the dilemmas faced by, and challenges before, Buddhist revival movements in contemporary Uttar Pradesh. A significant section of Dalits has moved to Buddhism as a result of its perceived anger towards Brahmanical caste order and the stigma of untouchability it suffered. It devised its own myths and counter-myths to claim that 'Buddhism was always our religion': 'only in the moment of defeat, Hinduism and untouchability were imposed on us'. At the ideological level, it found Buddhism quite attractive. But building institutions is taking its own toll of labour and skepticisms. The *Saṅgha* is yet to be revived on a full-fledged scale, yet some intellectuals are alarmed at the emerging trends of 'pontification' and 'superstition' within the Saṅgha. So, there are hopes as well as apprehensions and disappointments.

One may also have to watch out for two more issues: (a) whether this Buddhism will become a victim of the success of the Dalit movement, and (b) whether it will be able to revive monastic Buddhism in a full-fledged way.

The first issue is of more fundamental importance. As we have seen in the previous pages, anti-upper caste rhetoric is one of the most fundamental features of the Dalit political, social and cultural mobilization. In some cases, this rhetoric and the resultant mobilization has been so successful that a question has emerged: why should the Dalits follow the religion propagated by a Kṣatriya (the Buddha)? Besides, why should the Dalits follow a religion (Buddhism) in which Brahmanas had such an entrenched presence in the past? These questions, originally put forward by the Ājīvika adherents of a section of Dalit population, is creating some fundamental dilemmas.[122] A distinct unease is discernible among some Ambedkarite Buddhist intellectuals vis-à-vis this complex question. A way out has been attempted by claiming that the Buddha was a *mūlanivāsī* born in the Nāgavaṁśa or Chamaravaṁśa. One may not be sure if this attempt will be successful. The issue of the Kṣatriya origin of the Buddha may haunt this movement in future as well.

Similarly, it will be interesting to watch out if this Buddhism will be able to revive monastic Buddhism in a full-fledged way. Dr

Ambedkar's Navayāna had reservations about the prevalent forms of monastic Buddhism in different parts of Asia. His Navayāna was deeply driven by lay initiative and the situation has not changed much even today despite the repeated attempts of revival of monastic Buddhism. In the countries where Buddhism has continued as a living tradition, the *Saṅgha* does not face much problem in attracting new recruits to its fold. But in India, where monastic Buddhism has practicallty ceased to exist many centuries ago, its full-fledged revival may not be an easy task either. In most of the previous and contemporary versions of Buddhism across Asia, the *Saṅgha* invariably provided the institutional nucleus of the faith. We will have to keep guessing if the absence of a strong monastic tradition in this Buddhism will result in a drift.

Vigorous attempts are indeed being made to revive monastic Buddhism. If monastic Buddhism is indeed successfully revived on a large scale, what will be the form and nature of the same? What will be the resource base of the *Saṅgha* and what kind of reciprocal relationship will it have, if any, with the society? Will this Buddhism be able to handle the Ājīvika criticism? Or, with an increasing assertion among a section of Dalits, will Ājīvika-dharma become the only, or at least the dominant, religion to channelize their assertions, hopes and anger? Time will tell.

NOTES

1. This paper is based on two invitation lectures delivered by me: 'Revival or Reinvention: Dalit Discourses on Buddhism in Contemporary Uttar Pradesh, *c.*2005-2011 CE', invitation lecture delivered at the Nalanda Srivijaya Centre, National University of Singapore, on 15 December 2011; and 'Recent Buddhist Revival Movements in Uttar Pradesh', invitation lecture delivered at an International Conference titled 'Buddhism Rejoins the Great Conversation in India', jointly organized by the Oxford Centre for Buddhist Studies, University of Oxford; and Indian Institute of Buddhist Studies, Pune, on 22 November 2014. I am thankful to Prof. Tansen Sen, Prof. Peter

van der Veer and Prof. Richard Gombrich for their comments on my lectures.

2. Donald S. Lopez, Jr. (ed.), *Buddhism in Practice,* Princeton University Press, New Jersey, 1995, p. 3; M. Spiro, *Buddhism and Society: A Great Tradition and its Burmese Vicissitudes*, George Allen & Unwin, London,1971, pp. 7-13; Birendra Nath Prasad, 'Major Trends and Perspectives in Studies in the Functional Dimensions of Indian Monastic Buddhism in the Past One Hundred Years: A Historiographical Survey', *Buddhist Studies Review* (Journal of the UK Association for Buddhist Studies, London), vol. 25, no. 1, 2008, p. 89; Birendra Nath Prasad, *Monasteries, Shrines and Society: Buddhist and Brahmanical Religious Institutions in India in Their Socio-Economic Context*, Manak Publications, Delhi, 2011, p. 16.
3. Birendra Nath Prasad, 'Major Trends and Perspectives in Studies in the Functional Dimensions of Indian Monastic Buddhism in the Past One Hundred Years: A Historiographical Survey', *Buddhist Studies Review* (Journal of the UK Association for Buddhist Studies, London), vol. 25, no.1, 2008, pp. 76-89; Birendra Nath Prasad, *Monasteries, Shrines and Society: Buddhist and Brahmanical Religious Institutions in India in Their Socio-Economic Context*, Delhi, 2011, Manak Publications, Delhi, pp. 1-7.
4. A preliminary analysis of the diverse patterns may be seen in Upinder Singh, 'Exile and Return: The Reinvention of Buddhism and Buddhist Sites in Modern India', *South Asian Studies*, vol. 26, no. 2, pp. 193-217.
5. Trevor Ling, *Buddhist Revival in India: Aspects of the Sociology of Buddhism,* Palgrave Macmillan, London, 1980, pp. 132-4.
6. For an interesting analysis of this process, see Himanshu Prabha Ray, *The Return of the Buddha: Ancient Symbols for a New Nation*, Routledge, London and New York, 2014.
7. The patterns of pre-Ambedkar Dalit appropriation of Buddhism as a religion offering a perceived escape from *varṇa-jāti* system in different parts of India have been analysed by B.R. Mani, *Debrahmanising History: Dominance and Resistance in Indian Society*, Manohar, Delhi, 2007 (reprint); and G. Omvedt, *Buddhism in India: Challenging Brahmanism and Caste,* Sage Publications, Delhi, 2003. For the pre-Ambedkar Dalit appropriation of Buddhism by the *Ezhāvās* in Kerala,

see B.R. Mani, op. cit., pp. 307-8; G. Omvedt, op. cit., pp. 240-2. For a pre-Ambedkar Dalit appropriation of Buddhism by Iyothee Thassar (1845-1914) in Tamil Nadu, see B.R. Mani, op. cit., pp. 312-14; G. Omvedt, op. cit., pp. 236-40; G. Aloysius, *Dalit-Subaltern Emergence in Religio-Cultural Subjectivity: Iyothee Thassar and Emancipatory Buddhism*, Critical Quest Publications, Delhi, 2004, pp. 21-35.

8. G. Omvedt, op. cit., pp. 277-9. For a review of the approach of G. Omvedt, see Birendra Nath Prasad, 'Dilemmas of Revival of Buddhism in India', *Indian International Journal of Buddhist Studies*, vol. 7, 2006, pp. 171-5.
9. See Angane Lal, 'Vijayādaśamī Aur Bauddha Dharma', *Ambedkar In India*, October 2010, pp. 15-16.
10. G. Omvedt, op. cit., p. 262. With slight variations, these *pratijñās* have been mentioned in many journals and books referred to in the present chapter.
11. Eleanor Zelliot has observed in the 1960s that conversion to Buddhism in post-1947 CE Maharashtra has largely taken place within the Mahāra caste (Eleanor Zelliot, *From Untouchable to Dalit: Essays on the Ambedkar Movement*, Manohar, Delhi, 2019 (reprint), p. 126; p. 187). Later anthropological studies also indicate the continuation of this trend in the Buddhist revival movements of post-Ambedkar Maharashtra. See, for example, Johannes Beltz, *Mahar, Buddhist and Dalit: Religious Conversion and Socio-Political Emancipation in Contemporary Maharashtra*, Manohar, Delhi, 2005, pp. 97-103. Beltz has noted that 'In Maharashtra, only the Mahars converted to Buddhism' (p. 101). Other Dalit castes (the Chambhars, Dhor, Matang, etc.) 'rejected the idea that conversion was obligatory for all untouchable castes' (p. 102). Hence, 'with the exception of few rare examples, the Dhors, Chambhars and Matangs remained Hindus' (p. 102). These developments prompted Beltz to put a fundamental question: 'Even if Ambedkar wanted to unify the untouchables in the name of Buddhism, did not the Mahars isolate themselves even more by converting?' (p. 102).
12. Acharya Motiram Shastri was born in a village of Banaras district in 1927. An article published in the July-September 2009 issue of *Sanketa* provides some interesting information regarding his life and times.

We are informed that, after getting inspired by the ideology of Dr Ambedkar, he led a group of one thousand Dalits for an entry into the Viśvanātha Temple of Benares. He was arrested and sent to jail. When he was released from jail, he attempted the same again. In 1972, he formally embraced Buddhism at Sāranāth. In his native village, he donated one acre of land and his house, and mobilized money through public donations to construct a *vihāra*. Later, he established *vihāras* at Lumbini and Lucknow. His *samādhi* is in a Buddhavihāra at the locality called Takarohi in Lucknow. In him, we see most of the trends that culminate in Ambedkarite discourses on Buddhism in Uttar Pradesh now. He articulated that the Dalits are the *mūlanivāsī* of India; the Buddha was not a Kṣatriya but a *mūlanivāsī* Dalit; and Rāvaṇa was a great exponent of *śramaṇa* culture and he was a Buddhist. Acharya Motiram Shastri established a new political party called Rāvaṇarāja Samāja Party, claiming that in India, there are only two classes: Brahmanical class represented by Rāma and *śramaṇa* class represented by Rāvaṇa. He also argued that these 'two classes are in eternal conflict and Dalits must re-adopt the ideology propagated by Rāvaṇa'. To propagate this view, he wrote three books: *Buddha Aur Rāvaṇa; Rāvaṇa Nahīn Tathāgata; Rāvaṇa Lankā.* His life and contributions are yet to be researched in detail. For a brief summary, see S.K. Panchama, 'Ācārya Motirāma Śāstrī: Uttarī Bhārata Ke Mahāna Bauddha Dārśanika', *Sanketa*, July-September 2009, pp. 52-6.

13. Maren Bellwinkel-Schemp, 'From Bhakti to Buddhism: Ravidas and Ambedkar', *Economic and Political Weekly*, vol. 42, no. 23, 2007, pp. 2177-83.
14. Satanama Singh, *Mānyavara Kānśīrāma Aur Bauddha Dharma*, Samyaka Prakashana, Delhi, 2008, p. 11.
15. In Uttar Pradesh, the BSP began with the Bahujana plank, that is, it claimed it represented all Dalits, OBCs and Muslims. But it derived its main support from the different Dalit castes in general and the Jāṭava caste in particular. Among the OBCs, it cemented an alliance with the non-Yādava castes, particularly with the Maurya, Kuśavāhā, Śākya and Saini castes, who emerged as one of the most enthusiastic OBC supporters of the BSP. Maurya, Kuśavāhā, Śākya and Saini castes claim that both the Buddha and Aśoka Maurya were born in their caste. This feeling is most marked in the persons of the Maurya and

Śākya castes, and that has firmly gravitated them towards the BSP. Some members of the Maurya caste started their propaganda on an organized scale even before the Dalits. See, for example, Parasnath Maurya, 'Āpa Hindu Nahīn Bauddha Hain', *Ambedkar Today*, May-June 2006, pp. 45-46.

16. To the best of my knowledge, the role of journals in Dalit mobilization has not yet been attempted. But the role of the booklets in the same has been studied by Badri Narayana. See his, 'A Book Also Travels: Circulating Small Booklets in Dalit Poorva', *South Asian History and Culture*, vol. 2, no.1, 2011, pp. 1-15. This paper has been reprinted in Badri Narayana, *The Making of the Dalit Public in North India, Uttar Pradesh, 1950-Present*, Oxford University Press, Delhi, 2011, pp. 71-96.
17. The only aspect of Hinduism this Buddhist movement has tried to appropriate is the medieval *gurus* of the *Bhakti* movement in general and Guru Ravidāsa in particular. Barring this, this has shown least interest in appropriating any other aspect of the Hindu past of the Dalits. Ambedkarite discourses on Buddhism in contemporary Uttar Pradesh, on the other hand, prefer to treat Buddhism as the polar opposite to a 'decrepit' Hindu past.
18. Dr B.R. Ambedkar, 'Bauddha Dharma Swīkāra, Dharmāntarana Nahīn Gharavāpasī Hai', *Ambedkar Today*, October 2006, pp. 22-3. This article is a Hindi translation of his speech delivered at Kathmandu in 1930.
19. Mahendrapala Bauddhacharya, 'Dhammasenānāyaka Bhante Surei Susei Dwārā 30 Sitambara Se Hone Wālī Aśoka Dhammavijayadaśamī Kā Aitihāsika Mahatva', *Ambedkar Today*, September 2006, pp. 46-7; Rama Singh, 'Parivartana Ke Pachāsa Varṣa', *Ambedkar Today*, October 2006, pp. 24-5; Acharya Shubhanarayana Nand Yatharthi, *Ati-Pichhaḍe Śūdrasamāja Kī Gauravagāthā Dharmāyaṇa (Dharmanivāsa) Aitihāsika Rāmāyaṇa Bhāga-1,* Bauddha Seva Samstahana, Sant Kabiranagar, 2006, pp. 5-9.
20. Dr B.R. Ambedkar, 'Bauddha Dharma Swīkāra, Dharmāntarana Nahīn Gharavāpasī Hai', *Ambedkar Today*, October 2006, pp. 22-3.
21. Ibid., pp. 22-3.

The motif of a continuous conflict between Brāhmaṇa and Śramaṇa traditions in ancient India finds frequent mentions in contemporary

Ambedkarite discourses on Buddhism in Uttar Pradesh. See, for example, Hari Shankar Gautama, 'Aur Andherā Kāyama Rahe', *Ambedkar in India*, May 2010, pp. 4-5.

22. Om Praaksh Singh, 'Anusūchita Jātiyon Mein Pramukha Hai Bhārata Kā Mūla Chamāra Vaṁśa', *Buddha Sanketa*, January-March 2010, pp. 68-72. Om Praaksh Singh has argued that the people of this civilization worshipped Śiva. But he does not forget to mention that Śiva was an Anārya deity.
23. Swapna Kumar Biswas, *Bauddha-Dharma: Mohenjodaro-Harappā Nagaron Kā Dharma*, quoted in Rajiva Ratna, 'Buddha Kī 2550vī Jayanti Kaise', Editorial of *Ambedkar Today*, May-June 2006, p. 4.
24. Naval Kishore Viyogi, *Sindhu Sabhyatā Ke Sṛjanakartā Śūdra Evam Vaṇika*, Samyaka Prakashana, Delhi, 2006.
25. Satanama Singh, *Chamāra Jāti Kā Gauravaśālī Itihāsa*, Samyaka Prakashana, Delhi, 2009, pp. 32-40; Om Praaksh Singh, 'Anusūchita Jātiyon Mein Pramukha Hai Bhārata Kā Mūla Chamāra Vaṁśa', *Buddha Sanketa*, January-March 2010, pp. 68-72.
26. Om Prakash Singh, op. cit.
27. Mahendrapala Bauddhacharya, 'Ādarśa Bauddha Samāja Banāne Ke Sūtra', *Ambedkar Today*, May 2007, p. 8; S.L. Sagar, 'Dalit Krānti Ke Liye Sahī Itihāsā Jānana Āvaśyaka', *Ambedkar Today*, February 2010, pp. 40-1.
28. Satanam Singh, 'Buddha Ārya Kṣatriya Nahīn, Nāgavaṁśī The', in Shanti Swaroop Bauddha (ed.), *Makkhali Gosāla Ke Mānasa Putra*, Samyaka Prakashana, Delhi 2010, pp. 182-92.
29. Satnam Singh, *Chamāra Jāti Kā Gauravaśālī Itihāsa*, Samyaka Prakashana, Delhi, 2009, pp. 129-31. He has also claimed that Chandragupta Maurya and Aśoka Maurya too belonged to this caste (pp. 131-6).
30. Dr Dharmavira, *Therigāthā Kī Striyān Aur Dr Ambedkar*, Vani Prakashana, Delhi, 2007, p. 21.
31. Here, one may have the impression that this view is the culmination of the pattern of political mobilization of the Dalits. Dr Ambedkar onwards, many Dalit leaders have claimed that only a Dalit can represent a Dalit. This argument has, apparently, moved into the spiritual sphere also.
32. An approximate meaning of this word will be: one who earns his/her livelihood righteously by performing some productive and legitimate

labour. This word is used by a significant section of Ambedkarite intellectuals for Dalit and OBC population, claiming that most of the Dalit and OBC castes are peasants/ landless agricultural labours or artisans. This consciousness is so deeply entrenched that some enthusiastic Ambedkarites have started publishing a journal with the title *Kamerī Duniyā.*

33. Dr Dharmavira, *Therigāthā Kī Striyān Aur Dr Ambedkar*, Vani Prakashana, Delhi, 2007, pp. 21-2.
34. Satanam Singh, 'Buddha Ārya Kṣatriya Nahīn, Nāgavaṁśī The', in Shanti Swaroop Bauddha (ed.), *Makkhali Gosāla Ke Mānasa Putra*, Samyaka Prakashana, Delhi 2010, pp. 182-92.
35. Satnam Singh, *Chamāra Jāti Kā Gauravaśālī Itihāsa*, Samyaka Prakashana, Delhi, 2009, pp. 129-31.
36. Much before the emergence of an organized Dalit appropriation of Buddhism in the post-colonial Uttar Pradesh, some sections of the Maurya caste emerged as the most enthusiastic champions of Buddhist revival movements in Uttar Pradesh. See note no. 15 of the present chapter.
37. Acharya Shubhanarayana Nanda Yatharthi, *Ati-Pichhaḍe Śūdrasamāja Kī Gauravagāthā Dharmāyaṇa (Dharmanivāsa) Aitihāsika Rāmāyaṇa Bhāga-1,* Bauddha Seva Sansthana, Khalilabad, Sant Kabira Nagar, 2006. The front cover of the book contains the heading 'Itihāsa Ke Pannon Par Nanda Vaṁśa Ke Sitāre', and contains the photographs of the Buddha, Upāli, Samrāṭa Jarāsandha, Samrāṭa Śiśunāga, Samrāṭa Mahāpadmananda, Aśoka Maurya, Karpuri Thakur (ex-Chief Minister of Bihar, who belonged to the Nāī caste) and Bhikhari Thakur (a famous singer of Bhojpuri folk songs). Here also, we see a selective appropriation of history: Aśoka Maurya finds a place, but not Candragupta Maurya or Bindusāra. Candragupta Maurya or Bindusāra did not show any particular favour to Buddhism.
38. See for example, Dharmakirti, *Buddha Dharma Nahīn Hai Hindu Dharma Kī Śākhā*, Samyaka Prakashana, Delhi, 2010. Dharmakirti has vehemently criticized Dr Sarvapalli Radhakrishnan for his claim that Buddhism is just a branch of Buddhism and it was not an independent social and religious system. Points of criticism are many, but one of the most important points is: 'Dr Radhakirshnan was so hostile to

Buddhism that he did not allow the publication of *The Buddha and His Dhamma* by Government of India on the occasion of the celebration of 2,500 years of Buddhism; instead, he became instrumental in the publication of a 'third rate' book on Buddhism edited by P.V. Bapat, namely, *2500 Years of Buddhism*' (p. 75).

39. See for example, a short story titled 'Phir Kyā Huā Mā', by Engineer B.S. Rana, *Ambedkar Today*, May 2010, pp. 6-8.
40. Bauddhacharya Shanti Swarup Bauddha, *Sachitra Buddha Jīvanī*, Samyaka Prakashana, Delhi, 2008, pp. 12-20.
41. B.S. Rana, op. cit., pp. 6-8.
42. Bauddhacharya Shanti Swarup Bauddha, op. cit.
43. One may see a selective appropriation of history in these discourses. Aśoka is lionized and care is taken to revise even those legends which claim that before his conversion to Buddhism, he was bad-looking and cruel. The photographs of this king, which generally accompany such writings, invariably depict him as a handsome, brave man with kingly grandeur. For example, see Satyendra Singh, 'Bauddha Dharma Ke Prabala Prasāraka Aśoka Priyadarśī Bhāvuka Rājā The Na Ki Kurūpa Aur Krūra', *Bayāna*, October 2010, pp. 33-4.
44. Mahendrapala Bauddhacharya, 'Santa Ravidāsa Ek Mahāna Vykatitva: Chamāra, Buddha-Aśoka Ke Asalī Vaṁśaja', *Ambedkar Today*, February 2010, p. 32.
45. B.R. Mani, op. cit., pp. 307-8; G. Omvedt, op. cit., pp. 240-2; G. Aloysius, op. cit., pp. 21-35.
46. Haradoi district borders Lucknow district in the west.
47. Janachetana Manch, Janapada Farrukhabad, 'Holī Bahujano Kī Hāra Aur Mātama Kā Din Hai', *Ambedkar Today*, February 2007, p. 41.
48. Ibid.
49. See, for example, Janachetana Manch, Janapada Farrukhabad, 'Holī Bahujano Kī Hāra aur Mātama Kā Din Hai', *Ambedkar Today*, February 2007, p. 41.
50. Milinda Bauddha, 'Dharmāntarana Ke 51 Varṣa Aur Hum: Brāhmaṇo Se Nahīn, Brāhmaṇavādī Daliton Se Khatarā Hai Ambedkaravāda Ko', *Ambedkar Today*, October 2007, p. 22.
51. Ibid.
52. Acharya Jugala Kishor Bauddha, *Aśokakālīna Dīpadānotsava Jo Dīvalī*

Bana Gayā, Samyaka Prakashana, Delhi, 2010, p. 7. For similar observations, see Satanama Singh, 'Hindu Tyohāron Kā Pardāphāśa Karatī Ek Pustaka', *Ambedkar in India*, May 2009, pp. 26-7.

53. Ramacharana Vikal, 'Bauddha Dharma Vaigyānika Dharma Hai', *Ambedkar Today*, October 2007, p. 47; Dr Satyendra Kumar, 'Rāvaṇa Mahāna: Mere Putale ko Jalākara Bhī Nā Māra Pāoge Mujhe Kabhī', *Ambedkar Today*, February 2007, p. 64; Professor Angane Lal, 'Vijayādaśamī Aur Buddha Dharma', *Ambedkar in India*, October 2010, p. 15.
54. Ramacharana Vikal, op. cit.; Dr Satyendra Kumar, op. cit.
55. Mahendrapala Bauddhacharya, 'Dhammasenānāyaka Bhante Surei Susei Dwārā 30 Sitambara Se Hone Wālī Aśoka Dhammavijayadaśamī Kā Aitihāsika Mahatva', *Ambedkar Today*, September 2006, p. 46.
56. Ibid., pp. 46-7.
57. Ibid.
58. Ibid., pp. 46-7.
59. A. Rana, 'Paryataṇa Sthala', *Ambedkar Today*, February 2007, p. 30.
60. Ibid.
61. Ibid. An essay in the February 2007 issue of *Ambedkar Today* has identified the site of Bairanjā with the famous archaeological site of Ataranjikheda in the Etah district of Uttar Pradesh. It has been claimed that the Buddha spent his 12th *vassāvāsa* at the site of Bairanjā. Some local enthusiasts have founded a 'Śākyamuni Buddha Vihāra' in the neighbourhood of the site to 'mark the site where the Buddha spent his 12th *vassāvāsa'*. This particular issue of *Ambedkar Today* contains the report on Bairanjā as its cover story, with the main aim of promoting pilgrimage to this site. See Rajiva Ratna, 'Pāvana Bhūmi Bairanjā', *Ambedkar Today*, February 2007, pp. 5-15.
62. Shanti Swaroopa Bauddha, 'Jayachandra Deśadrohī Nahīn Parama Desabhakta The', *Ambedkar In India*, November 2010, pp. 35-6.
63. Ibid. Recently, Giovanni Verardi has presented a similar view. Verardi argues that Muslim onslaught from the west and Sena attacks from the east (i.e. from Bengal-Bihar), who were ardent supporters of orthodox Brahmanism, 'drove Jayacandra towards Buddhism in his attempt to find support among its followers in the region – Magadha – that was becoming the magnet attracting all the contradictions of

India' (Giovanni Verardi, *Hardships and Downfall of Buddhism in India*, Manohar Publications, Delhi, 2011, p. 359).

64. 'Nakalī Ambedakaravādiyon Ke Ṣaḍayantra Se Bachen Bahujana Samāja', Interview of Bhante Dhamma Tejankaradipa taken by Rajiva Ratna, *Ambedkar Today*, October 2006, pp. 42-3.
65. 'Anāgarika Dhammapāla', *Ambedkar Today,* May-June 2006, p. 26.
66. After the implementation of the B.P. Mandal Commission's recommendation of the reservation of 27 per cent of government jobs for the persons belonging to the Other Backward Classes (OBC) category in the 1990s, northern India underwent great social and political churning. A prime manifestation of this churning was the gradual loss of upper caste hegemony in north Indian politics and increasing presence of some castes belonging to the OBC category in north Indian political and social landscape. This phenomenon is often referred to as the 'Mandalisation' of north India. The 'Mandalisation' of north India and the decline of the Indian National Congress (INC) party were coeval processes, indicating the inability of the INC to successfully negotiate the political rise of the OBCs and Dalits.
67. For an analysis of this pattern, see Christophe Jafferlot, *India's Silent Revolution, The Rise of the Low Castes in North Indian Politics*, Permanent Black, Delhi, 2011 (reprint), pp. 453-91. It may be noted that the Vishwa Hindu Parishad consciously selected Mr. Kameshwara Chaupal – a Dalit from Bihar – to lay the foundation stone of the Rāmajanmabhūmi Temple. This was to ensure the Dalit mobilization for the cause of Rāmajanmabhūmi movement. This strategy was largely successful in the case of the OBCs of Uttar Pradesh, particularly in the non-Yādava segment of the OBCs, but the attempts to woo the Dalits of Uttar Pradesh during the period of our study did not have much success, which is reflected in the meteoric rise of the BSP.
68. Dr Dharmakirti, 'Ayodhyā Mein Rāma Mandira Nahīn Thā, Ayodhyā Mein Bauddhon Kā Bāvarī Mahāvihāra Thā', *Ambedkar Today,* December 2009, pp. 18-29; Vinita Maurya, 'Nā Rāmajanmabhūmi Nā Bābarī Masjid, Yahān Banā Thā Bauddha Vihāra', *Bayāna*, October 2010, p. 38.
69. These claims on the part of Buddhists were subsequently dismissed

in the courts of law and the site was handed over to the Hindus for the reconstruction of the Rāmajanmabhūmi Temple.

70. Dr Dharmakirti, op. cit., p. 18.
71. Ibid.
72. Ibid.
73. Ibid.
74. Ibid., p. 29.
75. Dr Dharmakirti, 'Ayodhyā Mein Rama Mandira Nahīn Thā, Ayodhyā Mein Bauddhon kā Bāvarī Mahāvihāra Thā', *Ambedkar Today*, December 2009, p. 29.
76. For an analysis of the role of Bhakti movement in general and *nirguṇa* Bhakti movement in particular in Dalit history, see Gail Omvedt, op. cit., pp. 186-216; B.R. Mani, op. cit., pp. 134-87.
77. Mahendrapala Bauddhacharya, 'Ādarṣa Bauddha Samāja Banāne Ke Sūtra', *Ambedkar Today*, May 2007, p. 8.
78. Mahendrapala Bauddhacharya, 'Santa Guru Ravidāsa Ek Mahāna Vyaktitva: Chamāra, Buddha-Aśoka Ke Asalī Vaṁśaja', *Ambedkar Today*, February 2010, p. 32; Shilapriya Bauddha, *Bodhisattva Guru Ravidāsa Laghunāṭikā*, Samyaka Prakashana, Delhi, 2002; Swaroopachandra Bauddha, *Bauddha Virāsata Ke Purodhā Guru Raidāsa*, Samyaka Prakashana, Delhi, 2006; Dr Angane Lal, 'Sant Śiromaṇi Raidāsa Aur Bauddha Dharma', in Dr Mahesh Prasad Ahirwar (ed.), *Śramaṇa Paramparā Aur Guru Raidāsa*, Dalit Lekhaka Saṅgha, Varanasi, 2005, pp. 31-8; Bhadrashila Ravat, *Sant Raidāsa Kī Vāṇi Mein Bauddha Chintana,* Samyaka Prakashana, Delhi, 2005; Shyama Singh, *Santa Raidāsa Kī Mūla Vicāradhārā,* Samyaka Prakashana, Delhi, 2009 (third edition).
79. Mewalal Madhukar, 'Dharmāntarana', *Ambedkar Today*, October 2007, p. 17.
80. Dr G.L. Prajapati and A.K. Nand, 'Binā Bauddha Bane Hamārā Ārthika Vikāsa Sambhava Nahīn', *Ambedkar Today*, September 2006, p. 41; Mahendrapala Bauddhacharya, 'Ādarṣa Bauddha Samāja Banāne Ke Sūtra', *Ambedkar Today*, May 2007, p. 18.
81. Rama Singh, 'Parivartana Ke Pachāsa Varṣa', *Ambedkar Today*, October 2006, p. 42.
82. Mahendrapala Bauddhacharya, 'Ādarṣa Bauddha Samāja Banāne Ke Sūtra', *Ambedkar Today*, May 2007, p. 15; Bhante Dhamma Tejankaradipa, 'Nakalī Ambedakaravādiyon Ke Ṣaḍayantra Se Bache

Bahujana Samāja', *Ambedkar Today*, October 2006, pp. 42-3. This paper is the publication of the interview of Bhante Dhamma Tejankaradipa, in *Ambedkar Today*.

Another paper states that nobody should claim the status of a missionary for the cause of the propagation of the ideology of Dr Ambedkar and Buddhism unless he starts observing the 22 *pratijñas*. See Dr Kamal Singh, 'Hindu Dharma Mein Rahakara Na Maranā, Yaha Tumhāre Vaśa Mein Hai', *Ambedkar Today*, May 2007, p. 21.

83. Milinda Bauddha, 'Dharmāntarana Ke 51 Varṣa aur Hum: Brāhmaṇo Se Nahīn, Brāhmaṇavādī Daliton Se Khatarā Hai Ambedkaravāda Ko', *Ambedkar Today*, October 2007, p. 23. For similar views, see Professor Angane Lal, 'Vijayādaśamī Aur Bauddha Dhamma', *Ambedkar in India*, October 2010, pp. 15-16.
84. Bhante Dhamma Tejankaradipa, 'Nakalī Ambedakaravādiyon Ke Ṣaḍayantra Se Bachen Bahujana Samāja', *Ambedkar Today*, October 2006, p. 42.
85. Ibid.
86. Ibid.
87. Bhāratīya Bauddha Mahāsabhā, Mahānagara Āgarā, 'Bauddhon Ke Liye Āvaśyaka Mārgadarśana', *Ambedkar Today,* October 2007, p. 21.
88. Ibid.
89. See Bhante Dhamma Tejankardip, op. cit., p. 43. He has discouraged such practices, saying that not even the closest disciples of the Buddha – Ānanda and Upāli – could have this honour. One may also witness an incipient concern that the messenger does not become more important than the message. In an interesting paper, it has been suggested that every Buddhist household must have, besides the photograph or the statue of the Buddha prominently placed in the drawing room to make it visible to the maximum number of visitors, should have at least one photograph or statue of Ambedkar. The author has noted that nowadays, independent photos of Dr Ambedkar (i.e. those photographs in which only Dr Ambedkar is depicted, the photo of the Buddha is not shown in the background) are circulating. The author of this paper recommends that one should avoid these photos. See Bhāratīya Bauddha Mahāsabhā, Mahānagara Āgarā, 'Bauddhon Ke Liye Āvaśyaka Mārgadarśana', *Ambedkar Today,* October 2007, p. 21.

90. Thom Wolf, 'Buddhism in the 21st Century: Three Challenges', in B. Mungekar (ed.), *Buddhism and the Contemporary World: An Ambedkarian Perspective*, Bookwell Publishers, Delhi, 2007, p. 30; P.S. Jaini, 'The Disappearance of Buddhism and the Survival of Jainism in India: A Study in Contrast', in his *Collected Papers on Buddhist Studies,* Motilal Banarsidass, Delhi, 2001, p. 142. For a historiographical review of such arguments, see Birendra Nath Prasad, 'Major Trends and Perspectives in Studies in the Functional Dimensions of Indian Monastic Buddhism in the Past One Hundred Years: A Historio-graphical Survey', *Buddhist Studies Review* (Journal of the UK Association for Buddhist Studies, London), vol. 25, no. 1, 2008, pp. 54-89. Also see Birendra Nath Prasad (ed. with an introduction), *Monasteries, Shrines and Society: Buddhist and Brahmanical Religious Institutions in India in their Socio-Economic Context*, Manak Publications, Delhi, 2011, pp. 3-7; 57-8.
91. Jagata Narayana, 'Bhārata Mein Bauddha Dharma Kā Punarjāgarana Evam Dr Ambedkar Kā Yogadāna', *Ambedkar Today*, October 2006, pp. 26-8. This special issue of *Ambedkar Today* was published to commemorate the 50th anniversary of Dr Ambedkar's conversion to Buddhism.
92. Ibid., p. 28.
93. Ibid.
94. Ibid.
95. Ibid.
96. E. Zelliot, 'Buddhist Sects in Contemporary India: Identity and Organization', in *From Untouchable to Dalit: Essays on the Ambedkar Movement*, Manohar Publishers, Delhi, 2005 (reprint), p. 243.
97. Gail Omvedt, *Buddhism in India: Challenging Brahmanism and Caste,* Sage Publications, Delhi, 2003, p. 4; E. Zelliot, op. cit., pp. 187-96, 222-48.
98. Rajiva Ratana, 'Merī Ammī', *Ambedkar Today*, July 2008, p. 51.
99. Shanti Swaroopa Bauddha, *Bauddhacaryāprakāśa, Vivāha Vidhi Sahita*, Samyaka Prakashana, New Delhi, 2011, pp. 73-94. This book may be treated as the standard textbook for conducting different rites, from the time of conception of a child in his/her mother's womb to the last rites of a man/woman. This book recommends that these rites should be got performed by a monk/*Bauddhācārya*.

100. Shanti Swaroop Bauddha, *Bauddhacaryāprakāśa, Vivāha Vidhi Sahita*, Samyaka Praakshana, New Delhi, 2011, p. 135.
101. It is probably due to this reason that even *upāsaka*s are allowed to perform rites and rituals for other *upāsaka*s in some instances.
102. Dr Bhante Karunashila Dhammacharya, 'Dr Bodhisattva Bābāsāheb Ambedkar Kaisā Dhamma Chāhate The? Aur Unkā Sapanā Bhārata Ko Buddhamaya Karūngā 55 Sāla Mein Kyon Nahīn Pūrā Huā?', *Ambedkar Today*, May 2010, pp. 30-1.
    Shanti Swaroopa Bauddha, *Bauddhacaryāprakāśa, Vivāha Vidhi Sahita*, Samyaka Praakshana, New Delhi, 2011, pp. 124-30, has provided a list of ideal names for Buddhist children. He recommends that the names of children must never have the word 'Indra', so names such as Mahendra, Surendra, Rājendra, etc. (p. 124) should be totally avoided. It seems that the author considers them as the remnants of Hindu influence. Such is the level of reluctance to show even indirect Hindu influences.
103. Dr Bhante Karunashila Dhammacharya, op. cit., pp. 30-1. So far, we have not come across any example of exhortation for the revival of the order of nuns.
104. As per 2001 census of India, only 0.8 per cent of Indian population has formally declared itself to be Buddhist. That includes the Buddhist population of Arunachala Pradesh, Sikkim, Himachala Pradesh, Tripura, etc. Dalits constitute not less than 15 per cent of Indian population. So, it is apparent that an overwhelming section of Indian Dalits has not officially declared itself to be Buddhist.
105. Dr B. Suresh, 'What the Buddhists Should Do and What the Buddhists Should Not Do', *Ambedkar Today*, June 2009, pp. 43-4.
106. Vajramohana Bauddhacharya, 'Samrāṭa Aśoka', *Ambedkar Today*, May 2010, pp. 34-5.
107. A.N. Bhaskar, 'Prācīnatā Aur Ādhunikatā Kā Sangama Bauddha Dharma', *Ambedkar Today*, October 2006, p. 35. Another paper states that 'it is the duty of the *upāsaka*s to pay their respects to the monks and donate whatever they can as Bābāsāheb Dr Ambedkar refers to the monk as *Buddhaputra*' (Bhāratīya Bauddha Mahāsabhā, Mahānagara Āgarā, 'Bauddho Ke Liye Āvaśyka Mārgadarśana', *Ambedkar Today*, October 2007, p. 21). For similar observations, see

Mahendra Singh, 'Bauddha Dharma kī Sarvayugīna Prāsangikatā Evam Aparihāryatā', *Ambedkar Today*, May 2010, p. 42.

108. Mahendra Singh, 'Bauddha Dharma Kī Sarvayugīna Prāsangikatā Evam Aparihāryatā', *Ambedkar Today*, May 2010, p. 42.

109. 'Anāgarika Dharmapāla', *Ambedkar Today*, May-June 2006, p. 21. Dharmapala was born as David Hivaviratne in a Christian family of Sri Lanka. Later he became a Buddhist monk, assumed the name of Anāgarika Dharmapāla, came to India and played a signficant role in the revival of Buddhism in colonial India. He is particularly remembered for his struggle to establish an exclusive Buddhist control over the Mahābodhi temple of Bodh Gayā. This paper traces the journey of this *bhikṣu*.

110. Parasanath Maurya, 'Bauddha Dharma Āndolana Mein Agrani Janapada Jaunapur: Mohammed Dilaśāda Ahmed Bane Bhante Prajñāratna', *Ambedkar Today*, October 2006, pp. 44-6. In 1976, Mohammed Dilaśāda, a resident of Jaunapur district in eastern Uttar Pradesh, converted to Buddhism. After becoming Buddhist, he assumed a new name: Prajñāratna. To mark his conversion to Buddhism, a big procession was organized. The memoirs of Mr. Maurya regarding this procession and the conversion of Mr. Mohammed Dilaśāda were published in the October 2006 issue of *Ambedkar Today*. One may gauge the symbolism of this paper by recalling that this particular issue of *Ambedkar Today* was published to mark the 'fifty years of change', i.e. to commemorate the fiftieth year of acceptance of Buddhisṃ by Dr Ambedkar.

111. Dr Dharmakirti, *Jāṭa Jāti Pracchanna Bauddha Hai*, Samyaka Prakashana, Delhi, 2005 (second edition), p. 58.

112. Ibid., p. 66.

113. Ibid., pp. 102-13.

114. Dr Dharmakirti, *Samasta Muṇḍā Jāti Bauddha Thī*, Samyaka Praakshana, Delhi, 2003, pp. 23-40.

115. Ibid.

116. Ibid.

117. For an analysis of this process, see Badri Narayan, *Fascinating Hindutva: Saffron Politics and Dalit Mobilization*, Sage Publications, Delhi, 2008.

118. Eleanor Zelliot, *From Untouchable to Dalit: Essays on the Ambedkar Movement*, Manohar, Delhi, 2019 (reprint), p. 126; p. 187; Johannes Beltz, *Mahar, Buddhist and Dalit: Religious Conversion and Socio-Political Emancipation in Contemporary Maharashtra*, Manohar Publishers, Delhi, 2005, pp. 97-103.
119. Kanshiram, 'Yadi Bauddha Dharma Ko Āge Badhānā Hai to Jāti Ko Bauddha Dharma Se Dūra Rakhanā Jarūrī Hai', *Bahujana Sangaṭhaka*, New Delhi, 28 May-3 June 2001; reprinted in Satanama Singh, *Mānyavara Kānśīrāma Aur Bauddha Dharma,* Samyaka Prakashana, Delhi, 2008, pp. 54-8.
120. Milinda Bauddha, 'Dharmāntarana Ke 51 Varṣa Aur Hama', *Ambedkar Today*, October 2007, p. 23.
121. Ibid.
122. This line of argument was initially advanced by Dr Dharmavira. His later writings are more assertive. See, for example, his *Mahāna Ājivaka Kabīra, Raidāsa and Gosāla*, Vani Prakashan, Delhi, 2017, in which he goes one step ahead of his earlier criticism of Buddhism. It is pertinent to quote him here: 'It is irrelevant to state that Buddhism was started by the Buddha. The reality is that Buddhism was run by the *brāhmaṇas*. Only the Buddha was a *kṣatriya*, all other Buddhist philosophers were *brāhmaṇas*. Śāriputra, who was the *dharmasenāpati* of the Buddha, was born in a *brāhmaṇakula*. The second *Bṛhaspati* of Buddhism – Mahāmaudagalyāyana – was also born in a *brāhmaṇa* family. We may count the names of other Buddhist philosophers and *dharmapuruṣas* who were born in *brāhmaṇakula*: Mahākāśyapa, Moggaliputra Tiṣya, Nāgasena, Aśvaghoṣa, Nāgārjuna, Āryadeva, Buddhayaśa, Buddhaghoṣa, Asanga, Vasubandhu, Dignāga, Paramārtha, Dharmakīrti, and Śāntirakṣita' (p. 3). He argues that Buddhism, started by a *kṣatriya*, was captured from within by the *brāhmaṇas*. (p. 3). Buddhism, as per his assessment, did not challenge the conceptual validity of *varṇa* system as the organizing principle of social order. But '*Ājīvakas* did not accept *varṇa* system': 'they were *avaṇṇavādī*' (pp. 3-4).

Bibliography

Ahir, D.C. 2005. *Buddhism Declined in India: How and Why*. Delhi: B.R. Publishers.

Ahmed, N. 1984. *Discover the Monuments of Bangladesh.* Dhaka: University Press Limited.

Alam, A.K.M. Shamsul. 1982. *Mainamati*. Dhaka: Dept. of Archaeology and Museums, Govt. of the Peoples' Republic of Bangladesh.

Aloysius, G. 2004. *Dalit-Subaltern Emergence in Religio-Cultural Subjectivity: Iyothee Thassar and Emancipatory Buddhism*. Delhi: Critical Quest Publications.

Amar, A.S. 2012. 'Buddhist Responses to Brāhmaṇa Challenges in Medieval India: Bodhgayā and Gayā'. *Journal of the Royal Asiatic Society,* Third Series, 22(1): 155–85.

Appadurai, Arjun and Carol Breckenridge. 1976. 'The South Indian Temple: Authority, Honour and Redistribution'. *Contributions to Indian Sociology,* 10(2): 191–3.

Appadurai, Arjun. 1977. 'Kings, Sects and Temples in South India, 1350-1700 AD'. *Indian Economic and Social History Review,* 14(1): 47–73.

Asher, Frederick M. 1972. 'The Bodh Gaya Image of the Year 64: A Reconsideration'. *The Journal of the Bihar Research Society,* LVIII: 151–7.

______. 1980. *The Art of Eastern India, 300-800.* Minneapolis: University of Minnesota Press.

______. 2000. 'An Image at Lakhi Serai and its Implications'. *Artibus Asiae,* 59(3–4): 296–302.

Bakker, Hans T. 2007. 'Monuments to the Dead in Ancient North India'. *Indo-Iranian Journal,* 50(1): 11–47.

Banerjee, Priyatosh. 1953. 'Two Medieval Inscriptions'. *Journal of the Asiatic Society Letters*, XIX: 105-7.

_____. 1973-74. 'Some Inscriptions from Bihar'. *Journal of Ancient Indian History*, VII(1-2): 102-11.

Banerji, R.D. 1915. *Pālas of Bengal*. Memoirs of the Asiatic Society of Bengal No. 3. Calcutta: Asiatic Society.

Banerji-Sastri, Ananta Prasad. 1940. 'Ninety-Three Inscriptions on the Kurkihar Bronzes'. *Journal of the Bihar and Orissa Research Society*, 26(3): 236-51.

Basu, Chandreyi. 2006. 'Patronage and Representation at the Huvishka Vihāra, A Kuṣāṇa Period Buddhist Monastery'. *Studies in History*, 22(2): 157-79.

Bauddha, Acharya Jugala Kishor. 2010. *Aśokakālīna Dīpadānotsava Jo Dīvalī Bana Gayā*. Delhi: Samyaka Prakashana.

Bauddha, Bauddhacharya Shanti Swarup. 2008. *Sachitra Buddha Jīvanī*. Delhi: Samyaka Prakashana.

Bauddha, Shanti Swaroopa. 2010. 'Jayachandra Deśadrohī Nahīn Parama Desabhakta The'. *Ambedkar in India*, November 2010: 35-6.

_____. 2011. *Bauddhacaryāprakāśa, Vivāha Vidhi Sahita*. New Delhi: Samyaka Prakshana.

Bauddha, Shilapriya. 2002. *Bodhisattva Guru Ravidāsa Laghunāṭikā*. Delhi: Samyaka Prakashana.

Bauddha, Swaroopachandra. 2006. *Bauddha Virāsata Ke Purodhā Guru Raidāsa*. Delhi: Samyaka Prakashana.

Bauddhacharya, Vajramohana. 2010. 'Samrāṭa Aśoka'. *Ambedkar Today*, May 2010: 34-35.

Bautze-Picron, Claudine. 1996. 'From God to Demon, from Demon to God: Brahmā and Other Brahmanical Divinities in the Late Buddhist Art of Eastern India'. *Journal of Bengal Art*, 1: 109-35.

_____. 1998. *The Art of Eastern India in the Collection of the Museum Für Indische Kurst, Berlin: Stone and Terracotta Sculptures*. Berlin: D.R. Verlag.

_____. 2010. *The Bejewelled Buddha: From India to Burma*. New Delhi: Sanctum Books in association with Centre for Archaeological Studies and Training-Eastern India, Kolkata.

Beal, S. 1884. *Si-Yu-Ki, Buddhist Records of the Western World: Translated from the Chinese of Hieun Tsiang*, vol. II. London: Trubner & Co.

Bhattacharya, A. 1977. *Historical Geography of Ancient and Early Medieval Bengal.* Calcutta: Sanskrit Pustak Bhandar.

———. 1998. 'Trade Routes of Ancient Bengal'. In A. Dutta (ed.), *History and Archaeology of Eastern India*: 200–12. Delhi: Books and Books.

Bhattacharya, G. 1993. 'An Inscribed Metal Vase, Most Probably from Chittagong'. In A.J. Gail and G.J.R. Mevissen (eds.), *South Asian Archaeology 1991*, Proceedings of the Eleventh International Conference of the Association of South Asian Archaeologists in Western Europe held in Berlin 1-5 July 1991: 323-38. Stuttgart: Verlag.

———. 1996. 'A Preliminary Note on the Inscribed Metal Vase from the National Museum of Bangladesh'. In D. Mitra (ed.), *Explorations in the Art and Archaeology of South Asia: Essays Dedicated to N. G. Majumdar*: 237-46. Calcutta: Directorate of Archaeology and Museums, Govt. of West Bengal.

———. 2000. *Essays on Buddhist Hindu Jaina Iconography and Epigraphy*. Dhaka: The International Centre for Study of Bengal Art.

———. 2003. 'An Inscribed Stone Image of the Buddhist Deity Aparājitā'. *Journal of Bengal Art*, 8: 95–101.

Bhattacharyya, N.N. 2005. 'The Cult of Tara in Historical Perspective'. In N. N. Bhattacharyya (ed.), *Tantric Buddhism: Centennial Tribute to Dr Benoytosh Bhattacharya*: 190-207. New Delhi: Manohar.

Bhattasali, N.K. 1945. 'New Light on the History of Assam'. *Indian Historical Quarterly*, XXI: 19-28.

———. 1923-24. 'Some Image Inscriptions from East Bengal'. *Epigraphia Indica*, XVII: 349-62.

Bhowmick, Atul Chandra. 1983. 'A Note on Jaina Sculptural Remains at Sitalpur, Bhangra, Harup and Deoli Villages in Purulia District'. *Jain Journal: A Quarterly on Jainology*, 18(1): 38-42. Calcutta: Jain Bhawan.

———. 1984. 'Jaina Sculptures from Bhavanipur, Hatuyara and Golamara'. *Jain Journal: A Quarterly on Jainology*, 18 (4): 165-70.

Bellwinkel-Schemp, Maren. 2007. 'From Bhakti to Buddhism: Ravidas and Ambedkar'. *Economic and Political Weekly*, 42(23): 2177-83.

Cecil, Elizabeth A. 2020. *Mapping the Pāśupata Landscape: Narrative, Place, and the Śaiva Imaginary in Early Medieval North India.* Leiden: E.J. Brill.

Chakrabarti, D.K. 1987. 'Pakbira: A Jaina Site in Purulia District, West Bengal'. In B.M. Pande and B.D. Chattopadhyaya (eds.), *Archaeology and History: Essays in Memory of Shri A. Ghosh*, 1: 351–7. New Delhi: Agam Kala Prakashan.

______. 1993. *Archaeology of Eastern India: Chhotanagpur Plateau and West Bengal*. Delhi: Munshiram Manoharlal.

Chakrabarti, Kunal. 2001. *Religious Process: The Purāṇas and the Making of a Regional Tradition*. New Delhi: Oxford University Press.

Chakravarti, Ranabir. 1990. 'Monarchs, Merchants and a *Maṭha* in Northern Konkan, *c.*900–1053 AD'. *Indian Economic and Social History Review*, 27(2): 189–208.

______. 1996. '*Vaṅgasāgara-saṁbhāṇḍāriyaka*: A Riverine Trade-centre of Early Medieval Bengal'. In Debala Mitra (ed.), *Explorations in Art and Archaeology of South Asia: Essays Dedicated to N.G. Majumdar*: 557–72. Calcutta: Directorate of Archaeology and Museums, Govt. of West Bengal.

______. 2002. *Trade and Traders in Early Indian Society*. Delhi: Manohar.

Chatterjee, Rama. 1985. *Religion in Bengal during Pāla and Sena Times: Mainly on the Basis of Epigraphic and Archaeological Sources*. Calcutta: Punthi Pustaka.

Chattopadhyay, R.K. et al. 2012. 'In Search of the Jaina Identity: A Study of the Sculptural Remains of the Vishnupur Region'. *Journal of the Indian Society for Oriental Art*, 28: 119–52.

Chattopadhyay, Rupendra Kumar and Dipsikha Acharya. 2010. 'Contexts of Early Medieval Remains of Purulia: Researching Ideologies'. *Pratnatattva*, 16: 9–31.

Chattopadhyay, Rupendra Kumar et al. 2010. 'Archaeology of the Lower Ganga Valley: Some Aspects of Cultural Sequence'. In Vibha Tripathi and Prabhakar Upadhyaya (eds.), *Archaeology of the Ganga Valley, Paradigm Shift*, 2: 314–47. New Delhi: Sharada Publishing House.

Chattopadhyay, Rupendra Kumar. 2010. *Bankura: A Study of its Archaeological Sources*. Kolkata: Platinum Publishers.

Chattopadhyaya, B.D. 1993. 'Historiography, History and Religious Centres: Early Medieval North India, circa A.D. 700–1200'. In Visakha N. Desai and D. Mason (eds.), *Gods, Guardians and Lovers:*

Temple Sculptures from North India, A.D. 700-1200: 33-47. Ahmedabad: Mapin Publishing Company.

——. 1994. *The Making of Early Medieval India.* Delhi: Oxford University Press.

——. 2004. 'State Perception of the "Forest" and the "Forest" as State in Early Medieval India.' In B. B. Chaudhury and Arun Bandopadhyaya (eds.), *Tribes, Forests and Social Formations in Indian History*: 23-37. Delhi: Manohar.

Chaudhury, Sukomal. 1982. *Contemporary Buddhism in Bangladesh.* Calcutta: Atisha Memorial Publishing Society.

Cohen, Richard S. 1998. 'Nāga, Yakṣiṇī, the Buddha: Local Deities and Local Buddhism at Ajantā'. *History of Religions,* 37(4): 360-400.

Cousins, L.S. 2003. 'Sākiyabhikkhu/Sakyabhikkhu/Śākyabhikṣu: A Mistaken Link to the Mahāyāna ?'. *Nagoya Studies in Indian Culture and Buddhism,* 23: 1-27.

Cunningham, A. 1892. *Mahābodhi or the Great Buddhist Temple under the Bodhi Tree at Buddha-Gaya.* London: W.H. Allen.

Das, D.R. 1992. 'An Early Brick Temple at Kantabera'. *Pratna Samiksha,* 1: 191-3.

Dasgupta, P.C. 1991. 'The Early Medieval Art and Architecture of Purulia.' In Asok Datta (ed.), *Studies in Archaeology: Essays in Memory of P.C. Dasgupta*: 203-7. New Delhi: Books and Books.

Davidson, Ronald M. 2002. *Indian Esoteric Buddhism: A Social History of the Tantric Movement.* New York: Columbia University Press.

DeCaroli, Robert. 2004. *Haunting the Buddha: Indian Popular Religions and the Formation of Buddhism.* New York: Oxford University Press.

Dehejia, Vidya. 1992. 'The Collective and Popular Basis of Early Buddhist Patronage: Sacred Monuments, BC 100-AD 250'. In Barabara S. Miller (ed.), *The Powers of Art: Patronage in Indian Culture*: 35-50. Delhi: Oxford University Press.

Dhammacharya, Dr Bhante Karunashila. 2010. 'Dr Bodhisattva Bābāsaheb Ambedkar Kaisā Dhamma Chāhate The? Aur Unakā Sapanā Bhārata Ko Buddhamaya Karūnga 55 Sāla Mein Kyon Nahīn Pūrā Huā?'. *Ambedkar Today*, May 2010: 30-1.

Dharmakirti, 2003. *Samasta Muṇḍā Jāti Bauddha Thī.* Delhi: Samyaka Praakshana.

——. 2005. *Jāṭa Jāti Pracchanna Bauddha Hai.* Delhi: Samyaka Prakashana.

_____. 2009. 'Ayodhyā Mein Rāma Mandira Nahīn Thā, Ayodhyā Mein Bauddhon Kā Bāvarī Mahāvihāra Thā'. *Ambedkar Today,* December 2009: 18–29.

_____. 2010. *Buddha Dharma Nahīn Hai Hindu Dharma kī Śākhā.* Delhi: Samyaka Prakashana.

Eaton, Richard M. 1994. *The Rise of Islam and the Bengal Frontier, 1204-1760.* Delhi: Oxford University Press.

_____. 2001. 'Who are the Bengal Muslims? Conversions and Islamisation in Bengal'. In Richard M. Eaton, *Essays on Islam and Indian History*: 249-75. Delhi: Oxford University Press.

_____. 2009. 'Shrines, Cultivators, and Muslim 'Conversion' in Punjab and Bengal, 1300-1700'. *Medieval History Journal,* 12(2): 191–220.

Geddes, Arthur. 1982. *Man and Land in South Asia,* edited with an Introduction by A.T.A. Learmonth et al. Delhi: Concept Publishing Company and Indian Council for Social Science Research.

Gellner, David N. 2003. *The Anthropology of Buddhism and Hinduism, Weberian Themes.* Delhi: Oxford University Press.

Ghose, Benoy. 1961. 'Cultural Profile of Purulia'. In B. Roy (ed.), *Census 1961, West Bengal, District Census Handbook: Purulia*: 3–14. Calcutta: Government Printing Press.

Ghosh, A. 1939-1940. 'A Bronze Image Inscription from Nālandā'. *Epigraphia Indica,* 25: 334–5.

Gupta, Chitrarekha. 1993–4. 'Jainism in Bengal: Beginning of the Study, Problems and Perspectives'. *Pratna Samiksha,* 2–3: 216–25.

_____. 2002. 'Bengal Art and Bengal Inscriptions: An Approach towards Co-relation – A Case Study with Punchra, a Village in the Vardhaman District, West Bengal'. *Journal of Bengal Art,* 7: 83–100.

Gupta, K.K. 1967. *Copper Plates of Sylhet,* vol. 1: *7th–11th centuries AD.* Sylhet: Lipika Enterprises.

Gupta, P.L. 1965. *Patna Museum Catalogue of Antiquities.* Patna: Patna Museum.

Gupta, Sudarshan. 2011. 'Temples in Their Wider Context: A Study of Temples of Early Medieval Assam'. In Birendra Nath Prasad (ed.), *Monasteries, Shrines and Society: Buddhist and Brahmanical Religious Institutions in India in their Socio-Economic Context*: 181-219. New Delhi: Manak Publications Pvt. Ltd.

Haque, Enamul. 1992. *Bengal Sculptures: Hindu Iconography up to c. 1250 A.D.* Dhaka: Bangladesh National Museum.

Husain, A.B.M. and Rashid, M. Harunur. 1997. *Mainamati-Devaparvata: A Survey of Historical Monuments and Sites in Bangladesh.* Dhaka: Asiatic Society of Bangladesh.

Holt, John Clifford. 2005. *The Buddhist Viṣṇu: Religious Transformation, Politics and Culture.* New York: Columbia University Press.

Hoque, M.M. and Seema Hoque. 1997. 'Ancient Human Settlement Pattern of Bangladesh: A Preliminary Study'. *Journal of Bengal Art,* 2: 283-300.

Huntington, S.L. and John C. Huntington. 1990. *Leaves from the Bodhi Tree: The Art of Pāla India (8th-12th Centuries) and Its International Legacy.* Dayton, Ohio: Dayton Art Institute in association with the University of Washington Press.

Huntington, Susan L. 1984. *The 'Pāla-Sena' Schools of Sculpture.* Leiden: E.J. Brill.

Imam, Abu. 2002. 'Samataṭa, Mainamati: Some Observations'. In G. Sengupta and Sheena Panja (eds.), *Archaeology of Eastern India, New Perspectives*: 613-23. Kolkata: Centre for Archaeological Studies and Training-Eastern India.

Jafferlot, Christopher. 2011. *India's Silent Revolution, The Rise of the Low Castes in North Indian Politics.* Delhi: Permanent Black.

Jaini, P.S. 2001. *Collected Papers on Buddhist Studies.* Delhi: Motilal Banarsidass.

Khan, A. M. 1999. *The Maghs: A Buddhist Community in Bangladesh.* Dhaka: University Press Limited.

Khan, Akabar Ali. 2001. *Discovery of Bangladesh: Explorations in the Dynamics of a Hidden Nation.* Dhaka: University Press Limited.

Khan, F.A. 1963. *Mainamati: A Preliminary Report on the Recent Archaeological Excavations in East Pakistan.* Karachi: Dept. of Archaeology, Govt. of Pakistan.

Kim, J. 2012. 'Unheard Voices: Women's Roles in Medieval Buddhist Artistic Production and Religious Practices in South Asia'. *Journal of the American Academy of Religion,* 80(1): 200-32.

Kinnard, Jacob N. 1996. 'Reevaluating the 8th-9th Century Pāla Milieu: Icono-Conservatism and the Persistence of the Śākyamuni'. *Journal of the International Association of Buddhist Studies,* 19(2): 281-300.

Kosambi, D.D. 1986. 'The Decline of Buddhism in India'. In his *Exasperating Essays: Exercises in the Dialectical Method*. Pune: Peoples' Publishing House.

Kulke, Hermann. 1995. 'The Early and Imperial Kingdom: A Processual Model for Integrative State Formation in Early Medieval India'. In Hermann Kulke (ed.), *The State in India 1000–1700*: 233–62. Delhi: Oxford University Press.

_____. 1999. 'Rivalry and Competition in the Bay of Bengal in the Eleventh Century and its Bearing on Indian Ocean Studies'. In Om Prakash and Denys Lombard (eds.), *Commerce and Culture in the Bay of Bengal, 1500–1800:* 17–36. New Delhi: Manohar.

Kumar, Sudhir. 2006. *Mānyavara Kānśīrāma Kī Asalī Śikṣā, Chāra Karoṛa Logon Kī Hogī Dīkṣā*. Delhi: Samyaka Prakashana.

Lahiri, Nayanjot and Bacus, Elisabeth A. 2004. 'Exploring the Archaeology of Hinduism'. *World Archaeology,* 36(3): 313–25.

Lal, Dr Angane. 2005. 'Santa Śiromaṇi Raidāsa Aur Bauddha Dharma'. In Dr Mahesh Prasad Ahirwar (ed.), *Śramaṇa Paramparā Aur Guru Raidāsa*: 31–8. Varanasi: Dalit Lekhaka Saṅgha.

Ling, Trevor O. 1980. *Buddhist Revival in India: Aspects of the Sociology of Buddhism*. London: Palgrave Macmillan.

Linrothe, Rob. 1997. 'Beyond Sectarianism: Towards Reinterpreting the Iconography of Esoteric Buddhist Deities Trampling on Hindu Gods'. In C.P. Sinha (ed.), *Art, Archaeology and Culture of Eastern India, Dr B. S. Verma Felicitation Volume*: 193–8. Patna: The Bihar Purāvid Pariṣad.

Lopez, Donald S. (ed.). 1995. *Buddhism in Practice.* Princeton, NJ: Princeton University Press.

Majumdar, R.C. (ed.). 1943. *The History of Bengal,* vol.1*: Hindu Period.* Dacca: University of Dacca.

Majumder, Shubha. 2012. 'Newly Discovered Jaina Antiquities from Cheliyama, District Purulia, West Bengal: An Archaeological Perspective'. *Proceedings of the Indian History Congress,* 73: 1250–60.

_____. 2014. 'Understanding the Archaeological Contexts and Iconic Details of Jaina Antiquities from Rakṣatpura and Śaṅkā, District Puruliā, West Bengal'. *International Journal of Jaina Studies,* 10 (1): 1–32.

———. 2016. 'Recent Explorations at Balarampur (Purulia District, West Bengal)'. *Puratattva,* 46: 236–41.

———. 2017. 'A Rare Icon of Tīrthaṅkara Mallinātha from Purulia, West Bengal: An Analytic Approach'. *Pratnatattva,* 23: 1–6.

———. 2017. 'Some Newly Documented Tīrthaṅkara Ṛṣabhanātha Sculptures from Pakbirra, Purulia District of West Bengal'. *Heritage: Journal of Multidisciplinary Studies in Archaeology,* 5: 419–32.

Majumder, Shubha et al. 2017. 'An Iconographic Study of Jaina *Chaumukha*s from the Eastern Fringe Areas of the Chhotanagpur Plateau'. *Kosala,* 10: 98–110.

Mani, B.R. 2007. *Debrahmanising History: Dominance and Resistance in Indian Society*. Delhi: Manohar.

Maurya, Parasanath. 2006. 'Bauddha Dharma Āndolana Mein Agrani Janapada Jaunapur: Mohammed Dilaśāda Ahmed Bane Bhante Prajñāratna'. *Ambedkar Today*, October 2006: 44–6.

McCutchion, D. 1961. 'Notes on the Temples of Purulia District'. In B. Roy (ed.), *Census 1961, West Bengal, District Census Handbook: Purulia*: 33–41. Calcutta: Government Printing Press.

Mishra, Umakant. 2009a. *Vajrayāna Buddhism: Study in Social Iconography*. Delhi: Pratibha Prakashan.

———. 2009. 'Imitation or Syncretism or Selective Appropriation?: Studying Religious Equations between Brahmanical Religions and Buddhism in the Poly-religious Landscape of Early Medieval Orissa'. *Lokaratna: An E-folklore Journal:* 65–85.

Misra, R.N. 2005. 'Beginning of *Śaiva-Siddhānta* and its Expanding Space in Central India'. In Sadananda Das and Ernst Furlinger (eds.), *Sāmarasya: Studies in Indian Arts, Philosophy, and Interreligious Dialogue*: 275–306. Delhi: D.K. Printworld.

Mitra, Debajani. 2004. *A Survey of Jainism and Jaina Art of Eastern India with Special Emphasis on Bengal from the Earliest Period to the Thirteenth Century*. Kolkata: R.N. Bhattacharya.

Mitra, Debala. 1969. *Telkupi: A Submerged Temple-Site in West Bengal*. Memoirs of the Archaeological Survey of India, No. 76. Delhi: Archaeological Survey of India.

Mitra, R.C. 1954. *The Decline of Buddhism in India*. Calcutta: Vishva Bharati Studies.

Mitra, R.L.1880. 'Transcripts and Translations of Two Inscriptions from Buddha-Gayā'. *Asiatic Society of Bengal Proceedings:* 76–80.

Morrison B.M. 1974. *Lālmāi: A Cultural Centre in Early Bengal*. Seattle, WA: University of Washington Press.

_____. 1970. *Political Centers and Cultural Regions in Early Bengal*. Tucson: University of Arizona Press.

_____. 1980. *Political Centres and Cultural Regions in Early Bengal*. Jaipur: Vikash (Indian edition).

Mukherjee, Rila. 2004. 'Rice Culture of Divine Right in a Celestially Ordered Zone: A Case Study of South Asian and South-East Asian Ideologies and Hegemonies from *c.*2000 BC to *c.*1800 AD with Specific Reference to Bengal'. *Revista Lusofona de Ciencias Sociais,* 1: 49–72.

_____. 2006. *Strange Riches: Bengal in the Mercantile Map of South Asia*. Delhi: Foundation Books.

Mukherjee, B.N. 1982. 'Commerce and Money in the Western and Central Sectors of Eastern India (c. AD 750–1200)'. *Indian Museum Bulletin,* XVII: 65–83.

Mukherji, R.R. and S.K. Maity. 1967. *Corpus of Bengal Inscriptions Bearing on History and Civilisation of Bengal*. Calcutta: Firma KLM.

Narayana, Badri. 2011. 'A Book Also Travels: Circulating Small Booklets in Dalit Poorva', *South Asian History and Culture,* 2(1): 1–15.

_____. 2011. *The Making of the Dalit Public in North India, Uttar Pradesh, 1950-Present.* Delhi: Oxford University Press.

Narayana, Jagata. 2006. 'Bhārata Mein Bauddha Dharma Kā Punarjāgarana Evam Dr Ambedkar Kā Yogadāna'. *Ambedkar Today*, October 2006: 26–8.

Nicholas, Ralph. 2001. 'Vaisanvism and Islam in the Environs of Rural Bengal'. In Rafiuddin Ahmed (ed.), *Understanding Bengal Muslims*: 52-70. Delhi: Oxford University Press.

Omvedt, Gail. 2003. *Buddhism in India: Challenging Brahmanism and Caste.* Delhi: Sage.

Panchama, S.K. 2009. 'Ācārya Motirāma Śāstrī: Uttarī Bhārata Ke Mahāna Bauddha Dārśanika'. *Sanketa*, July-September 2009: 52–6.

Patil, D.R. 1963. *The Antiquarian Remains of Bihar*. Patna: K.P. Jayaswal Research Institute.

_____. 1982. 'The Origin of Memorial Stones.' In S. Settar and Gunther

D. Sontheimer (eds.), *Memorial Stones: A Study of Their Origin, Significance and Variety*: 47-58. Dharwad: Institute of Indian Art History, Karnataka University.

Prasad, Birendra Nath. 2006. *Dilemmas of Revival of Buddhism in India* (A combined Review of Gail Omvedt, *Buddhism in India: Challenging Brahmanism and Caste,* Delhi, 2003, and D.C. Ahir, *Buddhism Declined in India: How and Why,* Delhi, 2005). *Indian International Journal of Buddhist Studies,* Varanasi, 7: 171-5.

———. 2008. 'Major Trends and Perspectives in Studies in the Functional Dimensions of Indian Monastic Buddhism in the Past One Hundred Years: A Historiographical Survey'. *Buddhist Studies Review,* London, 25(1): 54-89.

———. 2008. 'Monarchs, Monasteries and Trade on an 'Agrarian Frontier': Early Medieval Samataṭa-Harikela, Bengal'. *South and Southeast Asia: Culture and Religion,* Journal of the South and South-East Asian Association for the Study of Culture and Religion, 3: 160-77. Reprinted in Prasad 2011: 116-36.

———. 2009. 'Urbanisation at Early Historic Vaiśālī, *c.*600 BCE-*c.*400 CE'. *Social Science Probings*, Delhi, 21(1): 21-46.

———. 2010. 'Votive Inscriptions on the Sculptures of Early Medieval Samataṭa–Harikela, Bengal: Explorations in Socio-religious History'. *Religions of South Asia,* 4(1)*:* 27-43.

———. 2010. 'Votive inscriptions on the Sculptures of Early Medieval Aṅga, South Bihar: Explorations in Socio-religious History'. Paper presented at the National Conference of Indian Association for Buddhist Studies. Ahmadabad, 17-20 September 2010.

———. 2009. 'The "Hindu Buddha" and the "Buddhist Viṣṇu": Divergent Trends in Buddhist Encounters with Brahmanism' (A combined Review of Allen Trevithick, *The Revival of Buddhist Pilgrimage at Bodh Gayā: Anagaraika Dhammapala and the Mahabodhi Temple,* Delhi, 2006; and John Clifford Holt, *The Buddhist Viṣṇu: Religious Transformation, Politics and Culture,* Columbia University Press, 2005). *Indian International Journal of Buddhist Studies,* Varanasi, 10: 189-94.

———. 2010. 'Patronage and Societal Linkages: Buddhist Monasteries in Early Medieval Bihar and Bengal'. Paper presented at the International Conference on Buddhist Heritage – Gujarat, 15-17 January, M.S. University, Vadodara.

_____. 2010. 'Nālandā Mahāvihāra in its Archaeological Landscape: Archaeology of Religious Transformation in Early Medieval Bihar'. Paper presented at the Twentieth World Congress of the International Association for the History of Religions, University of Toronto, 15-21 August 2010.

_____. 2010. 'Art and Archaeology of a Village *Pratibaddha* to the Nālandā Mahāvihāra: A Note on the Socio-economic and Cultural Dynamics in the Hinterland of Nālandā Mahāvihāra'. Paper presented at the National Seminar on 'Recent Researches in Buddhist Art', The Bihar Purāvid Pariṣad, Patna, on 19 December 2010.

_____ (edited with an Introduction). 2011. *Monasteries, Shrines and Society: Buddhist and Brahmanical Religious Institutions in India in their Socio-Economic Context*. Delhi: Manak Publications Pvt. Ltd.

_____. 2011. 'Cultural Processes in the Hinterland of the Monastery: A Case Study of a Village in the Neighborhood of Nalanda'. Paper presented at the National Seminar on 'Heritage of Nalanda: Icons and Symbols, Thoughts and Literature', Nava Nalanda Mahāvihāra (A Deemed University), Nalanda, on 13 February 2011.

_____. 2012. 'Brahmanical Temples, *Maṭhas*, *Agrahāras* and a Buddhist Establishment in a Marshy and Forested Periphery of Two "Frontier" States: Early Mediaeval Surma Valley (Sylhet and Cachar), *c*.600 CE–1100 CE'. *Religions of South Asia*, London, 6(1): 33-60.

_____. 2012. 'Recent Archaeological Explorations in the Neighbourhood of Nalanda'. Paper presented at the ICHR sponsored National Seminar on Recent Archaeological Excavations and Explorations in the Ganga valley, organized by The Bihar Purāvid Pariṣad, in collaboration with the Archaeological Survey of India, Excavation Branch III, Patna, on 28 February 2012.

_____. 2013. 'A Folk Tradition Integrated into Mahāyāna Buddhism: Some Observations on the Votive Inscriptions on the Sculptures of Puṇḍeśvarī/Pūrṇeśvarī/Puṇyeśvarī Discovered in the Kiul-Lakhisarai Area, Bihar'. *Berlin Indological Studies*, 21: 299-306.

_____. 2013. 'Rethinking the Decline of Buddhism in the Nālandā Area: An Analysis in the Light of Some Recently Discovered Sculptures'. Paper presented at the 10th International Congress of Bengal Art, Patna, 21-24 February 2013.

_____. 2014. 'The Socio-Religious Dimensions of Dedicatory Inscriptions on Sculptures Donated to a Buddhist Establishment in Early Medieval Magadha: Kurkihar, *c.*800–1200 CE'. *Journal of the Oxford Centre for Buddhist Studies*, 7: 116–52.

———. 2019. 'A Viṣṇu Temple and Its Social Linkages in 11th–12th Century AD, Comilla, Bangladesh: A Study in Some Copper-Plate Inscriptions'. In D.P. Dubey (ed.), *Sanskrit Epigraphy in South Asia: Proceedings of the Epigraphy Section of the 16th World Sanskrit Conference, Bangkok, 2015*: 139–48. Delhi: D.K. Publisher.

———. 2019-20. 'Some Observations on the Inscribed Stone Sculptures of Aparājitā and Trailokyavijaya from Early Medieval Magadha'. *Kalā* (Journal of Indian Art History Congress), XXV: 77–82.

———. 2021. *Archaeology of Religion in South Asia: Buddhist, Brahmanical and Jaina Religious Centres in Bihar and Bengal, c.AD 600–1200.* London and New York: Routledge.

———. 2021. *Rethinking Bihar and Bengal: History, Culture and Religion.* London and New York: Routledge.

——— (edited with an Introduction). 2021. *Social History of Indian Buddhism: New Researches*. New Delhi: Research India Press.

——— (edited with an Introduction). 2022. *Studies in the History and Culture of Ancient Indian Buddhism*. New Delhi: Research India Press.

Prasad, Birendra Nath et al. 2009. 'Bārā: A Recently Discovered Site in Nālandā District and Its Bearings on the Decline of Indian Buddhism' in B. Labh (ed.), *The Ocean of Buddhist Wisdom,* 4: 225–34. Delhi: New Bharatiya Book Corporation.

Ratna, Rajiva. 2006. 'Buddha Kī 2550vī Jayanti Kaise'. Editorial of *Ambedkar Today*, May-June 2006: 4.

———. 2007. 'Pāvana Bhūmi Bairanjā'. *Ambedkar Today*, February 2007: 5-15.

Ravat, Bhadrashila. 2005. *Santa Raidāsa Kī Vāṇi Mein Bauddha Chintana.* Delhi: Samyaka Prakashana.

Ray, H.P. 1986. *Monastery and Guild: Commerce under the Sātavāhanas.* Delhi: Oxford University Press

———. 1994. 'Kanheri: The Archaeology of an Early Buddhist Pilgrimage Site in Western India'. *World Archaeology,* 26(1): 35–46

Ray, Swati et al. 2015. 'Exploring the Jaina Sculptural Remains in Ancient Manbhum.' *Berlin Indological Studies,* 22: 205–36.

Rana, Engineer B.S. 2010. 'Phir Kyā Huā Mā'. *Ambedkar Today*, May 2010: 6-8.

Roy, Kumkum. 1988. 'Women and Men Donors at Sanchi: A Study of the Inscriptional Evidence'. In L.K.Tripathy (ed.), *Position and Status of Women in Ancient India*: 209-23. Banaras Hindu University: Department of Ancient Indian History, Culture and Archaeology.

Sagar, S.L. 2010. 'Dalit Krānti ke Liye Sahī Itihāsa Jānanā Āvaśyaka'. *Ambedkar Today,* February 2010: 40-1.

Saha, Sharmila and Sanyal, Rajat. 2013. 'Templescape and Culture under the Mallas of Medieval Bengal: A Case Study'. In Ratnabali Chatterjee (ed.), *Urbanity and Economy: The Pre-Modern Dynamics in Eastern India*: 168-79. Kolkata: Setu Prakashani.

Sahai, B. 1983. *The Inscriptions of Bihar from Earliest Times to the Middle of 13th Century A.D.* Delhi: Ramanand Vidya Bhavan.

Sanyal, Rajat. 2016. 'Dhuluri (Purulia, West Bengal) Rock Inscription.' *Pratna Samiksha* (n.s.), 7: 55-71.

Sarao, K.T.S. 2012. *The Decline of Buddhism in India: A Fresh Perspective*. New Delhi: Munshiram Manoharlal.

Sastri, A. 1919. 'Ruins of Gholamara'. *Journal of the Bihar and Orissa Research Society,* 5(2): 283-7.

Sastri, H. 1942. *Nālandā and Its Epigraphic Material*, Memoirs of the Archaeological Survey of India, No. 66. Delhi: Manager of Publications.

Schopen, Gregory. 1979. 'Mahāyāna in Indian Inscriptions'. *Indo-Iranian Journal,* 21: 1-19.

_____. 1984. 'Filial Piety and the Monk in the Practice of Indian Buddhism: A Question of "Sinicization" Viewed from the Other Side'. *T'oung Pao,* Second Series, 70, Livr. 198, 1(3): 110-26.

_____. 1987. 'The Inscription on the Kuṣān Image of Amitābha and the Character of Early Mahāyāna in India'. *Journal of the International Association of Buddhist Studies,* 10: 99-137.

_____. 1988-1989. 'On Monks, Nuns and "Vulgar" Practices: The Introduction of the Image Cult into Indian Buddhism'. *Artibus Asiae,* 49(1/2): 153-68.

_____. 2005. *Figments and Fragments of Mahayana Buddhism in India: More Collected Papers*. Honolulu: University of Hawaii Press.

———. 2010. *Indian Monastic Buddhism: Collected Papers on Textual, Inscriptional and Archaeological Evidence*. Delhi: Motilal Banarsidass.

Sengupta, Gautam and Shambhu Chakraborty. 2002. 'Locale, Material and Monuments: Begunia Group of Temples, Barakar, West Bengal'. In G. Sengupta and Sheena Panja (eds.), *Archaeology of Eastern India, New Perspectives*: 389-418. Kolkata: Centre for Archaeological Studies and Training-Eastern India.

Sengupta, Gautam et al. 2014. *Vibrant Rock: A Catalogue of Stone Sculptures in the State Archaeological Museum, West Bengal*. Kolkata: Directorate of Archaeology and Museums, Govt. of West Bengal.

Sengupta, Gautam. 1999. 'Hero-Stone of West Bengal: A Preliminary Study'. *Journal of Bengal Art,* 4: 77-97.

Settar, S and F.A. Ganihar. 1982. 'Artists of Memorial Stones: Cāḷukya-Hoysaḷa'. In S. Settar and Gunther D. Sontheimer (eds.), *Memorial Stones: A Study of Their Origin, Significance and Variety*: 319-38. Dharwad: Institute of Indian Art History, Karnataka University.

Singh, Om Praaksh. 2010. 'Anusūchita Jātiyon Mein Pramukha Hai Bhārata Kā Mūla Chamāra Vaṁśa'. *Buddha Sanketa,* January-March 2010: 68-72.

Singh, Satyendra. 2010. 'Bauddha Dharma Ke Prabala Prasāraka Aśoka Priyadarśī Bhāvuka Rājā The Na Ki Kurūpa aur Krūra'. *Bayāna*, October 2010: 33-4.

Sharma, R.S. 1987. *Urban Decay*. Delhi: Munshiram Manoharlal.

Sharma, Shanta. 2003. 'Rulers, Urban Milieu and Temple Patronage: Shifting Contours in Rajasthan, *c.*AD 700-1000'. *History Today,* 4: 9-21.

Shaw, J. 2004. 'Nāga Sculptures in Sanchi's Archaeological Landscape: Buddhism, Vaiṣṇavism and Local Agricultural Cults in Central India, First Century BCE to Fifth Century CE'. *Artibus Asiae,* 64(1): 5-59.

Singh, Rama. 2006. 'Parivartana Ke Pachāsa Varṣa'. *Ambedkar Today*, October 2006: 24-5.

Singh, Satanama. 2008. *Mānyavara Kānśīrāma Aur Bauddha Dharma*. Delhi: Samyaka Prakshana.

———. 2009. *Chamāra Jāti Ka Gauravaśālī Itihāsa*. Delhi: Samyaka Prakashana.

———. 2009. 'Hindu Tyohāron Kā Pardāphāśa Karatī Ek Pustaka'. *Ambedkar In India,* May 2009: 26-7.

_____. 2010. 'Buddha Ārya Kṣatriya Nahīn, Nāgavaṁśī The'. In Shanti Swaroop Bauddha (ed.), *Makkhali Gosāla ke Mānasa Putra*: 182-92. Delhi: Samyaka Prakashana.

Singh, Shyama. 2009. *Santa Raidāsa kī Mūla Vicāradhārā*. Delhi: Samyaka Prakashana.

Singh, Upinder. 1996. 'Sanchi: The History of Patronage of an Ancient Buddhist Establishment'. *Indian Economic and Social History Review*, 33(1): 1-35.

_____. 2010. 'Exile and Return: The Reinvention of Buddhism and Buddhist Sites in Modern India'. *South Asian Studies*, 26(2): 193-217.

Sircar, D.C. 1951. 'Copper-Plate Inscription of King Bhavadeva of Devaparvata'. *Journal of the Asiatic Society, Letters*, XVII(2): 1-13.

_____. 1951. 'Some Inscriptions from Bihar'. *Journal of Bihar Research Society*, XXVII(3-4): 1-13.

_____. 1952. 'Pāla Rule in the Tippera District'. *Indian Historical Quarterly*, XXVIII: 51-7.

_____. 1973. *Epigraphic Discoveries in East Pakistan.* Calcutta: Sanskrit College.

_____. 1983. *Select Inscriptions Bearing on Indian History and Civilization*, vol. II: *From the Sixth to the Eighteenth Century*. Delhi: Motilal Banarsidass.

Sontheimer, G.D. 1994. 'The *Vana* and the *Kṣetra*: The Tribal Background of Some Famous Cults'. In G.C. Tripathy and H. Kulke (eds.), *Religion and Society in Eastern India*: 117-64. Delhi: Manohar.

Spiro, Melford E. 1971. *Buddhism and Society: A Great Tradition and its Burmese Vicissitudes.* London: George Allen & Unwin.

Stein, Burton. 1977. 'Introduction' to the special issue on South Indian Temples. *Indian Economic and Social History Review*, 14 (1): 1-9.

Talbot, Cynthia. 1991. 'Temples, Donors and Gifts: Patterns of Patronage in Thirteenth-Century South India'. *Journal of Asian Studies*, 50(2): 308-40.

_____. 2001. *Precolonial India in Practice: Society, Religion and Identity in Medieval Andhra*. Delhi: Oxford University Press.

Tarafdar, M.R. 1995. *Trade, Technology and Society in Medieval Bengal.* Dhaka: University Press Limited.

Thapar, Romila. 1992. 'Patronage and Community'. In Barbara S. Miller (ed.), *The Powers of Art: Patronage in Indian Culture*: 19-34. Delhi: Oxford University Press.

———. 2005. *Cultural Pasts: Essays in Early Indian History*. Delhi: Oxford University Press.

Upasaka, C.S. 1977. *Nālandā: Past and Present.* Nalanda: Nava Nālandā Mahāvihāra.

Verardi, G. 2011. *Hardships and Downfall of Buddhism in India.* Delhi: Manohar.

Viyogi, Naval Kishore. 2006. *Sindhu Sabhyatā Ke Srijanakartā Śūdra Evam Vaṇika*. Delhi: Samyaka Prakashana.

Weber, Max. [1916] 1992. *The Religion of India: The Sociology of Hinduism and Buddhism*, ed. and tr. H. H. Gerth and D. Martindale. Delhi: Munshiram Manoharlal.

Wink, Andre. 1999. *Al-Hind: The Making of the Indo-Islamic World*, Vol. II. Delhi: Oxford University Press.

Wolf, Thom. 2007. 'Buddhism in the 21st Century: Three Challenges'. In B. Mungekar and A.S. Rathore (eds.), *Buddhism and the Contemporary World: An Ambedkarian Perspective*: 29-48. Delhi: Bookwell Publishers.

Woodward, Hiram W. Jr.1990. 'The Life of the Buddha in the Pāla Monastic Environment'. *The Journal of the Walters Art Gallery*, 48: 13-27.

Zelliot, E. 1992. *From Untouchable to Dalit: Essays on the Ambedkar Movement.* Delhi: Manohar.

Index